372·21

# LEADERSHIP
# IN EARLY
# CHILDHOOD

*For my husband,*

*Gerry Gray,*

*forever my leading man*

# LEADERSHIP
# IN EARLY
# CHILDHOOD

### 3rd edition

## JILLIAN RODD

Open University Press

Open University Press
McGraw-Hill Education
McGraw-Hill House
Shoppenhangers Road
Maidenhead, Berkshire
England SL6 2QL

email: enquiries@openup.co.uk
world wide web: www.openup.co.uk

and Two Penn Plaza, New York, NY 1012–2289, USA

First published 2006
Reprinted 2006, 2007 (twice), 2008 (twice)

A catalogue record of this book is available from the British Library

ISBN 0 335 21969 1 (pb)
ISBN 9 8 0 335 21969 8 (pb)

Library of Congress Cataloging-in-Publication Data

CIP data has been applied for

Published simultaneously in Australia and New Zealand by Allen & Unwin

Set in 10.5/13 pt Sabon by Midland Typesetters, Victoria, Australia

Printed by Bell & Bain Ltd., Glasgow

# Contents

# Acknowledgments

The continuing interest in the issue of leadership in early childhood has encouraged the preparation of this third edition, which is the product of over 30 years' experience in the early childhood field and a reflection of my opportunities to meet and work with many of the gifted and dedicated women and men who make up the profession. The structure and content of the book have been revised and updated in the light of recent research, literature and feedback from students, colleagues and reviewers. However, the basic intention of the book remains the same: to give current and intending early childhood practitioners a better understanding of the nature of leadership in the early childhood profession and its impact on professionalism. The content of the book reflects the area of leadership and the associated skills that are considered to be essential for effective leadership in early childhood.

During my career, I have been privileged to work in a number of countries, and I have drawn on the expertise and experience of childminders, family day care providers and coordinators, nursery nurses, childcare workers and coordinators, pre-school, nursery and early childhood teachers, head teachers and directors, government administrators, advisers, academic educators and parents. Without their willingness to share their experiences and knowledge with me, this book could not have been written.

My ideas about leadership have evolved since writing the earlier editions, particularly through discussions with students, colleagues and friends in the United Kingdom, Australia, Singapore, the United

States, Canada, Korea, Egypt, Nigeria and Finland. I wish to express my appreciation for the feedback, ideas and inspiration that they have given me.

One dilemma that I encountered in writing this edition was accounting for the different terminology used in various countries to describe the roles, positions and jobs undertaken by early childhood practitioners. For example, the period and field is known as 'early years' in England, whereas in Australia and the United States it is referred to as 'early childhood'. Similarly, in England, adults who care for children in their home are known as childminders, whereas in Australia, they are known as family day care workers and in the United States as home workers. In England, there are nursery nurses and nursery teachers. However, their Australian and American counterparts are referred to as childcare workers and kindergarten, pre-school and early childhood teachers. The organisation and delivery of provision for children and families in Europe is very different to that in Asia and Africa. Given the diversity and interchangeability of terminology and structures, I have used descriptors typically employed in international contexts.

This edition incorporates many quotations drawn from a qualitative study entitled 'Voices of Early Childhood Practitioners' that I undertook with early childhood practitioners from several countries during 2004. Their insights are inspirational and have infused the text with the richness of their experience.

I especially wish to thank members of the Cornwall Early Years Development and Childcare Partnership, Early Years Team and Advisers for their creativity, support and friendship.

Finally, I would like to acknowledge the unstinting support and encouragement for writing this third edition given to me by my husband Gerry Gray at a time when all of his energy needed to be focused on living with very advanced cancer. My love and thanks to you, Gerry.

## DISCLAIMER

Every effort has been made to acknowledge the source of material that is not original in this book. However, many of the terms and concepts are so commonly used that the original source is uncertain. The author and publisher would be pleased to hear from copyright holders to rectify any omissions or errors.

# Preface

As someone who is deeply engaged in leadership matters of interest to early childhood practitioners, the contents of this book evoked intensely personal touch points. We are living through a period where there is increasing public interest in and promotion of leadership. However, there are conflicting and confusing signals about the place of leadership study within the early childhood training agenda. As I continue to struggle to find direction and focus through the complex and contested minefields of early childhood research, teaching, policy and practice, Rodd's book is at once timely and empowering.

Consider the following observation made by Kofi Annan, the Secretary General of the United Nations: 'Of all the lessons in the past decade, the critical role of leadership is perhaps the most important one to take with us into the new century. Leadership is imperative if we are to improve the lives of children, their families and communities.' (Annan, 2002, p. 6)

The passage of time in revising theory, practice and policy is slow. Now more than ever, there is a sense of urgency in meeting the needs of the children and families we seek to serve as early childhood professionals. This book has been structured so as to provide readers with a range of qualities, skills and strategies required of contemporary leadership. Imbued in the language used by Rodd is a sense that in seeking to resolve challenges faced in everyday practice, as early childhood leaders, we can make a difference.

This third edition of Rodd's book builds on the success of the previous editions by extending the balance between theory and practice with the integration of voices from the field. In revising and updating this edition, there is increased coverage and emphasis on strengthening the nexus between research and practice, as well as between training and pracice. When taken together, this new orientation highlights the urgent need to review and reflect on current understandings about early childhood leadership and its impact on the effectiveness of our professional endeavours. A challenge identified in the first edition of this book, it remains an enduring theme.

Following in Rodd's pioneering footsteps, there is now a growing body of early childhood researchers invested in exploring leadership matters. There is also more recognition and acceptance of the importance of leadership in the development and delivery of excellent quality services. There is no doubt that Rodd's research and publications have contributed to this cultural shift, and to growing attempts to reconceptualise our understandings of leadership practice and theory. The reformulation of higher education programs in early childhood during the 1990s saw the introduction of administration, management and leadership matters to undergraduate training. However, the momentum and impetus to continue this work appears to have become somewhat muted. This edition will provide a much-needed injection in rekindling serious debate in the field.

Rodd laments that leadership is not yet a mandated responsibility of practitioners involved in service delivery. As with the previous editions, Rodd re-establishes the importance of having qualified leaders in early childhood. Inclusion of a new chapter on supervision, mentoring and coaching signifies the importance of retaining the balance between academic scholarships and experiential teaching and learning. This renewed and expanded focus on adult learning also signifies an important departure from the familiar child-centred working environments that focus attention on becoming better teachers of young children, to being effective leaders who can administer, manage and lead small-business enterprises. Though some of us may not be ready for this reorientation, it is a refreshing and necessary rerouting in the exploration of leadership in early childhood.

Leadership also requires a commitment to both the acquisition and the dissemination of knowledge. There is no doubt that this edition too will be widely read and sourced by novice and experienced early childhood practitioners alike. It also has wider appeal beyond the early childhoood audiences to those interested in community capacity building, where early childhood policy and practice provide focus and leadership. In synthesising the essentials of leadership, Rodd brings together findings from a wealth of leadership literature, articulated in clear language accessible by anyone interested in early childhood leadership.

In reading this book, one can easily visualise an early childhood leader in practice. This has been achieved because Rodd herself is an effective leader. This book is her canvass, where she makes explicit her vision for the professionalisation of the early childhood field. Through her scholarship and writing, Rodd is able to inspire, influence and motivate, and thereby achieve positive change in nurturing leadership developments in the field. These characteristics are hallmarks of effective leadership. As such, this book is living proof that leadership in early childhood is achievable. As the challenges of aligning early childhood education and training programs with anticipated employment demands continue, this publication will once again place Rodd at the centre of professional discourses and praxis on leadership training and development.

**Associate Professor Manjula Waniganayake**
**Institute of Early Childhood, Australian Centre for Education Studies**
**Macquarie University, Australia**

# Introduction

*Leadership within early childhood has been and continues to be one of the major issues for debate. There is an identified need for strong leadership at government level and within local communities.*

Director, early learning centre

**THIS CHAPTER EXPLORES**
- **the role of leadership in the context of the early childhood profession**
- **the changing context of early childhood service provision**
- **the need for early childhood practitioners to identify more closely with the leadership role**

Dynamic and visionary leadership continues to be regarded as an important professional issue for early childhood practitioners around the world in the twenty-first century. In the quest for increasing quality in service provision for young children and families, and for recognition as professionals with unique expertise who are different yet equal to professionals in other fields, many early childhood practitioners consider leadership to be the key element.

*The early childhood profession needs visionary and effective leaders so it can best position itself to meet future challenges.*

Early childhood lecturer

Pugh (2001:1) identifies a number of features of early childhood practice that may be considered to define essential aspects of leadership by early childhood professionals. Applying Pugh's features to leadership, leadership in early childhood is considered to be about: the experiences and environment provided for children; the relationships between adults and between adults and children; meeting and protecting the rights of children and adults; and working collaboratively, crossing existing artificial boundaries to meet the needs of all concerned with the care and education of young children.

*Young children need good leaders.*

**Primary adviser**

Early childhood usually refers to a developmental period ranging from birth to approximately eight years of age. In many countries, two independent systems operate to provide care and education for young children. Professionals who work in the early childhood field can be employed in a range of settings in one or both of the systems. Childcare practitioners are usually restricted to settings that provide home or centre-based care for children from about six weeks of age until they enter primary school. Childcare practitioners also work with children up to twelve years of age in 'out of school hours' settings. Early childhood practitioners who are trained teachers may work in child care, but are qualified to work as teachers in early childhood settings, such as pre-school, kindergarten, nursery school and infant grades in primary schools, with children aged from three to eight years.

*Leadership is important as early childhood settings have many responsibilities to many different people—different staff, parents and children.*
**Pre-school development worker**

Despite continued calls to bring care and education together, these two systems still are not fully integrated. However, the increasing professionalisation of early childhood has broken down some of the artificial barriers between care and education in the field.

*This brings increasing responsibilities because graduates are expected to rise to leadership roles and responsibilities.*
**Senior lecturer, early childhood education**

It is widely acknowledged that the last century saw major changes in the provision and delivery of services for children and families. However, those who work in the early childhood profession continually need to be responsive to accelerating demographic and social change—for example aging societies, changes in family and employment patterns and, sadly, increasing numbers of children living in poverty (Pugh, 2001).

*The current political agenda with ongoing initiatives has affected many settings and the services they offer.*

**Head teacher, early excellence centre**

Early childhood has been high on the political agendas of governments in many countries, and early childhood practitioners are regularly expected to respond to new initiatives. For example, in England the focus on inter-agency liaison and multi-disciplinary collaboration as a way of more effectively meeting the combined care and education needs of children and families has demanded that early childhood practitioners work in ways that may be unfamiliar to them. In addition, early childhood practitioners are leading the inclusion of children with special needs into mainstream settings. Early childhood practitioners in a number of countries are interested in exploring aspects of the Reggio Emilia pre-school organisations with a view to modifying and implementing relevant approaches in settings. The municipal infant–toddler centres and pre-schools of Reggio Emilia are distinguished by the participation of staff, parents and community members, which is effected through actions related to organisation and the physical environment. Children's developmental potentials are carefully nurtured through a systematic, project-based focus on symbolic representation (Edwards, Gandini and Forman, 1994), and daily practice is characterised by emphasis on relationships and communication based on dialogue, exchange and reciprocity (Giudici, Rinaldi and Krechevsky, 2001). Such changes require strong leaders of high calibre who are capable of leading and meeting the interpersonal professional challenges of multi-professional teams.

This changing context has precipitated an expansion of flexible services for children and parents, which in turn has changed the roles that early childhood practitioners undertake (Pugh, 2001). One of these key roles is the ability to provide sensitive and skilled leadership (Caldwell, in Ebbeck and Waniganayake, 2003). In one of the searches to define quality in early childhood, Barbour (1992) argues that early childhood practitioners have moved beyond asking questions such as 'Should we ... ?' to pursue questions of 'How can we ... ?' This book addresses the still fundamental and pressing question of how early childhood practitioners provide leadership as a means to ensure quality services for young children and their families. Research continues to reveal that the leadership style and performance of administrators of early childhood services impact upon policy and practice and determine the development and implementation of innovative programs (Ebbeck and Waniganayake, 2003; Sylva and Siraj-Blatchford, 2003).

While change continues to be recognised as a hallmark of the early childhood profession, the concept of leadership—which is a necessary condition for effective change—has received only intermittent attention by early childhood theorists and researchers over the past three decades. The fundamental question of what is meant by 'leadership' in the early childhood profession still has to be answered in a way that is meaningful and credible for practitioners.

> *We, in early childhood, need to have conversations with each other about what it is we expect of our leaders ...*
>
> **Senior lecturer, early childhood**

Leadership is a term that is bandied about in numerous arenas and professions, but it is one which still is discussed infrequently in relation to early childhood. The media constantly remind us of the shortcomings of and the need for political leadership. The need for leadership in business and manufacturing industry continues to be highlighted. Politicians and current affairs commentators in many countries throughout the world continue to call for better educational leadership. Yet, when the problems associated with rapid change in the early childhood field are examined, early childhood practitioners make little reference to the absence of leadership within the profession that could facilitate the gradual and systematic implementation of appropriate changes. Caldwell (in Ebbeck and Waniganayake, 2003) comments that early childhood practitioners can be strongly resistant to new ideas and change. Therefore, the need for effective, socially and politically active leaders who understand the role played by administration and management in achieving quality provision has become even more pressing.

*It would appear that only a small number of early childhood teachers build leadership/advocacy into their positions, consequently there is not a strong united voice that communicates to the wider community.*
**Director, early learning centre**

Muijs et al. (2005) review the current research concerning leadership in early childhood and point out that there still is a paucity of research in this area. Despite the potential for exercising leadership in early childhood, the existing research findings and professional publications have not yet caught the interest and imagination of those working in settings, nor have they drawn attention to the evolving thinking about leadership—a result of the changing world of leadership in general and the nature of leadership in the early childhood field in particular. This may be attributed, at least in part, to the apparent vagueness and haziness about what is meant by leadership in early childhood and its practical relevance. Bowman and Kagan (1997) point out that the field does not have a commonly accepted definition of leadership, nor has it engaged in a systematic debate about the properties of, opportunities for and barriers to leadership. Ebbeck and Waniganayake (2003:17) support this view, and also assert that there are few publicly acknowledged leaders and no set of common expectations for leaders in early childhood.

Clark and Clark (1996) argue that a crucial component of leadership is choice. They believe that no matter how extensively a person is trained in leadership or how deeply they are thrust into a position of leadership, it is essential that they make a conscious choice to accept that role. Unfortunately, evidence shows that many early childhood practitioners do not, for various reasons, choose to accept a leadership role. Some of these reasons include low rates of payment, low status, poor working conditions, lack of understanding of employment rights and the stressful and physically demanding nature of the work itself (Rosier and Lloyd-Smith, 1996; Sumison, 2002). Leadership in early childhood appears to be a phenomenon that has been delved into off and on for the past 30 years, yet it continues to be an enigma for many early childhood practitioners.

Findings from numerous research studies into leadership in early childhood reveal that the majority of practitioners are not yet comfortable with, and choose not to respond to, the leadership demands of their work, including the managerial and supervisory aspects of working with adults (Ebbeck and Waniganayake, 2003). Caldwell (2003:iv) comments that 'professionals in the field of early childhood education and care . . . have been loathe to see themselves in these roles'.

Early childhood practitioners in a range of countries still appear to hold a narrow conceptualisation of the professional role as one where the focus is on direct care of and interaction with children (Hujala and Puroila, 1998). Although many practitioners understand that there is a need to be 'professional' in their job, and some are motivated to 'improve the image of the field', many still report that they are not comfortable with activities that might contribute to the achievement of these goals, such as managing programs, marketing, influencing policy, lobbying, making speeches, fundraising and research. Practitioners in many countries continue to identify minimally with Vander Ven's (1991) attributes that underpin the instrumental, professional and entrepreneurial dimensions of leadership, and they still appear to tag themselves with the attributes that Almy (1975) highlighted 30 years ago. For example, many students and some early childhood staff continue to define a good practitioner as one who displays patience, warmth, a capacity for nurturing and high energy levels. However, unless there is an active and strong identification and recognition of the leadership role and a broader conceptualisation of their professional role and associated skills, members of the early childhood field will not be able to meet increasing demands for competent administrators, supervisors, trainers, educators, researchers and advocates.

## REFLECTIONS ON LEADERSHIP IN PRACTICE

I have always been passionate about the principles of good early childhood practice. I was fortunate to have two head teachers who were sympathetic to my views and allowed me autonomy in my nursery. I was given further responsibility in the school—Key Stage 1 Coordinator and then Early Years Coordinator, and later became a member of the Senior Management Team. So I gradually learned new roles and took on more responsibility. Now I lead a team of eight early childhood teachers who support children and families in the county.

**Early education team leader**

While the need for increased professionalism and professional self-confidence has been recognised, early childhood practitioners still need to develop a clearly delineated understanding about the breadth and depth of their leadership roles and responsibilities (Rodd, 1996, 1997). In a conference presentation in 2003, Moyles argued that the role of the early childhood practitioner was not well understood, and neither were the depth and complexity of early childhood practice. She contended that improvement in understanding and practice comes from scrutinising and questioning traditional and accepted practice. For early childhood practitioners to gain a better understanding of and greater confidence to engage in leadership roles, there needs to be more extensive professional discourse in supportive, non-threatening and non-judgmental arenas.

The development of leadership skills continues to be a vital and critical challenge for early childhood practitioners around the world if the provision of socially and culturally responsive services for young children and their families is to be successful. It will no longer be acceptable (or feasible), as it was in the past, to rely on colleagues from other fields such as primary teaching, social work or nursing to provide leadership models and initiatives which can be adapted to the needs and contexts of early childhood services. Nor will it be seen as appropriate for the professional status currently being sought to adopt leadership mentors from outside disciplines. If early childhood is to achieve professional status equivalent to that of similar or related occupations, it is necessary to nurture and train individuals who will emerge as leaders from *within* the profession. Empowerment of the early childhood field has to begin with people who feel comfortable in and choose the leadership role at the program level, and who will progress to leadership at perhaps government and policy levels. The basis of such empowerment lies in a reconceptualisation of the professional role from the 'grass roots' up.

The restructuring of several training courses and awards in a number of countries is an attempt to break down the artificial dichotomy between care and education (Abbott and Hevey, in Pugh, 2001). However, the terminology that is used to denote the leader of an educational setting and that which is used to signify the leader of a childcare setting has acted to maintain the unproductive division between care and education. Regardless of the form of childcare and early education that parents choose, the needs of the child remain the same. A four-year-old has the same needs and is entitled to the same quality experience whether that child is placed in a childcare, family day care or a pre-school setting. In an attempt to overcome the nomenclature issue, the terms 'early childhood professional' or 'early childhood practitioner', as well as 'the leader', will be used in this book to denote the person who is responsible for the administration of an early childhood service or setting. Depending on the area, co-ordinators of family day care schemes can be responsible for the work of up to a hundred or so family day care providers. The terminology which is necessary to describe both centre-based and home-based care becomes cumbersome in the presentation of some ideas. Therefore, the term 'setting' will be used to include centre-based and home-based care and education programs. With the current move to incorporate early education programs within childcare services, it is hoped that early childhood teachers will be motivated to perceive any changes as opportunities to expand and modify their considerable expertise in education and to take up positions of leadership in the range of settings that will emerge over the next decade. This will benefit children, parents and early childhood staff.

# CHAPTER ONE

# UNPICKING LEADERSHIP IN THE EARLY CHILDHOOD CONTEXT

*Leadership is best defined as a process of engagement, the leader engages fellow professionals in best meeting the needs of children and families . . . in early childhood there is an expectation that leaders will be consultative in their approach.*

Lecturer and researcher

**THIS CHAPTER EXPLORES**
- **definitions of leadership for early childhood**
- **general concepts about leadership**
- **dimensions of leadership**
- **differences between leadership and management**
- **leadership as it relates to the early childhood profession**
- **the role of vision in leadership**
- **why leadership works in some situations and not others**

Despite the subject being addressed to at least some degree in pre- and in-service training programs, early childhood practitioners in many countries are noted for their reluctance to identify with the concept of leadership as part of their professional role (Caldwell, 2003; Solly, 2003). Indeed, Katzenmayer and Moller (2001) describe the need for leadership development as 'awakening the sleeping giant'.

This reluctance of early childhood practitioners to see themselves as leaders is an interesting phenomenon because, historically, traditionally and currently, they—as teachers, childcare staff and managers—have been and are trained to demonstrate high levels of autonomy and independence in policy and practice. This professional requirement for independent decision-making and problem-solving skills stems from the physical isolation of early childhood care and education settings (in which the majority of early childhood personnel are employed) as well as the small number of staff who are required to deliver programs for groups of children in such settings. With the lack of access to immediate support and backup, early childhood practitioners have developed autonomous styles and skills for meeting the demands of their situation which, in other working environments, might be called 'leadership skills'. The lack of an adequate model of leadership in early childhood practice is a gap that still needs to be addressed (Geoghegan et al., 2003).

For early childhood practitioners, leadership has been, and will continue to be, defined in terms of improving program quality (Alvarado et al., 1999). However, recognition of the concept of individual leadership potential, which exists at a personal and setting level, appears not to have been translated into aspirations for more general organisational or professional leadership which could advance the professionalisation of the early childhood field and achieve still much-needed advances in community credibility and status.

> *Leaders are people who have a public face through professional activities . . . who have been mentored by recognised early childhood leaders to assume these roles . . . it does not necessarily mean someone who is a centre director, coordinator or manager . . .*
> **Associate professor, early childhood**

In reviewing the literature on leadership in general, it is evident that the traditional themes and ideas about leadership are not really applicable to early childhood. Kagan (1994) identifies the shortcomings of three traditional approaches to understanding leadership: personal characteristics and traits; style, behaviour and strategies; and the nature of the task and work culture. She concludes that these approaches ignore important features of early childhood settings, which are the emergence of the multiple, shared and joint forms of leadership conventionally preferred by women; the need for intimacy, flexibility and individualisation of organisational strategies and processes; and an ethos of collaboration and collective success for all.

Whalley (1999) suggests that women as leaders in early childhood settings use a more facilitating than authoritative approach, and are more concerned with influence than authority. Such factors produce a kind of leadership that seems to be especially suited—and perhaps is even unique—to early childhood.

## WHAT IS LEADERSHIP?

Looking through the vast collection of literature related to leadership in educational and other fields, it is clear that many concepts and ideas are in fact applicable to leadership in early childhood. In general, leadership is about vision and influence. It can be described as a process by which one person sets certain standards and expectations and influences the actions of others to behave in what is considered to be a desirable direction. Taylor (2005) argues that a leader's words, actions, decisions, interactions and styles affect the beliefs, values, feelings and behaviour of the people they work with and are critical in determining how others respond in a team. Leaders are people who can influence the behaviour of others for the purpose of achieving a goal. They can encourage colleagues to change their behaviour, take a new approach to work and build new mind sets.

Leadership can be displayed in different ways and takes many forms. Davies (2005) presents eleven different authors' perspectives on leadership in school settings. Many of these perspectives are useful for building a model of leadership appropriate for early childhood contexts, such as strategic, transformational, ethical, learning-centred, constructivist, emotional, distributed and sustainable leadership.

Research into leadership has been criticised as being too focused on exploring what leaders do (Mitchell, 1990) and the attributes they possess rather than what is actually involved in leadership itself. The key leadership theories that centre on the trait, behavioural and situational aspects are examples of such approaches. However, these models of leadership, while useful in deconstructing some key components, do not offer insight into the complex process of leadership, which is multifaceted and based on reciprocal relationships (Morgan, 1997). Style theories attempt to clarify the ways in which leaders undertake their roles in different situations in order to successfully achieve their goals. Research findings by Geoghegan et al. (2003) reveal that early childhood practitioners rely on multiple rather than single leadership styles to conduct their day-to-day activities. They acknowledge the multi-faceted nature of leadership by identifying the need to explore the relationship and interaction between the various leadership styles.

Leaders do appear to possess a special set of somewhat elusive qualities and skills, which are combined into an ability to get others to do what the leader wants because they want to do it. Sarros and Butchatsky (1996) argue that leadership is purposeful behaviour intended to influence others to contribute to an agreed goal aimed at achieving positive outcomes for the organisation or individuals. Leaders are able to balance the concern for work, task, quality and productivity with concern for people, relationships, satisfaction and morale. They combine an orientation towards innovation and change with an interest in continuity and stability for the present. Leadership is a dynamic activity, rather than a set of static attributes. Dynamic leaders draw upon personal qualities which command respect and promote feelings of trust and security in others, and they engage in activities that help drive the organisation into the future. These activities include setting and clarifying goals, roles and responsibilities; collecting information and planning; making decisions; and involving members of the group by communicating, encouraging and acknowledging commitment and contribution.

There are many contemporary definitions of good leadership. In deconstructing leadership, this book focuses on leadership strategies for early childhood settings rather than leadership style for early years practitioners. Leadership is understood as a shared process where effective leaders draw on a range of strategies to achieve positive and ethical outcomes for members of the group or the organisation.

The key to effective leadership is the ability to interact with others in ways which:

- offer inspirational and credible values, vision and mission;
- encourage open communication;
- develop a team culture;
- set realistic and achievable goals and objectives;
- monitor and celebrate achievements; and
- facilitate and foster the development of individuals.

Such approaches to leadership do not constrain leadership to positional status but open leadership opportunities to those early childhood personnel who choose to take up purposeful activities aimed at improving quality and moving the field forward.

*There is usually a defined role of leader, for example, headship but other roles have an element of leadership which when supported enhances services and allows for effective cooperation between different professionals and services . . .*

**Head teacher, early excellence centre**

*Leadership can be undertaken for an hour, a day or a year . . .*

**Teaching assistant**

Leadership can be displayed in a range of early childhood contexts by people who have vision, drive, energy, commitment and positive relationships with others. People who are apathetic, inactive and out of touch with others are not leaders in the eyes of those they work with and for. Effective leaders understand that individual characteristics and contributions of members of the group are crucial but can be unpredictable in their impact, that systems are important but can become static, and that management is complex and can be difficult due to changing circumstances. Effective leaders know when to use professional judgment, when to support, when to push and when to give others opportunities to lead (Law and Glover, 2000). They help move individuals, the group and the organisation forward by being reflective and sharing with others what they have learned.

Every early childhood practitioner can choose to become a leading professional by demonstrating increasing competence in their work; becoming a critical friend to colleagues; supporting the development of others, including children, parents and colleagues; and acting as an ambassador and advocate for the profession. In fact, Sullivan (2003) claims that every early childhood practitioner shares in the leadership process each day. Improved professionalism in early childhood will come about when early childhood practitioners define themselves as 'leading professionals' who choose to take up the challenge of creating and delivering high-quality services for children and families.

## DIMENSIONS OF LEADERSHIP

As part of a project to encourage innovative approaches to leadership training and support for early childhood practitioners, Morgan (1997a) attempts to tease out some of the dimensions related to the term 'leadership' when applied to the early childhood context. She points

**13**

out that many of the commonly accepted definitions of leadership raise particular issues for the early childhood field. For example, Morgan suggests that when leadership is defined as positional—that is, tied to the position or office of a leader, such as a manager, coordinator or director—certain implications about expectations of leadership follow which can work to exclude other members of staff, such as teachers and childcare workers, from access to and responsibility for leadership. When leadership is defined as a capacity, ability or set of strategies to lead, every early childhood practitioner can choose to develop such skills in areas of particular interest to them. However, numerous studies (Ebbeck and Waniganayake, 2003; Moyles and Yates, 2004; Rodd, 1996) indicate that members of the profession have yet to identify and agree on what capacities, abilities, competencies and strategies are related to leadership in early childhood.

## REFLECTIONS ON A DAY IN THE LIFE OF A LEADER

I'm the director of a large childcare centre and my work is extremely complex. Let's take last Thursday for example. I begin my day at 8 a.m. I'm at the supermarket buying a cake for afternoon tea to say goodbye to a member of staff. I remember that I sent the card around for signing last week—did it come back to me, I wonder. By 8.30 a.m. I'm at my desk and a staff member has called in sick so I need to sort out the staffing ratios. Children and parents started to arrive at 8.00 a.m. and one mother is still waiting to talk to me about her child's behaviour at home. As I chat to the mother, the phone rings again. Fortunately, another staff member picks it up. The mail has arrived so I begin to sort out the correspondence—urgent for attention today, needs attention at some time, needs to be put in the staff room and the rest (meaning I'll get to it some time). It is now close to 9.30 a.m. and, because I don't have any teaching responsibility this morning, I visit a couple of the rooms to chat to the children and offer moral support to the staff. That gives me a chance to observe what is going on regarding learning, teaching and individual needs. By 11 a.m. I'm back at my desk, emails to read and respond to. How many today, only 34! It's midday, some parents are starting to arrive again, I've got reports to write—but I think that I should be visible and accessible to parents, so I wander out to reception to chat again.

It's lunchtime for some staff members, one has made an appointment to see me, that sounds official—could it be regarding a complaint about another staff member, a parent, a request for training or a request for a change of shift? It's a request for training, for permission and funding to go on a course related to equal opportunities. I agree subject to checking the available funding and making sure that the staffing can be covered. I need to remember to get back to her next week so that she can book it. I take the opportunity to give some feedback about the quality of her work. She seems to appreciate it. I can now eat a sandwich at my desk while I try to read and assimilate the latest government publication. I respond to some waiting correspondence.

Afternoon tea: it's time to say goodbye to a staff member who is moving on. Many of the children have been collected so those staff who don't have responsibility for children gather together and we have an informal chat. It's important to be sociable and listen to what they want to say. It then occurs to me that I could use the opportunity to talk to the staff about their work. I have been thinking about the elements of passion and creativity in early years practice so I introduce the themes and finish by asking whether people would be interested in talking more about them in a staff meeting. I want to stir up a couple of staff who seem to be a bit complacent about their practice. I realise that I may have to talk to them individually at another time.

The last of the children have left for the day. I meet with a couple of the teachers who have an idea about introducing a new initiative into the setting. We discuss how to put the suggestion to the rest of the staff who may be reluctant to take on any more work. One of the teachers offers to take responsibility for organising a presentation.

It's 4.30 p.m. and I am going to a meeting with other directors in my area. It is a fifteen-minute drive. I check with the remaining staff that all is under control for tomorrow, as Friday can be a hectic day, and I leave. This meeting finishes at 6 p.m. and I leave for home. In my briefcase I have a draft of the budget. I must check it tonight because I have a meeting tomorrow with the council's financial administrator. I tackle that at 9 p.m. That's a typical day for me.

When leadership is defined as the product of the endeavours of an interconnected group of individuals, the possibility of shared or collaborative leadership is opened up. This type of leadership appears to be attractive to early childhood practitioners, who perceive diversity as a strength for responding to the constantly changing demands in the early childhood field. Shared or collaborative leadership also addresses the difficulties that many early childhood practitioners experience about authority (Ebbeck and Waniganayake, 2003): some mistakenly align authority with power over others—that is, domination—and hence are averse to being seen in a position of authority. Authentic authority—that which is associated with effective leadership in early childhood settings—is conferred on people who are perceived as professional, possessing high levels of expertise, judgment, fairness and wisdom. Power—which also can be defined as influence and strength—is derived from working collaboratively with others.

## REFLECTIONS ON A DAY IN THE LIFE OF A LEADER

I am an early childhood teacher with eight years' experience. Teaching three- and four-year-olds has been my main responsibility. Recently I attended a training day on the importance of the first three years. The significance of the parent as the child's first and foremost teacher was reiterated. I suddenly knew that I was extremely interested in this area and thought that my setting could offer an opportunity to help parents of young children under three years in our area. This would be advantageous to the setting because this would be a way of prospective parents getting to know us and what we offered before they enrolled their children. Also, parents could make a better choice if they knew the setting.

I made an appointment to talk to the manager about the idea and she was interested. She suggested that we take it to the next staff meeting and see who else would be interested. She suggested that I take the lead and I agreed to do this. At the meeting, only one other staff member was interested and willing to take the idea forward. That didn't matter—now there were two of us plus the manager when needed.

The two of us spent a couple of planning sessions and a couple of evenings together and then we put forward our plan to the manager. She thought that it was a way of our setting starting up an outreach initiative and that she could find us some funding from the budget because of the benefits for parents, children and the setting. We outlined the plan to the rest of the staff at a meeting and they were supportive and encouraging, probably because there was no extra work in it for them!

Within three months, we held the first of a six-meeting program with a group of parents and their under-threes. We had six topics to focus on but also listened to the parents about what they wanted to cover and talk about. It was a great success and we've run this program twice now.

We've written a report for our newsletter and the local news-paper did an article about the program. We've also spoken at our local early childhood forum about the program. It was scary at first to even bring up an idea like this, but working with another staff member and the manager has been terrific. I don't think I would have had the courage to take on such an initiative by myself, but working collaboratively gave me so much more confidence. We hope that our success will inspire other staff members to feel confident to put forward their ideas.

When leadership is defined as guidance and direction, it implies the presence of someone to provide such guidance and direction and points back to expectations about leadership that are associated with someone holding a special position or office. The exclusion of people who do not occupy positions formally associated with leadership is a major limitation of this interpretation. However, many early child-hood practitioners do identify with the concept of guidance because, for them, it does not embody unacceptable connotations associated with concepts of power, command and authority. Leadership in the early childhood field appears to be more a result of groups of people who work together to influence and inspire each other rather than the efforts of one single person who focuses on getting the job done (Jorde-Bloom, 1997; Morgan, 1997b). It is therefore imperative that all members of the early childhood profession are encouraged to share and discuss their different perspectives on leadership and have access to opportunities for professional training in leadership as well as preparation for its roles and responsibilities.

Unfortunately, the terminology used to distinguish between leaders of childcare and educational settings has not helped either the early childhood profession or the community to understand the complexities of the diverse leadership roles in the early childhood field (Caldwell, 2003; Moyles, 2003). The concept of a 'leader' who influences others in order to administer an efficient, accountable small business or organisation, which includes adult staff and consumers, has yet to be assimilated into the professional role. Early childhood practitioners' perception and comprehension of and confidence in their leadership role with staff, parents and other professionals are not clear or well developed. This limitation in professional development may explain in part the leadership difficulties encountered in service provision and the ongoing low credibility and status of early childhood practitioners compared with other services and professions. Community and industry's stereotyped perception about jobs dominated by females also contribute to the de-valuing of early childhood as a legitimate profession.

In addition, narrow definitions of professional development and career by many early childhood practitioners have left the profession without its own specialised advocates to guide its members through the political and economic processes which are influential in determining the continuation or otherwise of these services. Many members of the early childhood field appear to be content to confine their work and aspirations to basic or advanced levels of direct care of children rather than extending their interest and competence to the more indirect care and educational activities related to professional, entrepreneurial and leadership roles and responsibilities with adults.

## REFLECTIONS ON A DAY IN THE LIFE OF A LEADER

I am a childcare worker and I have never thought of myself as a leader. I always thought that the manager was the leader. In my appraisal, my manager suggested that I attend a course on Effective Leadership and Management in Early Childhood Settings. I didn't think that this was relevant to me but the manager said it was so I went. I didn't think that I would get anything out of it because I work with the children, I don't do much administration like reports and budgets. But after the course, I came away with a different understanding of what leadership in early childhood was and what the differences between management and leadership were. I learned that I could be and probably was already a leader and manager. So I thought about my job and where I could see that I was a leader.

The sorts of things I do that indicate leadership and management are showing parents around the setting, talking to them about our approach to learning and the opportunities we offer the children, making displays of children's work for the reception area—I really enjoy that—reading professional magazines like *Practical Preschool* and *Early Educator*—I get lots of ideas from those types of magazines—and I make sure that the two of us in the Under Twos room have a written plan for the week. Apparently, even going on a training course is leadership because it shows that you want to improve your skills and that helps raise the quality of child care.

Before going on the course, I didn't realise that I was a manager and a leader because I did those things. Now I see that I could learn a lot more about running a childcare centre and I could take on more responsibility for other things. If I did that, I would be preparing myself for getting a manager's job one day.

It is becoming increasingly evident that the future survival and growth of the services provided by specialised early childhood practitioners depend upon dynamic, visionary leadership emerging from within the profession. An increasingly sophisticated comprehension is growing amongst members of the early childhood field about what is involved in leadership, particularly the idea that there are many ways to approach leadership and different levels at which it can be exercised (Alvarado et al., 1999; Taba, 1999).

As the professionalisation of the early childhood field gathers momentum, people understand that it is not necessary to begin at the top with developing the highly sophisticated leadership skills of policy development and critical decision-making in all practitioners. It is more important to unravel what leadership is and to identify the roles and responsibilities within the early childhood profession, thus permitting leadership to be exercised at a more grass roots level. This will facilitate the development of practitioners who are able to grasp the complexities of the work that they perform and the opportunities for leadership that arise in their daily working environment. As individual staff members gain confidence in their leadership capability at the setting level, some will become interested in extending their leadership abilities to wider arenas such as active contribution in professional organisations, action research within settings, writing for the profession and perhaps becoming politically active on behalf of the field.

## HOW IS LEADERSHIP DIFFERENT FROM MANAGEMENT?

Part of the difficulty in understanding leadership in early childhood stems from confusion with the concept of management. Law and Glover (2000:13) point out that, 'although there has been much debate over the differences between leadership and management, the terms tend to be used interchangeably: agreement over definition . . . is not reached easily'. Hayden (1996) offers a helpful explanation of issues relevant to management of early childhood services. However, she does not link management explicitly to leadership. Even the definitions of the core elements of early childhood practitioners' work (National Association for the Education of Young Children, 1993) and the emerging profile of early childhood professionals in Europe

**Table 1.1  A comparison of what managers and leaders do**

| Managers | Leaders |
| --- | --- |
| *Plan*—set objectives, forecast, analyse problems, make decisions, formulate policy. | *Give direction*—find a way forward, communicate a clear direction, identify new goals, services and structures. |
| *Organise*—determine what activities are required to meet objectives, classify work, divide it up and assign it (i.e. decide who does what). | *Offer inspiration*—have ideas and articulate thoughts that motivate others. |
| *Coordinate*—inspire staff to contribute both individually and as a group to the organisation's objectives. | *Build teamwork*—use teams as the most effective form of management, spending their time building and encouraging collaboration. |
| *Control*—check performance against plans; develop people and maximise their potential to achieve agreed outcomes (i.e. they get the work done through and by other people). | *Set an example*—model what leaders do and how they do it. |
|  | *Gain acceptance*—act in ways that arouse acknowledgment of their leadership status in followers. |

*Source*: Law and Glover (2000:16, 17, 20, 21)

**20**

(Oberhuemer, 2000) fail to clearly differentiate leadership as a distinctive role and responsibility with specific skills that are different from those of management.

It is important to understand that leadership and management are inherently linked and interwoven. Effective leaders in early childhood need to be aware that their leadership role is more than routine management, which focuses on the present and is dominated by issues of continuity and stability. Waniganayake et al. (2000) argue that management and leadership are different dimensions of the work of early childhood setting directors and managers.

Leadership emanates out of vision that is based in philosophy, values and beliefs, which in turn guides policy, day-to-day operation and innovation. It is manifested through strategic planning that grows out of reflection. Management is distinguished by active involvement in pedagogy, positive relationships, effective communication and high expectations for increasing professionalism (Solly, 2003). Solly (2003) suggests that management is related more to maintenance tasks, concerned with carrying on, keeping up, perpetuating and sustaining.

## REFLECTIONS ON MANAGEMENT AND LEADERSHIP IN PRACTICE

When I think about my management tasks, they generally tend to be around day-to-day issues, such as checking that the rooms and bathrooms have been cleaned properly, that there are no hazardous items in the outdoor area, that the rooms have been properly set up before the children arrive, that the parents' newsletter is ready to go out, that the rosters are completed on time and that the staff are relaxed and prepared to enjoy the day with the children.

When I think about my leadership responsibilities, I focus on activities such as reading the latest government guidelines and other important literature so that I can raise current issues at staff meetings, matching new staff members with experienced staff as mentors, thinking about different ways to evaluate the curriculum and staff performance, planning for continuing professional development for all of the staff, working with or delegating responsibility to staff teams for developing specific policies, sharing my expertise with staff and thinking about the best ways to manage some of the changes we have to attend to.

**Head teacher, early excellence centre**

On the other hand, leadership is considered to be about enhancement where qualities, behaviours and values are improved and strengthened through inspirational, politically sensitive public relations, research and dissemination skills displayed by those who are sufficiently courageous to work with and challenge policy-makers where necessary. Solly (2003) warns that maintenance could become a distraction and lead to a preoccupation with staying safe and not advancing. She perceives leadership to be associated more with taking risks to improve quality. In the same way, Moyles (2003) urges early childhood practitioners to constantly scrutinise and challenge traditionally accepted practices. These views articulate the important point that leadership is about learning and that all effective leaders are learners.

Other writers point to further differences between leadership and management and suggest that leadership is more related to:

- strategic development rather than day-to-day problem-solving (Kotter, 1989);
- fostering a culture of trust, developing an openness to learning, encouraging and stimulating learning, communicating organisational aims and vision with clarity (Bennis and Nanus, 1985);
- mission, direction, inspiration rather than designing and implementing plans, getting things done and working effectively with other people (Fullan, 1991).

These characteristics point to the fact that successful leaders are more than efficient managers. Rather than focusing on the narrow and specific details of getting through the day and keeping the setting running, they tend to spend their time reflecting on, deliberating about and planning program administration more broadly around values, philosophy, policies and the need to be responsive to change. They utilise staff resources by delegating others to take care of the fine detail required at the management level. Effective administrators incorporate the future-oriented aspect of leadership to program administration where innovation and change are effected through:

- group goal-setting, where the wider the participation of staff, the greater the likelihood of commitment by staff to the goals;
- consensus-building, where a productive working environment is created by the group taking responsibility for implementing and adhering to decisions;

- personnel development, where staff and parents are helped to grow and develop; and
- program development, where initiative is taken to establish, review, evaluate and modify existing programs.

While it is true that, in order to be an effective leader, one also needs to be an efficient manager, management skills do not equate with leadership skills. A person with highly developed management skills is likely to have structured the administration of the program to give adequate time to devote to key leadership functions. A person with poorly developed management skills is unlikely to be sufficiently organised to free up the time needed to focus upon leadership issues. In any case, management skills are necessary but not sufficient for effective leadership. The knowledge, abilities and skills of management and leadership are different but overlapping (Law and Glover, 2000). Interestingly, Armstrong (1994) perceives leadership as a cohesive force, facilitating management 'because even simple management tasks are complex and involve a combination of elements' (Law and Glover, 2000:13). Armstrong gives management the same status as leadership by arguing that 'all managers are by definition leaders in that they can only do what they have to do with the support of their team, who must be inspired or persuaded to follow them' (Law and Glover, 2000:13). This view maintains that effective teamwork is the foundation of effective leadership and supports the model of shared leadership that is favoured by early childhood practitioners.

## WHAT IS LEADERSHIP IN THE EARLY CHILDHOOD PROFESSION?

While the study of management can be found as a compulsory subject in the training of early childhood practitioners throughout the world, the same cannot be said of leadership. The lack of opportunities for leadership training, coupled with limited access to experienced role models (Humphries and Senden, 2000; Ebbeck and Waniganayake, 2003) and the antithesis many women appear to have towards roles and responsibilities that involve authority and power (Cox, 1996), have acted to impede development of an understanding of leadership, particularly as it pertains to early childhood. Although levels of professionalism, accountability and credibility are increasing in the global early childhood profession, the concept of leadership as a means of advancing the field still appears not to be as well understood by practitioners. Some early childhood practitioners are thinking about leadership in new ways—for example, Kagan's (1994) notion of shared leadership, Jorde-Bloom's (1995) notion of participatory management, Nupponen's (2000) discussion of transformational leadership and Waniganayake's (2000) model of distributive leadership (in Ebbeck and Waniganayake, 2003). However, identifying with the concept of and need for leadership by and of women still appears to be problematic for many of those who work in early care and education.

Effective leadership in the early childhood profession is about working towards creating a community and providing a high-quality service. This involves:

- offering inspiration to others by sharing ideas and thoughts;
- setting an example and being a strong role model;
- influencing the behaviour of others, particularly staff and parents, to contribute to a creative early childhood service by giving direction, finding ways forward and articulating a clear sense of direction;
- administering the service efficiently by building teamwork, collaboration and inclusion;
- supervising staff and guiding parents in ways which will enhance their personal growth, empowerment and professional development and progress; and
- planning for and implementing change in order to improve organisational and professional effectiveness.

These characteristics are evident in the following definitions of leadership provided by a range of early childhood practitioners in qualitative research undertaken for this edition.

*Leadership means someone who has a vision about their future expectations for self and others . . . can articulate what this is to others . . . and can garnish the necessary expertise to push forward an agenda that has been jointly constructed . . .*

**Senior lecturer**

*Leadership refers to individuals and groups of people who are committed to the provision of high-quality education and care for all children throughout the world . . . these people and groups are imbued with a passion that is readily communicated to others . . . they are enthusiastic and feel empowered to speak out and work towards change even when the odds are against them . . .*

**Director, early learning centre**

*Leadership refers to people who instigate and initiate new practices that can stimulate and support others in personal development . . . who get commitment from staff and support from them . . .*

**Early childhood trainer**

*Leadership means a team that works towards common aims for settings by defining ethos and principles, setting aims with achievable targets, valuing every person's contributions and establishing good lines of communication . . .*

**Early education team leader**

*Leadership guides, supports and respects members of the team . . .*

**Deputy supervisor**

*Leadership sets a good example for everyone to follow . . .*

**Pre-school development worker**

There are four basic steps necessary for any leader to make things happen in an organisation:

- *The definition of organisational and individual goals and/or objectives.* This will provide a clarification of the service and its purpose, an outline of future directions, a description of procedures and identification of resource requirements and agreed roles and responsibilities for each team member.
- *The setting of individual standards and expectations.* Delegated tasks will be outlined in terms of the function of each individual and include measures or standards of performance.
- *The provision of support and feedback.* Assistance is provided to individual team members to develop their expertise with constructive feedback to ensure that performance is maximised.
- *The monitoring and evaluation of outcomes.* A process of regular review is essential to ensure that the organisation is meeting its

defined objectives in relation to professional standards and within the specified timeframe.

The early childhood leader has a professional responsibility to attend to child wellbeing, adult morale and goal attainment which are the concerns of all early childhood programs. Early childhood leaders should also work in a manner which encompasses three issues defined by Sergiovanni (1999) as essential in successful leadership:

- *empowerment*—where authority and obligation are shared by the leader to result in increased responsibility and accountability throughout the group;
- *enablement*—where the leader provides means and opportunities for, and eliminates obstacles to, individual and group growth and development; and
- *enhancement*—where leader and follower roles are interwoven to produce increased commitment and extraordinary performance.

These factors are important in creating and shaping the work environment for children, parents and staff, where the leader sets the tone and psychological climate which is the hallmark of a quality program.

## WHAT IS THE ROLE OF VISION IN LEADERSHIP?

While leaders are responsible for coordinating time, talent and task, one of their top priorities is to formulate and articulate vision, values, mission and strategic direction in a way that others accept and are willing to implement as part of daily practice. Vision is the means by which leaders captivate the imagination of their followers and engage loyalty and support. It is the philosophy that is spelt out by the leader and adopted by early childhood practitioners which provides the direction for and gives meaning to innovative decisions, the search for new programs, practices, and the policies to improve effectiveness or expand service delivery. Vision provides direction for and sustains action in the team, can boost morale and self-esteem, and acts as a buffer against stress during periods of change.

Sergiovanni (1999) developed a hierarchy of ideas and ideals that can guide the organisation of thinking when addressing the process of developing vision into an operational philosophy. Leaders need to appreciate that others have different value priorities at different stages of professional development. Therefore, the entire staff should participate in discussion about values, ideas and ideals so that they can contribute to the final philosophy statement. In this way, they are more likely to perceive and own the philosophy because it came about as a product of the group process.

The philosophy that a leader then uses to guide decision-making concerning policy and practice should include information about:

- the vision (the leader's hopes and dreams);
- the contract (the leader's, staff members' and parents' shared values and expectations);
- the mission (the leader's, staff members' and parents' sense of shared purpose);
- the goals (the strategies utilised to achieve the vision); and
- the objectives (the tactic and tasks appropriate for achieving the goals).

The vision should be clear and simple, based on underlying professional values, and should make priorities explicit and indicate expectations about participation.

A breadth of experience is likely to benefit the development and communication of a vision by a leader. Although any early childhood practitioner can display and gain acceptance as an authentic leader, visionary and inspirational leadership is associated more with experience. Boardman (2003) suggests that early childhood leaders face challenges arising out of significant, diverse and complex educational changes, organisational dilemmas surrounding time and difficulties associated with knowledge and relationships. Therefore, those early childhood practitioners who bring wide experience and a depth of knowledge will have greater resources to draw on for creating a vision which will inspire the support of the staff.

## WHY DOES LEADERSHIP WORK IN SOME SITUATIONS AND NOT OTHERS?

Sometimes a leader operates successfully in one setting but experiences difficulties in another. There are a number of reasons for this.

One is that the cultures of the group and the leader do not match or fit. For example, the psychological climate of the group may be focused upon people and their individual needs whereas the leader's style might be task-oriented, emphasising organisational needs. Another reason is incompatibility between the leader and significant members of the group. For example, the leader and the deputy or the president of the committee of management might espouse different values and consequently have conflicting goals for the centre. A third instance is where there is a need for task-specific leadership. In this case, there is a mismatch between the nature of the task and leadership style. For example, a task that has to be completed in a specific format and has a specific timeline, such as fee subsidies or funding submissions, requires task-oriented, goal-specific and goal-directed leadership. Other tasks such as program-planning can be completed in a number of different ways and therefore left to the professional discretion of the staff member.

To provide effective leadership in an early childhood setting, the leader has to articulate a clear vision of the future and a general plan of action for getting there. They need to be capable of maintaining a balance between getting the job done and meeting people's needs. Getting the job done involves providing vision by clarifying goals, aims, objectives, roles and responsibilities; gathering relevant information from the staff and parents; summarising, integrating and developing ideas as a way of building a philosophy to guide the group in achieving its goals; and monitoring the group's progress towards the goals through constant evaluation. Meeting people's needs involves clarifying the group goals to help people understand the purpose of the group and to help gain commitment; providing guidelines to help people know what is expected of them in group interaction; providing a sense of inclusion or belonging and acceptance in order to draw on the full resources of the group; keeping channels of communication open; and creating a warm and friendly atmosphere in the setting where group members are valued through encouragement and recognition. Motivation, commitment and contribution are stimulated in all adults concerned with the setting when the leader addresses the above issues.

## BRINGING IT TOGETHER

The uniqueness of each early childhood setting makes it difficult to specifically define leadership broadly and exclusively. However, it appears that supporting the development of relationships between the members of early childhood communities and teamwork appears to be of utmost importance in shaping effective leadership in early childhood settings (Morgan, 1997a). Notions of trust, sharing, collaboration and empowerment also appear to be central to successful leadership. The diverse and multi-functional nature of leadership called for in early childhood settings highlights the need for leadership to be viewed more appropriately as a continuum which reflects greater or lesser degrees of input from certain features as demanded by specific situations.

# CHAPTER TWO

## WHO ARE THE LEADERS IN EARLY CHILDHOOD SETTINGS?

*Those who feel passionate about early childhood and want to share their beliefs and good practice will become leaders . . .*

Early education team leader

**THIS CHAPTER EXPLORES**
- **gender and leadership in early childhood**
- **who follows the early childhood leader**
- **essential characteristics of leaders in early childhood**
- **the functions of leaders in early childhood**
- **who is a leader in early childhood**
- **who can become a leader in early childhood**
- **the relationship between leadership and professional career development**

An abundance of literature is available on leadership, including both theory and its practical application. However, there still is a paucity of literature written specifically for the early childhood context (Geoghegan et al., 2003). Early childhood leaders operate in distinct settings and lead groups of people with specific characteristics. Most early childhood settings, be they early childhood centres, training organisations or government departments, are characterised by staff groups that are primarily female, socially and culturally diverse, and multi-professional. In addition, many early childhood settings employ young, sometimes unqualified and inexperienced staff as well as a variety of paraprofessionals. The general literature on leadership evidences a sex role stereotype bias, in that the overwhelming majority of the research has been conducted with men in positions of leadership in groups that usually have a high proportion of men (Hall, 1996). Therefore, the general literature may not be appropriate or relevant for early childhood leaders, who need to be aware of and respond to the specific characteristics and demands of the field.

## GENDER AND LEADERSHIP IN EARLY CHILDHOOD

Up until the past decade, few research studies had explored the nature of gender in leadership. More recently, the representation of women in leadership positions and the interplay between gender and leadership have been examined. The traditional model of leadership is considered to be more masculine in orientation, characterised by attributes such as control, power, domination and competition. The feminine model is believed to differ, with its interest focused on relationships, consensus, collaboration and flexibility. A study conducted almost 30 years ago (Hennig and Jardim, 1976) suggests that women behave differently to men in management positions, indicated by lower scores on three crucial aspects of team leadership: risk-taking, tolerance and flexibility. Research conducted in the early childhood field (Kinney, 1992) argues that women perform the same leadership functions as men—for example, empowering, restructuring, teaching, acting as a role model, being open and questioning—but carry out these functions using a facilitating rather than authoritarian style. In other words, women seem to lead in a way that will keep the group functioning successfully while men's leadership style appears to be more concerned with power and authority.

Grant (1997:2) claims that recent studies have indicated that the future of management is 'female', with the more feminine attributes of cooperation, communication, diplomacy and insight preferred over the traditionally male attributes of competition, aggression, hierarchy and logic. Although evidence indicates that the 'glass ceiling' is still a very real barrier to women aspiring to and taking up leadership positions (Cox, 1996; Hall, 1996; Law and Glover, 2000), women seem to be more interested in becoming leaders in a specific range of arenas, among them politics, business and education. Particularly in education, there has been a sizeable increase in the number of women in senior management positions over the past ten years. However, women are still under-represented when compared with men (Law and Glover, 2000). Debate continues about whether leadership is a male preserve, with women displaying little inclination towards, interest in and/or aptitude for this area, or whether the reason women have not taken up their rightful role as leaders in a range of work environments is due to fundamental sex discrimination in hierarchical organisational structures and social justice issues.

The majority of research into women as leaders has been conducted with women in primary and secondary education systems, as well as in social service areas and businesses where the followers are made up of heterogeneous groups of men and women. The major issues investigated are whether women leaders shape their behaviour to conform to the traditional male stereotyped model of leadership or whether leaders who are women themselves engage in a gender-specific, feminine model of leadership.

Yet in early childhood, where women dominate the field and generally assume the leadership positions that are available, little research has been undertaken. Henderson-Kelly and Pamphilon (2000) argue that women's ability to speak about leadership styles is hampered by prevailing notions of leadership and management that emerge from traditionally organised settings. They suggest that women are developing their own perspectives, models and language of leadership based on principles of care, connection and dialogue. Their work suggests that the application of current leadership theory, research and practice to gender-specific leadership is not applicable to early childhood leaders, who lead groups composed almost entirely of women.

Looking at the current research findings concerning gender and leadership, an interesting picture emerges. Some studies report that women take and are developing a specific leadership repertoire, and some find no gender differences in leadership; however, numerous studies report that women engage in repertoires and styles different from those of men. Whether this is gender-specific or gender-related has yet to be established, although anecdotal evidence suggests that some men who aspire to leadership, particularly in early childhood, are attracted to what is termed a feminised approach to leadership characterised by collaborative, consensual, people-oriented and non-hierarchical leadership.

For leaders in early childhood—the majority of whom are women—the emerging picture is one of strong leadership within a collaborative framework (Hall, 1996; Henderson-Kelly and Pamphilon, 2000; Solly, 2003). Leadership is exercised in a climate of reciprocal relationships where the leader seeks to act *with* others rather than assert power *over* others. The leader works as a member of the team. With regard to the task, participation and shared decision-making is emphasised (Ebbeck and Waniganayake, 2003), and leadership becomes a holistic, inclusive and empowering process. Effective leaders in early childhood are interested in empowering, restructuring, teaching, acting as role models, encouraging openness and stimulating questioning. They display leadership in:

- *vision behaviour*—where they create a vision and take appropriate risks to bring about change;
- *values behaviour*—where they build trust and openness;
- *people behaviour*—where they provide caring and respect for individual differences; and
- *influence behaviour*—where they act collaboratively.

Effective leaders utilise communication and interpersonal skills effectively in their interactions with others. Their approach is cooperative and affiliative rather than controlling. They gain acceptance as a leader because they are flexible and adaptable, not complacent. This approach is more conducive to the development of early childhood settings as learning organisations. However, because of the poor public perceptions of women in leadership positions and other barriers, many early childhood practitioners still find taking on leadership roles difficult. There are very few role models and mentors for those interested in becoming a leader. Those who aspire to be, and who already are, leaders have to work harder to prove—both to themselves and the wider community—that they can successfully undertake leadership roles and positions.

It is important that early childhood practitioners who aspire to leadership do not suffer from unreasonable insecurity about their abilities or create for themselves unreasonable demands for perfectionism. Positive self-esteem is very important for assuming and holding leadership. Most existing leaders readily admit that they learned to be a leader and continue to learn while in the job. This means early childhood organisations need to ensure that mentoring and coaching opportunities are available to assist those with leadership aspirations and those already holding leadership responsibilities (Ebbeck and Waniganayake,

2003). Mentoring is one way of nurturing novice early childhood practitioners to perceive themselves as leaders in the profession.

In conclusion, it is inappropriate to understand who becomes a leader and the nature of leadership on the basis of gender stereotypes because it would appear that both men and women are likely to engage in leadership approaches that are relevant for the nature of group members, goal and context. The effective leader is one who chooses the right approach for the people, task and context involved. Aspiring leaders and those thrust into positions of leadership need to examine the attitudes, attributes and behaviours that are more conducive to effective leadership and to the development of learning people and organisations. Effective leaders will create a culture where the values and traits that underpin able leadership are endorsed, be they masculine- or feminine-stereotyped values and traits. In this way, it will be possible to develop training options that optimise understanding of and engagement in a leadership paradigm suited to the early childhood profession, thus avoiding gender-stereotyped approaches to leadership. It is the engagement in effective practice that is important, not the gender stereotype. This includes developing assertive communication skills and a confident style for appropriate interaction with a range of people.

## WHO FOLLOWS THE EARLY CHILDHOOD LEADER?

Leadership is about motivating others to followship (Law and Glover, 2000)—that is, effective leaders motivate, inspire and persuade others to realise their goals. Inspiring followship in others is based upon an understanding of who the followers are, what their needs are and what resources they can offer the group.

The nature of the group for early childhood leaders, especially those in centres, is complex. Apart from the children, early childhood organisations are made up of heterogeneous groups of adults who range in age, experience, qualifications; come from diverse social, cultural and religious backgrounds; and have different agendas and goals. There are young and inexperienced staff who may be completing part-time training courses; there are older, experienced staff who are able to draw on their own life perspectives but who can be unaware or unaccepting of the value of the professional perspective; there are qualified staff, both young and mature, with different types and levels of qualifications, expertise and experience; and there are professionals from different disciplines and parents who often have different assumptions, expectations and goals from those of qualified early childhood staff. In addition, students who are undertaking supervised practical experience regularly work alongside all staff members.

Therefore, the early childhood leader needs to reflect upon the type or style of leadership best suited to such a complex group; the personal and professional attributes required for effective leadership of such a group; and the strategies that are appropriate for managing the range of situations that arise from the dynamics of such a group. The development of such expertise requires specialist training that includes consideration of the nature of the group to be led as well as other features of early childhood context. In addition, other features of the group point to the need for the development of leadership capacity in every early childhood practitioner.

The considerable social complexity of the group, where early childhood practitioners work directly with parents and staff as well as with children, requires sophisticated and complex communication skills that enhance interpersonal relationships and productive social interaction. Team-building and conflict-resolution skills are essential, as well as understanding the specific expectations of, and requirements for, working with children and parents as well as with staff.

Because early childhood practitioners work with the youngest and most vulnerable of children, they carry enormous responsibility for the quality of the children's daily lives. At the same time, practitioners exercise considerable autonomy over how they fulfil their responsibilities. Because leadership underpins the quality of practice as well as children's experience, they need to understand how to meet leadership challenges and opportunities in ways that best suit the group and situation. They need to develop a range of organisational and management skills as well as a high degree of technical expertise.

The work context is characterised for many by physical isolation from peers and colleagues—for example, there may be only two adults working with a group of fifteen children. This means that professional judgment about children, families and program management must be exercised in many cases quickly, confidently and independently. Decision-making and problem-solving skills are essential. In addition, many of the problems encountered in daily practice present an ethical or moral dilemma for practitioners. Familiarity with standards of practice such as The Code of Ethics developed by national early childhood professional bodies, including the National Association for the Education of Young Children and the Australian Early Childhood Association, can provide guidelines and direction for many of the difficult decisions that early childhood practitioners face in their daily work.

Early childhood practitioners generally have contact with a wide range of children and families. The diversity of the client group means that all early childhood practitioners, including but not only formal leaders, must be motivated to be well informed about current research in child development and learning and government initiatives, and continually upgrade their knowledge and skills in order to make sound professional judgments that will improve service provision. Understanding the role of research is essential for innovative decision-making by early childhood practitioners, not only formal leaders. Possessing appropriate knowledge and skills enhances their ability to effect change and allows practitioners to make services responsive to current family and community needs.

The stage of personal and professional development at which individuals may be given the opportunity to become a leader varies. Katz (1995a) and Vander Ven (1988) recognise that it is possible for individuals to undertake positions of leadership at a young age or with little experience, and while they are still novices and in survival mode. This approach also implies that many early childhood practitioners share and/or undertake some leadership responsibility as part of their normal workload and/or in preparation to take on more formal leadership responsibility.

## ARE THERE ANY ESSENTIAL CHARACTERISTICS OF EARLY CHILDHOOD LEADERS?

Although much of the literature disputes the validity of the attribute approach to identifying who will become an effective leader, numerous authors argue that leaders of integrity in education exhibit certain characteristics. These characteristics illustrate an attitude towards life and learning that appears to have much relevance for leaders in early childhood. Southworth (2000) considers leadership to be essentially about learning and Solly's findings (2003) indicate that early childhood practitioners identify lifelong learning as a personal strength of effective leaders.

These characteristics, which are related to lifelong learning and the notion of a learning person, are as follows:

- curiosity (an interest in learning);
- honesty (principles and actions being open to public scrutiny and a willingness to speak the truth);
- courtesy (treating others with respect and dignity);
- courage (a willingness to risk and dare and a willingness to make mistakes and learn from them); and
- compassion (creating trust, empathy, high expectations, hope and inspiration and providing opportunities for individual, group, personal and professional development).

Claxton (2002) regards the development of dispositions for lifelong learning as fundamental for leaders who are responsible for enabling, encouraging and evaluating other people. Because effective leaders need to be better learners so that they can help others to learn more effectively, they need to strengthen their own learning power by developing what Claxton refers to as the 'four Rs of learning power' (2002:17):

- *resilience* (being ready, willing and able to lock on to learning);
- *resourcefulness* (being ready, willing and able to learn in different ways);
- *reflectiveness* (being ready, willing and able to become more strategic about learning); and
- *reciprocity* (being ready, willing and able to learn alone and with others).

Bennis (1989:37) argues that 'leaders learn by leading and they learn best by leading in the face of obstacles'. Leaders today operate in challenging socio-political contexts that demand inquiry-based, flexible strategies in a culture of cooperation (Greany and Rodd, 2003). Solly (2003) suggests that if leadership is linked to learning, early childhood practitioners will learn from one another because the leader subtly nurtures collaborative learning by acting as a model, learner and facilitator.

These characteristics are evident in the following leadership characteristics provided by a range of early childhood professionals in qualitative research undertaken for this edition.

*Leaders show a passion for learning, inspiration for those around them and the ability to be humble, caring and build the self-esteem of the community . . .*

Early childhood adviser

*Leaders have passion, enthusiasm, compassion . . . they are flexible in that they are prepared to work across roles, everything from pulling up their sleeves at working bees, scrubbing the floor if necessary, contributing to classroom teaching, counselling parents and staff, advising on policy, etc., all with a sense of humour . . .*

Director, early learning centre

*Leaders are hard workers, dedicated and enthusiastic . . . they have ideas and opinions, they believe that sharing these helps . . .*

Teaching assistant

*Leaders want to make a difference and are able and prepared to take action . . .*

Head teacher

*Leaders have a personality that generates respect, they are respected into the position of leader . . .*

Pre-school development worker

*Leaders have a desire to know more . . . and pass their knowledge widely to others in the early childhood field and/or the public arena . . .*

Associate professor, early childhood

*Leaders are respectful, fair and motivational . . . knowledgeable, forward thinking, decision-makers and problem-solvers, understanding, responsible and reliable . . .*

Nursery officer

The above characteristics and dispositions are the foundations for building positive relationships with others and are essential in order to effect leadership. These characteristics and dispositions are more important for effective leadership than being popular with and liked by members of the group. Unfortunately, many inexperienced in leadership often assume that it is important for leaders to be liked, to know, to be right, to be in control, to be invulnerable and to be rational. However, these assumptions are inaccurate and counter-productive, resulting in leaders who feel inadequate to the task. The above characteristics and dispositions are more likely to produce confident, trust-worthy and courageous leaders who are admired, respected and consequently supported by their followers. Development of such characteristics and dispositions is essential for anyone wishing to work in early childhood services, but is pivotal for effective leadership of the diverse groups of parents and staff that characterise the early child-hood field.

## WHAT ARE THE FUNCTIONS OF A LEADER IN THE EARLY CHILDHOOD PROFESSION?

Effective leaders focus on two key elements: task performance and work relationships. These must operate simultaneously to effect efficient progress at work while building morale.

It is the leader's responsibility to ensure that the group moves towards its goal, which in early childhood is the provision of high-quality services. This element is referred to as task performance and includes any aspect of productivity, getting the job done and anything related to quality of work or performance in pursuit of the aims and goals of the organisation.

At the same time, the leader needs to ensure that the pursuit of task performance is not at the expense of work relationships—or, in other words, the quality of life at work. It is also the leader's responsibility to consider the welfare of the other people at work and to ensure that group morale is kept high through building and maintaining construc-tive interpersonal relationships.

Neugebauer (1985) differentiates four major leadership typologies that can be found in early childhood settings. Characteristics related to such a typology have been described by Jorde-Bloom, Sheerer and Britz (1991). The styles outlined vary in terms of the degree of emphasis placed upon achieving the task or results and promoting relationships or morale. Neugebauer's styles of leadership are summarised below:

- The *Task Master* places heavy emphasis on the task or results and little emphasis on relationships or morale.
- The *Comrade* places heavy emphasis on relationships and morale but little emphasis on the task or results.
- The *Motivator* places strong emphasis on both the task and relationships.

- The *Unleader* places little emphasis on either results or relationships.

Neugebauer suggests that the situational context of leadership is less important than the style of leadership in early childhood settings. He cites studies of administration which indicate that the style of leadership in care and early education settings is related to teaching style, the tone of interpersonal relationships and staff involvement in decision-making. The Motivator is therefore the style of leadership thought to be the key to successful leadership in early childhood settings.

The Motivator includes the following characteristics:

- warmth and flexibility;
- sensitivity, creativity and encouragement;
- confidence in the abilities of the staff and their commitment to hard work;
- a supportive and non-judgmental approach;
- open, two-way communication channels;
- involvement and participation of staff in goal-setting and other important tasks;
- confident decision-making and problem-solving;
- frequent feedback;
- encouragement of self-evaluation of staff performance; and
- risk-taking.

The combination of such characteristics enables the early childhood leader to demonstrate concern for the personal and professional needs of the staff as well as confidence in their ability and responsibility. In this way, both the task (providing a high-quality program) and relationships (a harmonious work environment and high morale) can be accomplished.

Neugebauer suggests that, of the remaining three styles, only the authoritarian Task Master is relevant to leadership in early childhood settings. However, while this approach ensures that goals are set and an appropriate program is implemented, a number of disadvantages are inherent in this style of leadership: the staff may not agree with the leader's goals and overtly or covertly refuse to implement them; the lack of respect for staff ability to contribute to the decision-making can also result in frustration and hostility, which ultimately will diminish staff motivation to work hard.

Although it is useful to categorise leadership styles in order to clarify dimensions of leadership, it is not as helpful to evaluate one or other style as the 'best' for specific contexts. It must be recognised that leadership styles are not static and, despite Neugebauer's claim that situational leadership is less relevant for early childhood settings, there are many situations where one particular leadership style is more effective than another. An effective leader may be a person 'who knows when to act quickly and when to think and act slowly' (adapted from Sternberg, quoted in Claxton, 2002:55).

For example, if a setting has experienced a period of chronic change, staff morale might be low. A sensitive leader will emphasise relationships and work on building up group morale and staff self-esteem—that is, they will employ the Comrade style, rather than focusing heavily on the job at hand. Another setting might have a leader experiencing stress and 'burnout', who withdraws from active participation in the setting, becoming an Unleader. Staff may then decide to do what they like in the absence of direction from the leader. A new leader coming into this situation may well need to employ a Task Master style to ensure that goals are set and the quality of the service is improved. There is even a scenario where the Unleader style could be the most effective. This might be where the staff are experienced, highly self-motivated, address problems as they arise and have worked well together as a team. Given that the staff are productive and have good working relationships, the leader might decide to decrease their input and let things run by themselves for a while.

In many ways, it is not the style of leadership that the leader believes they are using but rather how the style is perceived and experienced by the group that matters. If the leader contends that their style is that of the Motivator but the staff experience the style as that of the Task Master, then the leader is really using the authoritarian Task Master style. The differences between the styles can be small, and can be a result of how the leader communicates with and relates to the staff. It is the responsibility of leaders to improve their social interaction with staff and parents. The communication style used can determine the tone and quality of interpersonal relationships and social interaction. The communication skills that are considered to be most effective for early childhood leaders to achieve the task while simultaneously promoting relationships are described later in Chapters 4 and 5.

## WHO IS A LEADER IN THE EARLY CHILDHOOD PROFESSION?

The early childhood profession is perhaps unique in terms of its access to designated positions of leadership that can be taken up, if in name only, by practitioners from the earliest stage of entering the field.

*Anyone can become a leader if they possess an interest in the area . . .*
**Nursery officer**

*Who becomes a leader varies hugely . . . leaders can be room supervisors or policy-makers but whoever they are they usually are committed to moving practice on . . .*
**Deputy supervisor**

*The routes into leadership are not planned . . .*
**Early childhood adviser**

*Leadership is not only present in positions of seniority . . .*
**Nursery officer**

It appears that the early childhood practitioners who become leaders are those who find meaning and significance in even the minutiae of their day-to-day work.

Qualified early childhood teachers—called directors, managers or coordinators—traditionally have been appointed as the formal leader of a range of early childhood settings and services, even though their teacher training contained little emphasis on knowledge about and skills for working with adults. Their responsibilities include the provision of an educational curriculum for young children, support to parents, financial administration, record-keeping, compliance with regulatory requirements, supervision and coordination of other professionals and paraprofessionals and evaluation.

However, as Jorde-Bloom's (2003) findings reveal, teaching experience (although valuable) does not adequately prepare a person for formal leadership, management and administrative roles. In some countries, owners of private provision who may hold no or only basic early childhood or relevant qualifications are the official leaders. One adviser observed:

*leadership in early childhood is generally weak . . . leaders are often young, bound by a fairly traditional vision . . . we need more leaders in their enchanted years . . .*

As increasingly diverse services for young children and their families are required, and as more multi-disciplinary, inter-agency settings are established, the mantle of official leadership will be worn by increasingly diverse individuals—for example, head teachers, directors, managers, teachers, nursery officers and playworkers.

Although these leaders are largely autonomous, they are accountable for the quality of policy and practice to a range of bodies, such as a committee of management, a governing body or a partnership auspiced by a local authority, and ultimately to the government departments which fund early childhood services. Because each early childhood service and setting is unique, who becomes a leader will depend on the type of structures that are in place (Ebbeck and Waniganayake, 2003). However, it is evident that in settings where there are clearly defined purposes, procedures, roles and responsibilities and clearly delineated lines of communication and decision-making, leadership can be distributed among a number of practitioners. Solly (2003) describes a number of early excellence centres in England where a range of early years staff undertook some and differing leadership responsibilities. In fact, official leaders often gain acceptance as leaders when they are perceived as distributing or delegating leadership responsibilities appropriately to staff.

A collaborative or collegiate approach to leadership appears to satisfy the need for a different type of leader in early childhood—one who is guided more by moral, rational and socio-emotional concerns than structural and systemic issues (Solly, 2003). Waniganayake et al. (2000) suggest that opportunities for early childhood practitioners to become leaders are restricted where power for real decision-making is retained by formal and hierarchical leaders. Rosemary et al. (1998) suggest that the way to help more practitioners to become leaders is to share tasks and distribute more opportunities to lead. Such opportunities to practise as a leader can help practitioners make a smoother transition to appointment as a formal leader.

Appointment or promotion to leadership in early childhood settings still appears to be based upon the personal qualities and style that an individual brings to a position, exemplary practice with children or longevity at a setting (Jorde-Bloom and Sheerer, 1992). While such appointment practices may have been workable in settings where there were only a small number of adults working together, the leadership demands of larger play, childcare and educational settings now call for more sophisticated knowledge and skills. Depending on the numbers and ages of the children using a particular service, the numbers of staff employed can be as high as fourteen or more. Quite apart from the demands of providing leadership for families, such a large and usually heterogeneous group of staff calls for a more informed and skilled approach to centre and staff management. It is essential that early childhood settings avoid the chaos and disruption to communication, decision-making and routines that can result from the appointment or promotion of an inappropriate leader.

There are few professions today that have not recognised the advantages in productivity and relationships from management and leadership training for suitable staff. The early childhood field recognises that increased professionalism and credibility in the community may be related to trained leadership at a centre level (Jorde-Bloom, 1997; 2003). However, the trend is still towards people being appointed to positions of leadership on the basis of their personal attributes, how well they work with children or how long they have worked in the field rather than on the basis of formal training in or specialised expertise in leadership (Jorde-Bloom, 2003). Jorde-Bloom (2003) argues that a systematic and comprehensive plan for leadership succession should be put in place in all settings. The consistent provision of high-quality services through expert leadership will lay the foundation for early childhood staff being acknowledged by the community as having the ability to make leadership contributions to the wider society.

## WHO CAN BECOME A LEADER IN THE EARLY CHILDHOOD PROFESSION?

One of the difficulties faced by the early childhood profession is identifying those individuals who, given opportunities for personal and professional career development, might emerge as future leaders. Because the field is dominated by women who (compared with men) place different emphases on family and career at different stages in their lives, it is not easy to assess who will exhibit leadership potential and the extent to which this potential will be developed as part of long-term career aspirations.

*Most staff in early childhood are women. For various reasons historically they have not been good at projecting themselves and taking leadership roles outside their settings . . .*

**Early years team leader**

The fact that women who enter the profession are likely to experience training and career interruptions due to time taken to establish and nurture a family means that there are structural obstacles to developing and retaining a professional workforce in the early childhood field. Many women will require access to flexible training programs and a career structure that can cope with them moving in and out of the system according to family commitments.

It is obvious that, for a large proportion of personnel in this field, a considerable number of years of full- and part-time work will be required to accumulate the knowledge, skills and experience which underpin leadership capabilities and contribute to increased professionalism.

*To become a leader you need expertise—for example, qualifications, skills and experience plus ideas and forward thinking . . .*

**Nursery officer**

*To become a leader you must have experience, not necessarily as a teacher, qualifications, a personality that gains respect and a proven track record . . .*

**Manager, childcare centre**

*Experience counts a lot in terms of who becomes a leader . . . there is an expectation that you need to pay your dues in order to maintain your credibility . . .*

**Early childhood lecturer**

All workers who enter the early childhood field need to be imbued with the belief that personal potential and aspiration for professional growth and leadership can be nurtured throughout their career even if it is disrupted.

*It also comes from the individual themselves, you may be initially reluctant to take on a position of leadership but you get drawn into the role and it becomes part of how you see yourself . . .*

**Early childhood lecturer**

Ordinary life experience as an adult can provide opportunities to refine the communication and interpersonal skills which are prerequisites for leadership and broaden one's understanding and perspective on life. This can help build a basis from which specific training in leadership can be undertaken.

*Individuals in more senior positions have a 'feel' for who will make a good leader and foster their leadership development by giving them more responsibility . . .*

**Early childhood lecturer**

In a study of the impact of leadership training, Bella and Jorde-Bloom (2003) highlight the power of leadership training in the early childhood field in terms of improved role perceptions and job performance, increased feelings of self-efficacy and enhanced ability to effect change.

Debate continues about the origins of leadership—that is, can people learn and be trained to be successful leaders, or is leadership dependent upon characteristics that are largely inherited? Three main schools of thought have emerged. First, there is the trait approach—do leaders possess certain traits that differentiate them from their followers? Are leaders born or are they made? Second, some advocate the behavioural approach—do leaders engage in certain behaviour or possess certain styles that influence other people? Third, in the situational approach, the situation and/or the structure of the task are considered to be influential in determining which style of leadership to use.

It is generally accepted that, although certain inherited personal attributes may be associated with leadership, specific leadership skills can be learned. In addition, it seems that leadership potential can emerge at any time during one's life. Therefore, all people are considered to be capable of leading at different times and in different situations. A person can be a leader in relation to a specific group or a specific task. The qualities, characteristics and skills required in a leader appear to be largely determined by the demands of the situation in which the person is to function as a leader. These include the structure of the task and the characteristics of the people in the group. The situational nature of leadership means that there is no exclusive list of personal attributes or styles that are associated with effective leadership. However, a thorough understanding of the needs of the situation, which includes the task and the people, will enable an effective leader to develop a repertoire of characteristics and skills that is essential for meeting the organisation's goals. Awareness of the needs, capabilities and interests of the group members will assist in the selection of the style of leadership to which the group will be receptive.

Situational leadership demands that leaders understand the requirements of the group members and the task in order to match relevant attributes and skills to the situation.

Waniganayake (in Waniganayake et al., 2000) proposes a model of distributive leadership where knowledge is the central focus of organisational learning. She suggests that knowledge provides the foundation for an early childhood practitioner's capacity to be a leader. Knowledge refers to both pedagogical and practical understanding, and this can be dispersed within early childhood organisations and fit with the various specialisations that may exist in settings. A number of authors have suggested different aspects of leadership specialisation. For example, Bowman and Kagan (1997) propose that specialised leadership opportunities exist in early childhood settings in relation to pedagogical, administrative, advocacy, community, conceptual and career development leadership. Schwahn, Spady and William (1998) suggest that educational leaders can develop specialised expertise in authentic, visionary, cultural and quality domains.

Such perspectives support the notion that leadership is a multifaceted, collaborative endeavour undertaken by effective teams which operate in an inclusive culture of learning and shared knowledge.

## WHAT IS THE RELATIONSHIP BETWEEN LEADERSHIP AND PROFESSIONAL CAREER DEVELOPMENT?

Analysing the stages of professional and career development for early childhood practitioners provides insight into the types of experience gained over time and the limitations that may constrain effective leadership if early childhood practitioners are appointed to positions of leadership before they are, in professional terms, developmentally ready and capable. Bella and Jorde-Bloom's research (2003) reveals that almost 75 per cent of their sample of early childhood directors reported that they were not prepared, or only somewhat prepared, for their formal leadership role. Yet strong leadership is necessary to ensure quality services. It is therefore essential that, in a profession where people can step into a leadership role at any stage in their career, appropriate professional support related to different stages of career development is available.

Katz (1995a) outlines four developmental stages for early childhood professionals:

1 *survival*—where the main concern literally is surviving and getting through the day in one piece;
2 *consolidation*—where the practitioner is ready to build on the experience gained in the first stage;
3 *renewal*—where the practitioner is very familiar and competent in the task of direct work with children and begins to look for new challenges and ways of extending expertise; and
4 *maturity*—where activities and interests are directed towards a meaningful search for professional insight, perspective and realism.

In an early model, Vander Ven (1988) proposed five stages of personal and professional development in early childhood careers that focused upon levels of cognitive understanding regarding the complexity of the practitioner's roles and the types of responsibilities associated with these roles:

1 *novice*—practitioners who function at non-professional (as distinct from unprofessional) levels, usually in direct care functions;
2 *initial*—practitioners in direct care and educational roles under close supervision by a senior staff member;
3 *informed*—practitioners who have completed formal training and who have made a strong career commitment to the early childhood field;
4 *complex*—experienced practitioners who have the option of following a career path that focuses on expert direct practice or leadership functions; and
5 *influential*—practitioners who, as a result of long experience in a range of roles and functions, hold composite, high-level, professional leadership roles.

Subsequently, Vander Ven (1991) modified this into the following three-stage model:

1 *direct care: novice*—the usually non-professional, affective and professionally immature orientation of young and inexperienced practitioners;
2 *direct care: advanced*—practitioners who are more able to demonstrate logical and rational behaviour, make choices and predict and explain outcomes of their behaviour. These practitioners have out-

grown Katz's stages of survival and consolidation and are moving into the renewal stage;

3 *indirect care*—practitioners who have moved beyond working directly with children and parents and possess the understanding and expertise to take up professional leadership roles and responsibilities.

Leadership potential is more likely to emerge in practitioners who are in Katz's stage 3—renewal or Vander Ven's stage 2—direct care advanced, and to be well developed in Katz's stage 4—maturity or Vander Ven's stage 3—indirect care. Appropriate professional support and socialisation—for example, through training, job shadowing (a work-based learning experience where practitioners gain insight into particular roles through following, observing and asking questions of an experienced colleague during a typical day), mentoring and coaching—needs to be available to support practitioners who are showing leadership aspirations and capacity in these stages of professional development.

## BRINGING IT TOGETHER

The continued professionalisation of the early childhood field has been linked to regular monitoring and evaluation—for example, through processes of quality assurance, accreditation or inspection, where early childhood services aim to achieve quality standards above minimum statutory or licensing requirements. These processes are likely to result in increased leadership responsibility for many early childhood practitioners, with improved quality resulting from on-the-job training and supervision of staff who may have had limited experience and formal education and training. This expanded responsibility, together with the opportunity to undertake leadership roles from the beginning of one's career in early childhood, means that all students and existing staff should be encouraged to acquire an understanding of the essentials of leadership in the field. The factors outlined above point to the need for leadership skills to be considered just as essential to the role of the early childhood practitioner as the fundamental skills of child observation, curriculum design and implementation and program administration.

# CHAPTER THREE
## THE PERSONAL QUALITIES OF EARLY CHILDHOOD LEADERS

*A caring and respecting human being who is emotionally intelligent . . .*
**Early years adviser**

**THIS CHAPTER EXPLORES**
- **the personal qualities of early childhood leaders**
- **typologies of leadership for early childhood practitioners**

The early childhood profession has been described as a 'pink ghetto' (Loane, 1997) because women dominate it. Traditional female stereotypes, the ideology of motherhood and the caretaking paradigm have contributed to distorted public and self-perceptions and assumptions about the capacity of early childhood practitioners to assume and display leadership. Solly (2003) describes the early years context as primarily female, socially and culturally diverse, multi-professional, varying in qualifications, experience, conditions of service and career structures. In addition, it is a field that is subject to the demands of constant change, a multitude of initiatives and pressure for innovation. To be a successful leader in such a complex context requires particular personal qualities and attributes.

Wonacott (2001) points out that transformational leadership, which is at present highly valued in educational settings, is based on stereotypically female traits such as communication, collaboration, consensus, nurturing and inclusion. Leadership is often described in terms of the relationships built up by the leader with team members. The quality of relationships tends to be evaluated in terms of attributes such as empathy, warmth, respect and genuineness—all of which are associated more with the feminine stereotype. Although men and women who are leaders display both masculine and feminine traits and behaviours, the traditional features of the female approach to leadership is argued to be more appropriate and successful in today's world generally, and in early childhood settings specifically. Consequently, effective leaders need to acquire and exhibit personal qualities that will achieve cooperation from and active participation by others.

Becoming a leader is much more than simply accepting a particular role or position. It is about personal values, beliefs and qualities. Maxwell (1999:1) writes: 'Leaders are effective because of who they are on the inside—in the qualities that make them up as people.' Leaders need self-awareness—that is, they need to understand their personal strengths and weaknesses. Hartle and Thomas (2003) argue that, although it is difficult to predict the future shape of specific leadership roles and appropriate profiles, one step in a six-step approach to leadership talent development is to define the leadership markers required and encourage personal growth in staff.

The key personal aptitudes of leaders identified by the early childhood practitioners who participated in the qualitative research for this edition were consistent with those associated with transformational leadership and included understanding, caring and respect for others, empathic, supportive and considerate, enthusiastic and approachable, open minded, flexible and fair.

## TYPOLOGIES OF LEADERSHIP FOR EARLY CHILDHOOD PRACTITIONERS

The identification of some of the characteristics, skills, functions and responsibilities of leaders is an attempt to assist leadership development. However, leadership is essentially a holistic concept in which the whole is more than the sum of the parts. Given that leadership is a complex construct and sometimes difficult to identify in early childhood settings, a typology of leadership for early childhood practitioners may help to simplify some of the factors that underpin effective leadership in these settings.

A typology is a means of, or framework for, classifying selected factors or features. It can be used as a summary or protocol for understanding the structure of a phenomenon. While it can be argued that a typology oversimplifies what may be a very complex concept, it can be helpful for understanding essential components, especially where it is believed that certain parts may be acquired through training. In relation to leadership, a number of inventories, profiles or typologies have been developed which attempt to describe leadership. They focus on different conceptions of leadership, but few have attempted to relate such profiles to a specific context. It is recognised that the context of leadership, including the nature of the group and the organisational setting, is a determining factor in effective leadership.

One advantage of a typology of leadership is that aspiring and formal leaders are alerted to significant features of effective leadership, thus avoiding a trial-and-error approach to learning how to be an effective leader. Given that few early childhood practitioners have access to specific training before taking up leadership responsibilities or while in the position, the typology may be an effective instrument for signalling important features, developing an understanding of what constitutes leadership in early childhood and enhancing self-perception as a leader.

## TYPOLOGY OF AN EARLY CHILDHOOD LEADER

A typology of leadership was developed from research undertaken with early childhood practitioners in Britain (Rodd, 1997) and Australia (Rodd, 1996) (see Table 3.1). Therefore, it is applicable specifically to early childhood practitioners and settings. However, it is important to recognise that leaders cannot always achieve the results they and the team want, and the desired results are seldom attributable to one person alone, as leadership in this context tends to be a collaborative and shared endeavour.

The typology includes three different aspects that were identified from survey and interview information in the research. The groupings of personal characteristics reflect understanding at different stages of professional development.

The grouping which describes a set of nurturing characteristics as essential for leadership tended to be identified by those with under three years' experience in early childhood—that is, the novices in the profession. For those with longer experience and in leadership positions, such characteristics were perceived as 'givens'—that is, all people working with young children and their families would be expected to display such characteristics. Being nurturing is considered to be a necessary but not sufficient characteristic of a leader. However, a nurturing approach to staff and adults associated with the setting was considered to be important in an early childhood leader's general approach.

The grouping of personal characteristics which reflect the rational, analytic use of a knowledge base tended to be identified by those with between three and ten years' experience, and those who were more informed about the complexity of the profession. Many of the respondents in this group were in fact designated leaders who were very concerned about quality improvement in their own setting.

The last grouping of personal characteristics, where vision, professional confidence and empowerment were perceived to be essential for effective leadership, reflected the knowledge and experience of those who had previous leadership experience and training and who took a broader perspective on leadership. These respondents were at more advanced stages of professional development, and they displayed an understanding of the complexity of their roles and responsibilities both within the setting and also within the wider community.

In relation to professional skills, five major generic areas were identified, with none taking priority over the others. The acquisition and display of technical competence were perceived as basic but essential because these were considered to be the vehicles of empowerment for staff as well as the organisation. General administrative ability was considered to be crucial, as was financial management because the viability and smooth operation of the centre were believed to hinge on these two functions. However, it was acknowledged that it was easy to be dominated by these two areas and to accept that effective leadership was simply a result of successful management of centre operations and the budget.

## KEY SKILLS FOR EFFECTIVE LEADERS

Effective leadership in early childhood involves two other key skills from which power and influence in the centre were derived. Effective communication, the ability to 'synthesise complex information and communicate that information cogently and succinctly to a variety of different audiences' (Jorde-Bloom, 1997:13) is a hallmark of an

**Table 3.1  Rodd's typology of an early childhood leader**

| Stage of professional development | Personal characteristics | Professional skills | Roles and responsibilities |
|---|---|---|---|
| Direct care: novice | Kind, warm, friendly<br><br>Nurturing, sympathetic<br><br>Patient | Technical competence as an early childhood practitioner to act as a model, guide, mentor | To deliver and be accountable for a quality service<br><br>To develop and articulate a philosophy, values and vision |
| Direct care: advanced | Self-aware<br><br>Knowledgeable<br><br>Rational, logical, analytical<br><br>Professional, professionally confident | General administration<br><br>Financial management<br><br>Effective communication<br><br>Human resource management | To engage in a collaborative and partnership approach to leadership<br><br>To engage in ongoing professional development and to encourage it in all staff |
| Indirect care | Visionary<br><br>Mentor, guide, empowering<br><br>Assertive, proactive<br><br>Goal-oriented | | To be sensitive and responsive to the need for change and lead change effectively<br><br>To act as an advocate for children, parents, carers, staff, the profession and general community |

effective leader. In addition, human resource management—that is, effective utilisation of the talents, skills, interests and abilities of the group by motivating, inspiring and empowering group members to pursue common goals—illustrates the more feminine approach to leadership by early childhood practitioners. The multifaceted nature of leadership is evident in the generic skills included in the typology.

While the roles and responsibilities of leaders in individual early childhood settings may vary considerably, a set of generic roles and responsibilities for leaders were identified. Again, no one role or responsibility was considered to take priority. Recognition of the interrelatedness of roles and responsibilities at the broader level characterised leadership. The delivery of a quality service was perceived as an obvious broad responsibility. The ability to develop and articulate a vision and to engage in a collaborative and partnership style of leadership were considered to be the means for achieving this broad responsibility. In addition, encouraging all staff to participate, and engaging oneself, in ongoing professional development was thought to be part of the empowerment process. Responsiveness to the need for change was considered to be a means not only for ensuring the survival of early childhood services, but also for the pursuit of quality. Finally, advocacy was recognised as a responsibility that leaders needed to fulfil, but it was thought that this would increase and improve as leaders became more self-assured and confident overall.

## PEDAGOGICAL EFFECTIVENESS IN EARLY LEARNING

The Department for Education and Skills in England commissioned the 'Study of Pedagogical Effectiveness in Early Learning' (Moyles, Musgrove and Adams, 2002), which concentrated on identifying attributes of effectiveness of early childhood practitioners. The study aimed to help practitioners develop the effectiveness of their practice, and thus benefit children and families. Key statements were offered regarding effective practice in:

- teaching and learning interactions;
- teaching and learning context;
- planning, assessment and evaluation;
- value and entitlement of children;
- teaching and learning practices;
- value and belief in the importance of one's own role;
- knowledge and understanding;

- reflection and thoughtfulness; and
- personal qualities.

Of particular interest for leadership in early childhood are the key statements regarding the personal qualities of effective early childhood practitioners. These include:

- self-motivation and the ability to motivate others;
- the ability to be reflective, questioning, analytical, committed to learning and professional development, welcome and initiate constructive critical engagement with peers and others;
- being confident and secure in the role of teacher;
- an informed interest in young children and their development, and caring about how children think, learn and behave;
- high expectations of self and staff;
- being positive and realistic about what can be achieved, and having positive attitudes and approaches to children and adults;
- friendly, amenable, open and welcoming relationships;
- a sense of humour, fun and enjoyment, and enthusiasm;
- a caring, nurturing, calm and sensitive approach;
- being intuitive, receptive, empathetic, responsive and able to 'tune in' to children;
- open-mindedness, adaptability and flexibility with children and adults;
- vision, innovation and imagination;
- having flair and bringing creative thinking to the professional role;
- being able to take initiative and use common sense;
- being organised and able to maintain an organised environment;
- fairness and consistency in handling children and adults;
- having patience and tolerance, but also the ability to set clear parameters;
- being articulate and an able communicator who understands the effects of body language and posture on others;
- having skills in being both an independent and collaborative worker;
- being reliable and emotionally stable in the working environment.

These are broad, overarching statements that are often difficult to evaluate. However, they are useful in helping early childhood practitioners consider the types of skills, characteristics and attributes that leaders may possess.

## PERSONAL STRENGTHS OF EARLY CHILDHOOD LEADERS

Solly's (2003) research into the personal strengths of early childhood leaders, although not a typology, showed that attributes such as enthusiasm, passion, inspiration and advocacy were rated as the greatest strengths. Being a lifelong learner and being part of a team ethos were also important. Trust and respectful relationships and clear and effective communication based on entitlement, shared philosophy and vision were essential.

## ADMINISTRATION, MANAGEMENT AND LEADERSHIP

Another recent typology developed by Ebbeck and Waniganayake (2003:32) integrates the relationships across dispositions, skills, roles and responsibilities of administration, management and leadership (see Table 3.2). This typology assists early childhood practitioners to appreciate the range of roles, responsibilities, skills and dispositions that they may need to develop in order to work towards becoming an effective administrator, manager and leader.

**Table 3.2  Ebbeck and Waniganayake's typology of administration, management and leadership**

|  | Administration | Management | Leadership |
|---|---|---|---|
| **Roles and responsibilities** | Maintain day-to-day tasks of data-collection | Monitor quality assessment and improvement | Facilitate staff development and training |
| These are expected behaviours of a particular job or position, and may be specified in one's duty statement or job description | Set up a system of records and files<br><br>Keep track of correspondence and financial dealings | Analyse the needs of children, families and staff every day<br><br>Oversee day-to-day financial upkeep | Analyse the needs of children, families and staff from a long-term perspective<br><br>Design and direct policy development |
| **Skills** | These are technicalities or | These are interactive skills | Leadership skills relate to macro-level |

**Table 3.2** *(continued)*

|  | Administration | Management | Leadership |
|---|---|---|---|
| **Skills** *(cont.)* | | | |
| Learnt competencies acquired through training and experience, necessary to work as administrators, managers and leaders | basic foundation competencies necessary for the organisation to function:<br>• Awareness of official guidelines and legal requirements<br>• Organisational skills such as documentation, correspondence and filing<br>• Follows policies and procedures precisely | necessary for maintaining a centre, and are concerned with immediate and short-term issues, mainly:<br>• Communication skills<br>• Staff supervision and support<br>• Marketing and promotion<br>• Assessment and evaluation of programs, services and staff | engagements, both inside and outside the centre, and are primarily concerned with the future:<br>• Delegation<br>• Research skills<br>• Advocacy and lobbying<br>• Liaison and networking<br>• Policy formulation and analysis<br>• Critical thinking |
| **Dispositions**<br><br>Personal attributes or qualities of early childhood practitioners that can affect their work | Organised: approaches work systematically<br><br>Eager to obtain sound information<br><br>Demanding in searching for accuracy<br><br>Follows set policies and protocols<br><br>Comfortable with use of technology | Understands the importance of accountability requirements<br><br>Enjoys working with staff and families<br><br>Concerned with risk assessment<br><br>Driven by efficiency and productivity<br><br>Entrepreneurial | Enjoys working with others, both within the centre and outside<br><br>Passionate about speaking out for children and families<br><br>Enjoys challenges<br><br>Visionary<br><br>Empowering<br><br>Articulate<br><br>Adaptable |

## EFFECTIVE LEADERSHIP AND MANAGEMENT EVALUATION SCHEME (EARLY YEARS)

The Effective Leadership and Management Evaluation Scheme (Early Years) was developed by Moyles and Yates (2004) together with a range of consultants, in recognition of the increasingly complex roles faced by leaders and managers in early childhood settings. It aims to provide guidance and support to practitioners in a managerial role, and enables them to evaluate their own skills and knowledge. This typology of skills and attributes identifies those which are essential and desirable in four broad areas: leadership skills; management skills; professional skills; and personal characteristics. The typology also offers four levels of operation, similar to stages of professional development: intuitive and pragmatic; reasoned and articulate; involved and collaborative; and reflective and philosophic (see Table 3.3).

Each of the skills and attributes below has been defined more precisely so that managers and leaders can evaluate themselves in order

**Table 3.3  A summary of Moyles and Yates' (2004) Effective Leadership and Management Evaluation Scheme**

| Leadership skills | Management skills | Professional skills | Personal characteristics |
|---|---|---|---|
| Visionary | Ensure effective human resource management | Encourage the formalisation of qualifications | Have knowledge and a natural enthusiasm for children, teaching and learning |
| Responsible | | | |
| Accountable | Ensure effective curriculum management | Be an effective problem-solver | |
| Charismatic | | | Have a strong commitment to the pre-school-to-school transition of the child |
| | | Understand the importance of shared values | |
| Integrity | Ensure effective interaction, involvement and intervention at micro (setting) meso (local) and macro (national) levels | | |
| Engage and involve others in ideas, innovations, goals and visions | | Have effective time-management skills | Have an attraction to the profession for intrinsic rather than extrinsic reasons |
| Command and offer respect | | Have good communication and discourse skills | |

**Table 3.3** *(continued)*

| Leadership skills | Management skills | Professional skills | Personal characteristics |
|---|---|---|---|
| Motivate staff | Ensure that all relevant people are empowered | Have good diplomatic and conflict resolution skills | Have status and rank as a culture-setter |
| Flexibility | | | |
| Knowledgeable | Ensure effective decision-making | Understand how to manage change | Have a continued commitment to and vested interest in onging child development |
| | Ensure effective planning and strategy-making | | |
| | Ensure effective implementation and monitoring of ideas | | Have a strong sense of ambition and a strong desire for improvement |
| | Ensure effective operation of basic procedures | | Have an approach advocating creative intelligence |
| | Ensure effective physical resource management | | Have an approach advocating emotional intelligence |
| | | | Have infectious self-awareness |
| | | | Have a good sense of humour and understand the importance of fun and play |

*Source:* Summarised with permission from Prof. J. Moyles

to work out where problems and weaknesses lie, which professional areas need developing and which areas are easy and enjoyable.

The research into the qualities of effective leaders in early childhood, although packaged differently in the different typologies, reveals many similarities and common ground in the qualities, skills, knowledge and capabilities considered to be associated with leadership. It is important not to interpret the lists as prescriptive. Their usefulness lies in the fact that they act as markers and points for reflection about how things are and what changes may be needed to enhance or improve the situation. The typologies reveal that effective leaders appear to demonstrate a capacity for:

- *emotional intelligence*—the ability to identify and respond sensitively to one's own and others' feelings (Goleman, 1996);
- *critical thinking*—the ability to influence others through logical and analytical reasoning);
- *directional clarity*—the ability to set, articulate and motivate people to commit to clear goals;
- *creative intelligence*—the ability to solve problems by integrating and applying knowledge, understanding and skills;
- *people enablement*—the ability to empower people by offering support and mentoring;
- *reciprocal communication*—the ability to listen empathetically and to network with others;
- *change orchestration*—the ability to lead change proactively and constructively;
- *perseverance*—the capacity to behave assertively, confidently and professionally.

The various typologies attempt to build a picture of leadership made up of qualities, skills, roles and responsibilities that are generic for early childhood leaders. However, it must be remembered that typologies tend to simplify what is a very complex and holistic responsibility. It is important for members of the profession to decide whether these are indeed requisite and/or desirable features for leaders. When assessing personal leadership potential or that of others, it may be helpful to check which of these features are either emerging or developed and whether or not specific features can be learned. The dimensions shown in Table 3.4 are helpful in determining the quality of leadership in early childhood settings.

**Table 3.4 Dimensions for determining leadership quality in an early learning setting**

| | |
|---|---|
| Shared goals | ('We know where we're going.') |
| Mutual respect | ('Everyone has something to offer.') |
| Lifelong learning | ('Learning is for everyone.') |
| Collegiality | ('We're in this together.') |
| Continuous improvement | ('We can get better.') |
| Responsibility for success | ('Together we can succeed.') |
| Risk-taking | ('We learn by trying something new.') |
| Support | ('There is always someone there to support me.') |
| Openness | ('We can discuss our differences.') |
| Celebration and humour | ('We feel good about ourselves and what we have achieved.') |

York-Barr and Duke (2004) undertook a meta-analysis of existing empirical research and literature related to teacher leadership. Although their analyses focus on teacher leadership, the information about who teacher leaders are is also relevant for early childhood practitioners. They bring together research evidence that describes key characteristics of leaders and argue that leaders possess qualities which enable them to:

- build trust and rapport, establish solid relationships and influence culture through relationships, working collaboratively;
- support colleagues and promote growth among colleagues;
- communicate, and especially listen effectively;
- handle conflict, negotiate and mediate;
- deal with group processes;
- assess, interpret and prioritise needs and concerns; and
- understand the big picture and envision the impact of decisions.

Leaders are also effective practitioners because they generally have:

- significant experience in their fields;
- extensive knowledge of learning and teaching;
- a clearly developed personal philosophy of education;
- individual responsibility for actions;
- the respect of colleagues;
- sensitivity and receptivity to the thoughts and feelings of others;
- cognitive and affective flexibility; and

- administrative and managerial skills that help them to manage the workload.

## BRINGING IT TOGETHER

Where such features can be learned or developed, it is important for individuals to gain access to professional training or development opportunities to practise, refine and extend them. In many ways, leadership is similar to the concept of quality. Our definition and understanding evolves as we learn more about the needs of those associated with early childhood settings. For all early childhood practitioners, leadership is about improving those qualities and skills that are related to quality in the profession.

# CHAPTER FOUR

## COMMUNICATION SKILLS: MEETING OTHERS' NEEDS

*People skills especially in communication are required to be an effective leader . . .*

Deputy head, early childhood centre

**THIS CHAPTER EXPLORES**
- **emotional intelligence and leadership**
- **skills for meeting others' needs**
- **sending accurate and unambiguous messages**
- **overcoming physical and psychological barriers**
- **listening for understanding**
- **appropriate responding**
- **managing feelings**

Human beings are social beings and as such have a need to belong and to find a place in the group (Adler, 1958). People—both adults and children—are motivated to behave in ways which help them achieve a sense of significance in the groups in which they live. When people believe that they belong, they also feel connected, capable and competent, willing to contribute to meet the needs of the group. Leadership plays an important role in determining and understanding human behaviour in groups. It is the leader who determines the psychological climate of the group and motivates individual members' level of performance in the achievement of the group's goals. Goleman (1996:148) argues that leading and 'managing with heart'—that is, the use of emotional intelligence—is essential for organisational survival and efficiency. For Goleman, leadership is the ability to use people skills in order to motivate colleagues to collaborate so that they can achieve a common goal.

Successful leadership in the early childhood field is a matter of communication more than anything else. Early childhood services are specifically 'people' services, where communication and interpersonal relationships are the building blocks on which other activities, such as developmental programs and curricula, are based (Rodd, 1989). Positive human relationships between adults and children and between adults themselves are regarded as both the basis of the service and an outcome of the service. Better relationships are considered to develop out of feelings of safety, security and trust and are characterised by openness and sharing between people. These qualities are created and maintained by the type of interaction that takes place between people (Johnson, 1996).

Leadership in the early childhood field is more than the style used, the personal attributes and psychological make-up of the individual in charge, the conditions where and the settings in which leadership emerges. It is about how communication skills, the early childhood professional's tools of trade, are used as a means of building more satisfying relationships. Such relationships contribute to enhanced development and learning by children, parents and the staff who are part of the service (Rodd, 1987). Given that it is the responsibility of the leader to ensure that the early childhood service meets a diversity of needs and expectations for a range of consumers, it is essential that the leader understands the importance of self-presentation and performance in the area of communication and their relationship to leadership.

Because every leader plays a unique part in setting the psychological climate of the organisation, the leader needs to demonstrate a certain level of self-awareness and understanding in order to be able to influence others, both children and adults, through interpersonal communication. To gain the basic trust and confidence of others—something which is fundamental for the operation of a quality early childhood service—leaders need to convey a specific set of attitudes and beliefs to others. In other words, leaders must create an image or profile that will be genuine, attractive and inspirational to the people they work with. The following attributes are regarded as essential for leaders in early childhood.

First, leaders must convey confidence in self and in the early childhood profession. The personal style of leaders can influence how they are perceived by children, adults, staff and other professionals, which in turn can determine how the overall community perceives the profession. Leaders who do not believe in their own ability to do the job well, perhaps as a result of limited self-understanding of values, attitudes, strengths, weaknesses, roles, responsibilities and goals, or a lack of valuing of importance of the profession, will convey these attitudes and beliefs in subtle, non-verbal ways and in more overt ways to those people with whom they interact. On the other hand, confident and enthusiastic leaders who communicate through beliefs, actions and words that they have a strong sense of self, and are committed to making an impact on the lives of the children and adults they interact with, will attract followers who are willing to be guided in the direction taken by the leader.

*We believe in our leader because she believes in herself . . .*
**Childcare worker**

For parents in particular, it is important that early childhood leaders convey confidence and a genuine acknowledgment of the importance of the job. Parents place their most important extensions of self—that is, their children—in the care of early childhood practitioners. The anxiety and mixed feelings reported by many parents can be exacerbated or diminished by the personal presentation of the leader. Confident leaders have the potential to reassure parents that they have the welfare of the child in mind and will ensure that the child spends a happy and productive day.

A confident leader can assist staff through displays of positive attitudes about their contribution to children's and parents' growth and development and model positive ways of coping with the daily demands of working with young children, relating to parents who may be vulnerable, stressed or have unrealistic expectations, and of simply getting through the day in this people-intensive working environment.

*The leader keeps things running smoothly by setting a good example for everyone to follow . . .*
**Childcare worker**

Second, leaders who are able to inspire the confidence and support of children, parents and staff will have a well-developed understanding of the positive aspects of themselves and will have taken the time to know themselves well. Successful leaders need to have a high level of proficiency in a range of skills—for example, motivating, delegating, financial management, planning and curriculum design—but will also accept that personal and professional growth takes time and is, in part, a result of experience. Such leaders will be able to make a realistic self-assessment of assets and limitations and will not understate or overstate what they bring to the early childhood setting. Nor will such leaders be harshly or overly critical of any shortcomings, but will accept that it takes time to develop the sophisticated and complex skills that are needed for working with and leading other people.

Third, effective leaders have positive attitudes to new experiences. The history of early childhood is a history of change with a tradition of action, with some daring and risk-taking and considerable persistence which has been produced by a combination of societal, cultural, political and economic forces. These forces necessitate leadership activities in the macro contexts of social development and change, the meso contexts of groups and organisations and the micro context of individual relationships. Given that change has been part of the fabric of the early childhood profession, leaders in the field need to develop a positive attitude to new experiences and change in general.

Individuals who perceive change as a challenge and therefore possess the power to create change have been described as lifelong learners (Claxton, 2001). Learning is regarded as a 'process of active engagement with experience that may involve an increase in skills, knowledge, understanding, a deepening of values or the capacity to reflect' (Lucas et al., 2002:15). Some of the core features of lifelong learners are robust self-esteem, openness of communication and a wide behavioural repertoire that promote confidence rather than crisis in the face of challenge, and a flexible problem-solving approach in response to new experiences. At the other end of the scale is the individual who is not open to new experiences and who is resistant to change. This type of person may exhibit low or inflated self-esteem, defensive communication and a routinised, inflexible behavioural repertoire that fosters an unwillingness to risk new experiences and a perception of change as threatening. A positive attitude to new experiences is an integral part of the process of the professional development and transformation of early childhood practitioners into leaders.

Fourth, effective leaders have a positive attitude to relationships with others and consider that the quality of relationships in the workplace is as important as the task-related aspect of goal achievement. They will place value upon activities that assist with really getting to know children, parents and staff. Such leaders are interested in the effects of their own behaviour upon others, use feedback to modify their own behaviour and are willing to try different ways of relating to other people. They can see the benefits of building and maintaining satisfying and harmonious relationships as a way of meeting children's and adults' need to belong and feel significant in the group, and as a way of providing mutual support between the providers and consumers of early childhood services.

### REFLECTIONS ON LEADERSHIP IN PRACTICE

In our day-to-day work, the way we treat other people shows our leadership qualities and skills. Leadership is shown through respect, understanding, caring and communication, especially listening.

**Deputy head, early childhood centre**

Developing positive attitudes to relationships with others is essential for leaders in the early childhood profession because children's optimum development and learning are dependent upon quality interpersonal relationships (Anning and Edwards, 1999), as is the quality of partnership that will develop between staff and parents. In addition, staff morale, commitment and performance levels are affected by attitudes to and expectations about relationships in the workplace. Positive attitudes to relationships can influence staff to interact with each other (and the leader) in a caring and constructive manner. The extent to which children, parents and staff feel trusted, accepted and respected by the leader will determine the quality of communication and interaction.

Finally, effective leaders maintain positive interaction with others. Even though individuals may have the best of intentions about interacting with others positively in the workplace, disagreement, dispute and conflict are inevitable. This is particularly likely in work contexts where individual and personal value systems can influence and determine professional policy and practice. The early childhood field is one to which individuals (parents and staff, trained and untrained, mature and young, experienced and inexperienced) bring their own subjective, highly personalised, socially and culturally determined beliefs and values about child-rearing, child care and early education. Effective leaders understand the destructive impact of inappropriate, negative interaction styles on levels of trust, feelings of security and safety and on performance, and actively model and promote mutually respectful, cooperative and collaborative interactions with others as a means of enhancing the general self-esteem and goal achievement of the group.

## EMOTIONAL INTELLIGENCE AND LEADERSHIP

While 'academically' intelligent and clever individuals often are appointed to positions of leadership, they will not necessarily become successful leaders if they have not developed considerable emotional intelligence. Emotional intelligence is similar to Gardner's (1983) earlier notions of intrapersonal intelligence (that is, self-awareness, self-control, persistence, self-motivation and energy) and interpersonal intelligence (social understanding and the ability to get things done with and through others), which constitute two of his original seven multiple intelligence definitions.

According to Goleman (1996), emotional intelligence is the master aptitude that deeply affects all other abilities, either enhancing or interfering with them. In fact, emotional intelligence as opposed to traditional notions of intelligence is considered to account for out-standing performance in top leaders (Sharp, 2002).

Emotionally intelligent leaders can raise standards, encourage personal and professional growth, and foster organisational sustaina-bility. They also appreciate the need to support staff to develop their emotional competence and, through them, contribute to the building of emotional competence throughout the organisation. In very simple terms, emotional intelligence (Goleman, 1996) involves:

- knowing your own feelings;
- being able to manage your own emotions;
- having a sense of empathy;
- being able to repair emotional damage in yourself and others;
- being emotionally interactive—that is, tuning into people so that you can interact with them effectively.

Effective communication skills are the tools that underpin the ability to act in an emotionally intelligent and competent manner. Emotionally intelligent leaders are able to identify and talk about their own feelings, are good listeners, ask appropriate questions and engage in meaningful dialogue.

Emotional intelligence also underpins enhanced job performance and satisfaction (Wong and Law, 2002). When people feel emotionally competent, they feel more positive about their job and how they perform it. Consequently, the workplace can be a source of personal and professional enhancement and empowerment for all.

MacGilchrist, Myers and Reed (1997) extended the concept of multiple intelligence to organisations such as educational settings. They argued that nine different intelligences could be found in successful educational settings, one of which is emotional intelligence. Intelligent settings use the full range of intelligences to address the quality of provision including teaching, learning, effectiveness and improvement. The collective capacity of early childhood settings to achieve their goals successfully depends on having an emotionally intelligent leader who in turn nurtures and values the emotional intelligence of staff, thereby enhancing the capacity of the setting to work in emotionally intelligent ways.

## COMMUNICATION SKILLS FOR EFFECTIVE LEADERSHIP

Communication is our link to others (Steiner, 1999). It is the way we represent our thoughts and feelings to others, transmit knowledge, solve problems and build relationships. Leaders gain personal power from the proficient use of communication skills because, regardless of the situation, they help others feel encouraged, rewarded and optimistic rather than diminished and pessimistic.

In analysing the responsibilities of leaders in early childhood settings, there appear to be two major areas that need to be balanced in order to survive at a personal level and effectively achieve the goals of the service. First, an early childhood practitioner must meet the needs of other people. There are specific communication skills which are helpful in meeting this responsibility. Second, it is essential that skills for meeting our own needs in the work context are developed. While there is some overlap between the two sets of skills, they can essentially be divided into two groups, as set out in Table 4.1.

**Table 4.1 Communication skills**

| Skills for meeting others' needs | Skills for meeting our own needs |
| --- | --- |
| Sending accurate and unambiguous messages | Appropriate self-assertion |
| | 'I' messages for 'owning' statements |
| Overcoming physical and psychological barriers | Conflict resolution |
| | Delegation |
| Listening for understanding | Time management |
| Appropriate responding | Stress management |
| Managing feelings | |

Many early childhood practitioners claim that they have no problem with communication—no difficulties in understanding others and being understood themselves. While this may be true at one level, there is always room to improve skill in this area. It is not sufficient for early childhood leaders to communicate at the basic 'get-the-message-across' level. More sophisticated and complex skills are required to deal with the variety of situations that present themselves when the job involves working with people. It would not be acceptable for a cabinetmaker to build a fine piece of furniture with a second-rate, blunt and rusty saw. In the same way, it is not acceptable for early childhood practitioners to consider fulfilling their roles and responsibilities with second-rate, unrefined communication skills.

Because the early childhood leader's primary responsibility is to meet the needs of others, such as children, parents and staff, the skills for meeting others' needs are described first. Chapter 5 examines the skills needed to meet our own needs.

## SKILLS FOR MEETING OTHERS' NEEDS

In many ways, effective communication in the early childhood context is dependent on the leader's sensitivity to other people's need to feel understood. Goleman (1996) challenges us to imagine what it would be like to work in a place where the staff were skilled in emotional competencies—where they were attuned to the feelings of others, able to handle disagreements and able to go with the flow when necessary. Leaders who are accomplished communicators can set the example and encourage early years practitioners to respond to the difficulties they encounter in the workplace in emotionally intelligent ways.

It is the leader's responsibility to create an emotional climate from which self-disclosure, empathy and honesty will emerge and foster the perception of 'being understood'. The skills that the leader employs to communicate with others on a day-to-day basis contribute to that process.

## SENDING ACCURATE AND UNAMBIGUOUS MESSAGES

Early childhood services are 'people' services where the business of the day is providing quality care and education programs for young children, understanding parents' needs and expectations, supporting them in their parenting role and utilising available staff resources effectively. Communication plays an important role in all of this. While early childhood practitioners who are trained in child development possess a good understanding of young children's language and communication abilities and limitations, and attempt to match the style and complexity of messages to children's developmental capabilities, this sensitivity may not extend to communication with adults. Given that it is the leader's responsibility to disseminate large amounts of information at different levels within the early childhood setting, it is important to consider the extent to which clear, accurate, unambiguous and non-toxic messages are constructed for the intended receiver.

Such messages are constructed from a consideration of the character-istics of the intended receiver, the need to have the message understood in the way that it was originally intended and an awareness of points of potential breakdown. Because verbal messages are usually sent only once and compete with all sorts of distractions, it is essential that care be taken with the construction of these messages and that the sender does not assume that the message was understood as it was intended. The communication styles used by sensitive early childhood practitioners are different for babies, toddlers and four-year-old children. Similarly, when constructing a message, a range of factors need to be taken into account—for example, the needs of parents versus staff, the fact that some people are from non-English speaking backgrounds, trained and untrained staff members, experienced and inexperienced people, as well as the importance of the message. Because people tend to hear what they want to hear, it is important to check the recipient's under-standing of the message. Early childhood practitioners do this with children, and need to ensure that they also use this skill in their communication with adults.

Subtle power plays can be identified in some of the messages communicated in some work environments. In early childhood settings, it is not uncommon to come across hurtful gossip, unkind humour, subtle insults, 'tiny lies' or omission of truth and covert pecking orders. Steiner (1999:181) calls them 'toxic transactions' and argues that they contribute to the development of uncooperative and even hostile work environments. It is important that leaders recognise such emotionally incompetent messages for what they are, understand their ultimately destructive outcome for all associated with the setting, and act to stop and/or prevent them from occurring.

## OVERCOMING BARRIERS TO COMMUNICATION

Since anything that competes for our attention can be a barrier to effective communication, clearly, early childhood settings are not conducive to effective communication. The physical setting with staff isolated in separate rooms, the staff roster system, the noise that young children make, the constant ringing of the telephone, the interruptions by parents who want staff attention immediately and the primary child supervisory responsibility of the staff all work against effective communication and increase the possibility of communication breakdown.

Although not all communication exchanges require high levels of skill, certain situations—such as dealing with a parent complaint, providing feedback to staff and obtaining information about the progress of a certain child—require discreet and tactful handling. The effective leader is aware of the range of barriers to communication within the setting and considers ways in which their impact can be eliminated or minimised. Barriers to communication that exist in physical settings can be manipulated and used by those who wish to sabotage communication efforts. For example, people may be using barriers to prevent effective communication taking place when they deliver an important message to a listener who is occupied with a group of children in a noisy toddler room, when they call a message out as the listener passes by the office or at the same time that they are involved in a telephone call or when they give unnecessary attention to distractors and interruptions.

The physical barriers in an early childhood setting can be handled relatively easily when compared with the psychological barriers to effective communication that may occur. These consist of the subjective attitudes, values, beliefs, stereotypes and prejudices that all of us bring to a communication exchange. It is interesting to note that many of the subjective and enduring attitudes we use to interpret the messages we receive are formed by the age of five. This is why it is important for early childhood practitioners to be aware of the sub-context of communication with children and adults. While on the surface it may appear that a particular message is being conveyed, an underlying value-laden or emotionally unintelligent communication can influence how the receiver interprets and understands the conversation.

Leaders in early childhood services need to be aware of their own and their staff members' values, attitudes, prejudices and stereotypes, and be conscious that they may influence how they understand and meet other people's needs. What we hear other people saying can be influenced by our own preconceived judgments. Take the example of a teenage mother who comes to discuss behaviour problems that she is experiencing with her four-year-old boy. Certain value judgments may spring to mind immediately—such as poor, uneducated, inexperienced, neglectful, incompetent, irresponsible, immoral and so on. In fact, none of these may apply to this person. However, if such value judgments dominate the way in which the leader or the staff perceive the mother, they will act as barriers to communication and influence how well the mother's need to be understood and supported is met. Sensitive leaders do not underestimate the power of psychological barriers to interpersonal interactions.

## LISTENING FOR UNDERSTANDING

One of the biggest criticisms that early years practitioners have of their managers and leaders is that they do not listen to them. This is possibly the greatest barrier to effective communication because it communicates lack of interest and preoccupation with other matters to the speaker. Early childhood practitioners consistently rate the ability to listen effectively as one of the key leadership attributes.

The most effective communicators are those who are able to put aside their own egocentric preoccupation with speaking and instead direct their attention and energy to listening for the meaning behind what the speaker is saying (West, 2004). This type of listening is different from simply hearing the words. While there are often many distracting noises in the background, such as cars passing by, doors banging or the radio next door, we do not specifically listen to them unless they are meaningful in some way. Goleman (1996) suggests that non-defensive listening (and speaking)—that is, listening to the *feelings* behind what is being said—is essential for helping receivers to be receptive to a message. When we listen, especially in a professional capacity, we are trying to meet others' need to be understood. Therefore, it requires that an effort be made to comprehend and use all the available information, including underlying feelings, to understand the meaning of the message as it was intended. This kind of listening is referred to as 'active listening' or 'reflective listening' in the literature on communication.

What is involved in listening for understanding? The listener first ensures that she or he has the appropriate time and space to devote to the speaker. If time is likely to be insufficient to meet the speaker's needs, the listener needs to convey interest in the speaker's issue and negotiate a more appropriate time to devote to the speaker. If the time is suitable, the listener needs to eliminate or minimise potential barriers to communication, such as redirecting telephone calls, preventing interruptions and sitting in positions that communicate positions of equality rather than power.

Second, the listener deliberately focuses attention on the speaker by using appropriate eye contact, body posture and non-verbal communication to indicate that she is interested in and following the speaker's issue.

Third, the listener gathers information from three sources from the speaker: the content, or the actual words heard; the speaker's body language, or non-verbal communication (which is a more reliable guide to the accuracy and importance of the verbal content); and the paralinguistics—how the speaker says the words (tone of voice, emphases, breathiness, fast or slow delivery).

Fourth, the listener uses all of these sources of information to interpret the speaker's message and reflects and clarifies understanding in a short recapitulation of the essence of the speaker's message.

Finally, the listener modifies understanding of the speaker's intended message in the light of the speaker's response to the listener's clarification. This process communicates interest, empathy and respect in meeting the speaker's need to be understood, and encourages further communication and interaction.

## APPROPRIATE RESPONDING

In the communication process, listening is the most important skill that needs to be developed in most people—children and adults. However, communication is a two-way process, and the way in which early childhood practitioners respond to children, parents and staff affects the quality of the interaction.

Carl Rogers (1961) delineates five response styles that account for approximately 80 per cent of the verbal communication that professionals engage within human service occupations. The other 20 per cent consists of the unintelligible grunts, groans and acquiescent noises that people scatter throughout their conversations. Rogers argues that all people develop preferred response styles, which tend to be produced automatically in the short space in which a timely response is expected to ensure the flow of human communication. Rogers believes that the use of one response style for 25 per cent or more of most communication results in the speaker being stereotyped by the listener as 'always' responding in that way. The effect of this stereotype is considered to diminish people's perception of being understood, blocking further communication and decreasing the possibility of the listener meeting others' needs.

The five response types Rogers describes are:

- *advising and evaluating*—typical responses are 'What you should do now is . . .' or 'If I were in your shoes, I'd . . .';
- *interpreting and analysing*—responses would be 'The problem you really have here is . . .' or 'You've missed the point! The real issue is . . .';
- *supporting and placating*—the aim is to diminish emotions in responses such as 'Don't worry, they all go through that stage!' or 'Forget it! He'll get over it.';
- *questioning and probing*—the intent is to gain additional information but this may turn into an interrogation, such as 'Did she have a disturbed night? Did anything unusual happen this morning? Is everything all right at home?'; and
- *understanding or reflecting*—the listener's response focuses on the underlying feelings as well as the content and indicates their understanding of the message to the speaker in a short paraphrase such as 'You're concerned about Sam's adjustment to child care' or 'You appear to be pretty pleased with how the program is developing!'

Rogers argues that, of the five response types, the understanding or reflecting response is the most under-developed and under-used, with professionals frequently and indiscriminately utilising the remaining four. The other four response types, while appropriate at times, can have detrimental effects upon communication if they are insensitively applied. That is, they can be received as emotionally unintelligent responses.

They also contain inherent disadvantages as an initial response in a communication exchange because they do not acknowledge the speaker's feelings, allow for the possibility of clarification of meaning or communicate that the intended full meaning of the message has been understood.

The understanding or reflecting response, in addition to overcoming these limitations, enables the speaker to explore the issue in greater depth and can be used to empower individuals to solve their own problems without having to rely on the expert professional. This is an important consideration for early childhood practitioners, whose role and responsibilities include supporting the personal development of parents and the professional development of staff.

Effective leaders in early childhood contexts will be aware of the advantages and limitations of the different response types and use their experience and expertise to determine which would be the most productive for meeting others' needs in the situation. The appropriateness of response type is the hallmark of a highly sophisticated and competent professional communicator.

## MANAGING FEELINGS

It is commonly acknowledged that people professions inherently contain work-related pressures that often result in work-induced stress. Early childhood leaders spend their working day immersed amongst people, their expectations, needs, problems and demands; consequently, they are required to respond to and deal with situations which can elicit emotional reactions on their part. While it is important to recognise and articulate personal reactions and emotional responses to events in our professional lives, it is essential that these are managed in a professional and emotionally intelligent manner which does not affect early childhood practitioners' ability to meet the needs of others and does not diminish others' sense of self-esteem.

Early childhood services around the world are dominated by women. In most societies, women have tended to be socialised to take the role of placator in emotionally arousing situations. In general, they have difficulty acknowledging the legitimacy of their emotions and expressing them in a constructive manner. The usual strategy is to deny and bury feelings until they build up to explosion point. There have been many anecdotal reports of early childhood staff avoiding issues by storming out, slamming doors, crying, name-calling, blaming and absenting themselves from work until 'things calm down'. It seems that it is still more the exception than the rule for women in the early childhood field to confront emotionally arousing incidents in an assertive manner. To add to this difficulty, early childhood leaders interact with a diverse group of people such as babies, toddlers and pre-schoolers, younger and older parents and staff, as well as professionals from other organisations who are pursuing their own agendas, who differ in their ability to manage their own emotions and who are experiencing various levels of stress and vulnerability in their own personal lives. It is therefore even more important that early childhood practitioners become emotionally competent and model emotionally intelligent ways of managing feelings.

## BRINGING IT TOGETHER

The effective leader in early childhood will be aware of the potential for emotional arousal in the interdependence of the group of children, parents and staff, and will understand the need to accept the emotional responses of other people. The emotionally intelligent leader will respond to these on a genuine and professional level and be aware of personal biases, resources and skills for managing personal feelings in the workplace. This is the point where the connection between meeting others' needs and meeting our own needs is made. In order to manage their own feelings in the professional situation, the early childhood practitioner must develop skills to meet their own needs.

# CHAPTER FIVE

# COMMUNICATION SKILLS: MEETING OUR OWN NEEDS

*Most workers in early childhood are women and we are not good at projecting ourselves and taking leadership roles both in and outside our settings . . . we need to gain more confidence, speak out and be heard in the community . . . I had to learn to stand up for myself and my beliefs.*

Manager, day nursery

**THIS CHAPTER EXPLORES**
- **skills for meeting our own needs**
- **appropriate self-assertion**
- **what is assertion**
- **'I' messages**
- **conflict resolution**
- **delegation**
- **time management**
- **stress management**
- **electronic communication**

The development of the early childhood profession has been shaped by the position of women in society (Ebbeck and Waniganayake, 2003) and is rooted in the tradition of philanthropy. The pioneer women of the profession wanted to improve the lives of young children and they were guided by an interest in child development and ways to promote it in order to rescue children from moral, spiritual and economic slums—that is, they were interested in meeting the needs of others. Their motivation to act as advocates for child-rearing, mothers and motherhood also stemmed from their desire to enhance the development and quality of their own moral, spiritual and intellectual lives—in other words, to meet their own needs.

It appears that, as the early childhood movement failed to achieve professional credibility in the community commensurate with its history and achievements, the continuing focus on nurturing, unselfishness and improving the quality of children's environments has been given undue prominence and used to absolve practitioners from their responsibility for meeting their own needs for economic and political improvement. In other words, early childhood practitioners have come to perceive themselves as powerless to meet their own professional needs. They have sublimated their own needs into an almost evangelical crusade to meet the needs of others, such as children, parents and staff. The dual goals held by the pioneer women should be restored for present early childhood practitioners so that they can have their own needs as professionals met as well as meeting the needs of the consumers of their services.

*The field needs stronger representation at government decision- and policy-making levels and within union movements to ensure the continuation of funding for early childhood services and parity of wages and conditions for early childhood staff that are commensurate with other educators . . .*

**Manager, children's centre**

Part of the ability to meet our own needs lies in the concepts of self and self-esteem. Early childhood leaders need to be able to value their occupation and its contribution to society, and have a realistic assessment of their own strengths and limitations in order to meet others' and their own needs. If early childhood practitioners perceive themselves or their job as inferior, inadequate or less worthy than other people or jobs, this will result in a loss of confidence about perceived and actual requirements which are necessary to discharge professional roles and responsibilities.

The tendency of early childhood practitioners towards nurturing and meeting the needs of others has resulted in the phenomenon of burnout, which continues to be associated with educational settings

(Law and Glover, 2000). Burnout can result from meeting the needs of others at the expense of one's own needs and, according to Faber (1991:35), can lead to:

- loss of enthusiasm and dedication;
- a growing sense of frustration and anger;
- a sense of triviality;
- withdrawal of commitment;
- a growing sense of personal vulnerability; and
- a sense of depletion and loss of caring.

Burnout leads to reduced performance, staff absenteeism and staff turnover—all of which diminish the quality of early childhood services. One way of avoiding this is to ensure that a balance is created between meeting the needs of others and meeting our own needs. Assertion is a skill that permits people to do this in a constructive way.

## APPROPRIATE SELF-ASSERTION

The most important skill that early childhood leaders can develop, both for themselves and for the consumers of their services, is appropriate self-assertion. This skill is useful in situations such as setting limits with children, communicating a request to a parent, expressing an opinion to a staff member, setting parameters with a committee, meeting their own needs to express feelings appropriately, being honest in their responses to other people and asking not to be interrupted. It is an appropriate skill for responding to feedback from quality assurance assessors and other external evaluators such as inspectors. It is important for other people with whom leaders interact because it is a skill that enables effective communication in ways that preserve others' sense of self-esteem.

### WHAT IS ASSERTION?

Very simply, assertion is a matter-of-fact statement that conveys rights, opinions, beliefs, desires and positive or negative feelings in a way that does not impact on the self-esteem of the other person (Ferguson, 2003). It is a professional technique for communicating with other people because it is a direct and honest expression that conveys personal confidence and respect for self and others. Being assertive does not guarantee that individuals get what they want. What it does do is enhance the professional relationship by being emotionally honest, confronting issues and problems and respecting the fact that other people are responsible for managing their own feelings and responses.

Assertion (or using fair play) is the position of balance between two other familiar behaviours: non-assertion (avoiding conflict) and aggression (winning at all costs). These three communication styles can be seen as a continuum from the passive, indirect, self-denying, non-assertive style to the confronting, inappropriately emotionally honest and self-enhancing at others' expense, aggressive style. Both non-assertion and aggression can have negative and destructive effects on further communication and ultimately in terms of future relationships, whereas assertion is considered to act as a facilitator to further communication and assists in building and maintaining relationships as well as personal confidence and self-esteem.

Most people have some difficulty in communicating assertively, either in certain situations or with certain people. Few people possess the level of self-confidence and skill necessary for consistent self-assertion. Inability to act assertively usually is related to lack of self-esteem, where our own needs are undervalued in relation to others' needs and consequently denied. Aggressive behaviour can result if our own needs are perceived as dominant and superior to those of others and self-righteously, aggressively pursued.

These differences explain why individuals can be seen to fluctuate between the three communication styles described above. For example, a person may be able to assert herself with young children when being interrupted by saying something like: 'Excuse me, John, I'd like to finish talking to Susan.' The same person might have difficulty being assertive in a similar situation with John's mother, and may respond non-assertively by permitting herself to be interrupted. It is likely that negative feelings of hurt, anxiety and guilt for not taking responsibility for one's own needs will be experienced later. Those individuals who persistently engage in non-assertive behaviour can build up levels of frustration, which ultimately result in an aggressive outburst—that is, the mouse turns into a lion and intimidates the surprised recipient of the emotional eruption.

On the other hand, the same person may only be able to confront an issue that is of concern to them by fuelling themselves first with anger. For example, the person may confront the issue of being interrupted by another staff member with an aggressive response such as: 'Well, that's just typical of you! You never let anyone finish what they are saying. I'm just not going to bother any more!' The person on the receiving end of this outburst is likely to feel attacked, angry and vengeful, which will affect the relationship at a later time.

In a professional setting, early childhood practitioners need to analyse their own obstacles to appropriate self-assertion. Continued non-assertion and disregard for personal needs might be a symptom of poor self-concept and low self-esteem, and will generally lead to anxiety and frustration. A tendency towards aggressive responses that infringe upon the rights of others also reflects problems with an un-realistically inflated or poor self-concept and self-esteem. This ultimately will lead to unmanageable relationships in the workplace. Individuals who are uncertain about their ability to be assertive in specific situations or with certain people usually do not believe that they are entitled to basic personal rights. In order to increase one's confidence in such situations, an examination of one's belief system in relation to personal rights is useful. All human beings have the right to make decisions about their body, property and time, and to be treated with respect by others. In addition, we all have the right to express appropriately our own opinions, feelings and wishes.

Another obstacle to appropriate self-assertion is fear of the consequences of assertive behaviour. Non-assertive individuals usually believe that people will not like them or will reject them if they express their feelings. In fact, the opposite is true. People generally respond well to appropriately assertive individuals and feel irritation with, pity and ultimately disgust for, chronically non-assertive individuals. Aggressive individuals usually believe that the use of power achieves their desired goals in relationships. This may appear so in the short term where individuals may defer to the demands of the aggressive person. However, the long-term consequences of aggression are that the support, cooperation and goodwill of the recipients of aggressive displays are lost and a desire to take revenge, get even and retaliate can emerge. This negative reaction can escalate into situations where the aim is to sabotage.

Assertive responses are usually appropriate for situations that occur frequently and with people with whom one wishes to continue a positive relationship. Therefore, there are usually many opportunities to practise assertive responses and to learn from the results. Learning any new skill takes time and practice, and learning to act assertively is no different. In order to be appropriately assertive in early childhood professional situations, the following steps can be followed.

- Identify what you actually want to accomplish—that is, the goal of the assertive situation. For example, you may wish to have a particular parent pay their fees on time each week.
- Clarify how being assertive will help you achieve this. In this instance, being assertive will permit you to explain your needs in the situation, such as the budget requirements.
- Analyse what you would usually do to avoid being assertive in this situation or with this person. In the past, you may have sent a note home with the child, left messages on the parent's answering machine or dropped subtle hints.
- Clarify what the likely advantages of being assertive instead would be. The direct expression of your needs and wishes will minimise misinterpretation and misunderstanding of your requirements and maximise the probability of the parent responding to your request to pay the fees on time.
- Identify what might be preventing you from being assertive here. Are you holding false notions about the consequences of being assertive? Could it be that your non-assertion is related to mistaken beliefs about the need for politeness in interactions about money? Do you fear an aggressive or tearful response from the parent?
- Identify any other sources of anxiety and think of how you will cope with and reduce them. Are you anxious about what the parent might say about you to the staff or other parents? Think about and reaffirm your own rights in the situation.
- Construct a model response that you would feel comfortable saying in the situation or to the person and practise it aloud several times. Refine the statement if necessary until you find one that feels genuine. You could say something like: 'I need to speak to you about the payment of fees. When the fees are not paid on time I become concerned that the setting will not have sufficient funds to meet its operational demands. I'd prefer it if you could let me know if your fees cannot be paid on time. That will give me time to assess my budget and give us an opportunity to negotiate some alternatives.'
- When the situation arises, have the courage to put your assertive response into practice, knowing that you will probably have another opportunity to try again.

- Reflect upon the results of your assertive statement in terms of what you liked about what you did, the outcome and what you would change in the next opportunity to be assertive. You may have liked that you were direct, explained your needs and responsibilities, that you stayed calm and didn't attack the parent, or that you opened up a chance for further discussion.

Using these steps will help to achieve the goal of assertiveness and increase self-confidence in managing the communication exchange. The way in which the assertive statement is phrased is the next important skill in meeting your own needs.

## 'I' MESSAGES

The aim of communicating assertively is to express honestly and directly personal opinions, feelings and wishes. Unfortunately—particularly when emotions are aroused—personal opinions can be turned into statements of blame. These are not conducive to productive relationships and can act as barriers to further communication. The use of the word 'you' to begin statements may arouse defensive tendencies and provoke a retaliatory attack. Consider the effects of these two statements on a staff member when you want to discuss the issue of punctual return from tea breaks. 'You're late back from tea again, Joan. You've got us all behind in the lunch routine! This had better not happen again!' An alternative is: 'I'm concerned about the effect of our breaks on the lunchtime routines, Joan. I'd like to discuss the issue when you've got some time.'

The first statement puts the blame for the problem squarely on Joan in a fairly threatening way, and does not lay any groundwork for problem-solving. Joan is likely to react in a defensive manner, become angry at the attack and find reasons why the problem is nothing to do with her but concerns other issues about which the speaker is obviously ignorant. In the second statement, the speaker is able to employ a matter-of-fact tone of voice to define the issue at point of discussion and provide a non-threatening framework to explore with Joan what factors could be contributing to the issue. Joan is less likely to perceive herself as the focus of blame and attack, and therefore more likely to discuss the issue openly and constructively.

In terms of owning personal statements, it is important to commence sentences and statements with the 'I' pronoun rather than generalised terms such as 'we', 'they' or 'some parents'. This subtle change in emphasis eliminates emotional overtones that can impede clear communication and reduces the likelihood of petty disputes about the source and intent of the message. The 'I' message allows the appropriate expression of feelings in a professional context, such as: 'I was annoyed to find that the kitchen was not cleaned after the staff meeting last night. I'd prefer it if we could come up with a satisfactory arrangement for the next meeting.' Using this framework, the early childhood practitioner can address issues and express opinions in a constructive manner and provide a model for professional communication exchanges in the setting.

## CONFLICT RESOLUTION

Disputes, disagreements, differences of opinion, friction, clashes, confrontations, dissension, quarrels and antagonism are examples of the range of conflict that can be observed in any typical early childhood setting. Conflict appears to be an inevitable part of living and working with other people and, because the early childhood profession is essentially about working with people, the potential for conflict is high. Boardman (2003) observes that the possession of sound conflict-resolution skills is crucial for effective leadership. The large number of requests from professionals in early childhood settings for assistance in dealing with and managing conflict indicates that this is an area of concern for their own personal survival and job satisfaction. It is an area where many early childhood practitioners regard themselves as having few skills. Conflict resolution is discussed in detail in Chapter 6.

## DELEGATION

One of the biggest problems that early childhood practitioners report is the amount and diversity of the work that is required in order to fulfil their roles and responsibilities. In terms of completing the workload, the effective leader will know when and how to delegate work to others so that the goals of the service are achieved. Effective delegation of authority and tasks can help to reduce administrative pressure and workload (Hayden, 1999).

Delegation is a skill. It is not simply asking or directing a staff member to complete a task. Delegation requires a match between the task to be undertaken and the skills, interests and characteristics of the staff member seen as an appropriate delegatee. In order to delegate successfully, the early childhood professional has to be willing to relinquish some of the duties and responsibilities that have previously been associated with her role. It is important that the tasks considered appropriate to assign to other staff include some of the pleasant, rewarding jobs as well as some of the more mundane and unpleasant jobs. Delegation is not simply getting rid of all the tasks that are unpleasant, unpopular or boring!

Delegation involves having confidence in the staff and their ability to act as responsible professionals. However, there are various barriers to delegation. These are illustrated in some typical comments overheard in early childhood settings.

*I don't want the staff to think that I can't do my job.*

*I've done this job for years. Nobody can do it as well as I can.*

*I'll only get the blame if someone else makes mistakes.*

*It will take less time if I do it myself.*

*The staff won't see me as part of the team if I don't do the job myself.*

Neugebauer and Neugebauer (1998) offer guidelines for assessing 'delegation phobia' and some ideas for effective delegation. The delegator first needs a clear understanding of the relative importance of the various tasks which are considered suitable for delegation and must be able to distinguish between key leadership functions which should always be retained by the leader (such as evaluation, policy development and reports for the committee of management) and other duties which could be undertaken by others (such as fee subsidies, petty cash and organising in-service programs).

There are two important issues in delegation: the selection of the appropriate person to delegate to and the way in which the nature of the task is communicated to them. When selecting the appropriate person to undertake a specific task, the early childhood leader needs to know the potential of the staff by being familiar with their strengths, weaknesses, personal characteristics and learning styles and their work aspirations. Maslow's (1970) hierarchy of needs is useful

**Figure 5.1 Maslow's hierarchy of needs**

in understanding why individual staff members come to work, their predominant motivation and their potential to undertake special delegated tasks.

This framework for understanding people's motivation describes lower level needs which, if fulfilled, permit the individual to progress to higher order needs. At the lowest level are physiological needs, such as the need for food, water and sleep. The financial remuneration gained through employment enables these needs to be met and is a basic motivation for all workers, regardless of how much they earn. When these physiological needs are met, the individual is able to pursue fulfilment at the next level of need—that is, safety needs. At this level, the worker is motivated by needs for security, stability, structure, law and order, protection and freedom from fear and anxiety. Casual employment status, such as casual relief work in early childhood settings, is unlikely to assist in meeting these needs. The employee will be interested in undertaking tasks that are perceived to contribute to their personal safety and security, such as meeting minimum work expectations and competency, detailing rosters of who is responsible for what tasks and any other activities that ensure predictability in the work environment and the continuation of employment.

Maslow's third level is characterised by belonging and love needs, where individuals are motivated to work in order to be part of a group, to extend their social network and to meet needs for affectionate relationships with others. Such individuals will be interested in tasks that build and maintain relationships. These are the people who will arrange the Christmas party, suggest staff dinners and organise the afternoon tea for staff farewells. Their need for harmonious relationships means that they may also take on the role of mediator when conflict between staff occurs or relationships are strained.

Maslow's fourth and fifth levels in the hierarchy of needs describe motivation typologies that are relevant to efficient delegation of important responsibilities. The need for esteem is the dominant motivator in relation to work at the fourth level. There appear to be two sub-levels of this need. First, individuals are motivated by the need to demonstrate mastery, competence, autonomy and self-confidence; and second, a need to feel appreciated and important and to gain a sense of respect from others emerges. Status, prestige and perhaps even fame become dominant motivators. Individuals who wish to demonstrate their competence and gain public recognition for a job well done generally respond well to delegation, particularly if the task is introduced with the phrase: 'I think you are the best person to undertake this important task.' However, if the task is perceived to be beyond the personal capability of the staff member and there is a chance of failure, it is unlikely that the individual will accept the delegation. In such a situation, assurance from the leader about access to support and assistance if required may help to convince a staff member to undertake the task.

The highest level of Maslow's hierarchy of needs is described as the need for self-actualisation. This is the level where the individual is motivated by the need for personal growth and development. Individuals at this level work because they want to develop their potential and become the best that they can be. This is the level where the greatest differences between individuals are evident. In terms of delegation, individuals at this level will be interested in challenging tasks that may demand the acquisition of new skills or knowledge. The individual at this level is truly a lifelong learner. The main difference between this level and the previous level is the role of demonstrated competence and public recognition versus personal standards of achievement, success and growth. A staff member's contribution is a result of intrinsic motivation rather than factors external to the self.

The effective early childhood leader will consider individual staff members' motivation in relation to their employment, and match this with the kind and level of task deemed suitable for delegation. Having decided that a particular task is suitable for delegation, and having selected a potential delegatee on the basis of characteristics, skills, interests and motivation type, the leader needs to invite the staff member to undertake the task. It is important that the leader explains:

- the nature of the task to be undertaken;
- the deadline by which the task must be completed;
- the level of authority and accountability that will be assigned to the person who undertakes the task; and finally
- the reasons why the staff member is considered to be the best person for the job.

The leader should also ask for some input from the staff member concerning any aspect associated with the performance and completion of the task. In effective delegation, leaders need to explicitly define their role as one of support and facilitation rather than supervision. A timeline and procedures for reporting back should be decided upon, as well as a means for evaluating the work.

In delegating tasks and duties to other staff members, it is important for early childhood leaders to keep in mind that other people are likely to approach and complete the job differently from the way that they would have done. Therefore, reasonable expectations of others and the final outcome are essential if staff are to perceive delegation as a means of staff development and a pathway to job satisfaction.

## REFLECTIONS ON LEADERSHIP IN PRACTICE

The best leaders in settings always delegate duties to people who will be able to perform them the best. This is because they know the staff, the setting and the children. Good leaders always give others the opportunity to share their ideas too and that helps them know what you are interested in and good at.

**Nursery nurse**

Inappropriate delegation can lead staff to feel exploited, misunderstood and frustrated in their work. It can also result in early childhood leaders losing confidence in the staff and themselves and retreating to the unproductive position of: 'If you want a job done well, then you have to do it yourself.' Delegation should result in an improvement of the morale and performance of the entire staff as well as ensuring that there is sufficient time for early childhood leaders to devote to their own work. If time is still a problem, then time-management strategies need to be investigated.

## TIME MANAGEMENT

One of the most pressing problems facing early childhood practitioners today is said to be insufficient time to complete the range of responsibilities that are associated with delivering services to young children and their families. Yet, when the topic of time management is mentioned to early childhood practitioners, the response is usually one of scepticism. It is evident that the demands of the jobs of coordinators and directors of early childhood settings have increased dramatically over the past decade and, with the ongoing changes in the early childhood field, this trend seems likely to continue. Time management is about how early childhood practitioners develop short-, medium- and long-term coping strategies to meet the demands of our professional roles and responsibilities.

The concept of 'time in the working day' in early childhood settings is difficult to define because working with young children involves 'duty of care'—that is, children's needs must be met regardless of whether or not staff are officially on duty—and because, for many staff, there are no or very liberally interpreted rules about overtime. No early childhood practitioner would leave a child abandoned outside a setting if the parent were not on time to collect them. Many practitioners, because of split shifts, attend staff and other meetings outside their allocated hours. Therefore, for many practitioners, the job takes as long as it does to get done regardless of statutory working hours. This can place pressure on work–life balance. A number of early childhood practitioners have commented on the strain that the long and often unpredictable hours required to do their job properly puts on their relationships and leisure pursuits.

Although many tasks—especially those involving paperwork—can be taken home and completed outside work time, the impact of such a practice conducted on a regular basis is likely to be destructive in terms of increased personal stress levels and less time for individual pursuits and family life. While the work may get done, it is often at a personal cost. The effects of poor time management will be taken up in the next section on stress management.

Time management is simply a strategy that can be used to assist early childhood practitioners to meet all the demands that are placed upon them during a typical day. It must be remembered that there are also many activities that take place during the evening and on weekends, such as evening staff meetings, weekend workshops and conferences, fundraising functions and maintenance working parties. A 40-hour working week is not the norm for those who work in early childhood. In addition, because early childhood staff are 'public figures' in that their performance is observable by the consumers of their service, it is essential that they are seen to handle the variety of demands on their time and also do this in a manner which presents an image of competence and efficiency. At this point, a distinction needs to be made between 'being busy' and 'being efficient'. A 'busy' leader might well analyse their willingness to delegate some duties and responsibilities to other appropriate staff. It may be that the leader's difficulties with delegation interfere with efficient task accomplishment and leadership.

Time management is merely a means of getting things done as quickly as possible and with as little stress as possible. It essentially involves setting goals in one's personal and professional life, and establishing priorities for the tasks to be undertaken in order to achieve these goals. The major obstacle to time management in early childhood services is interruption. Therefore, skill in dealing with this problem must be developed. Appropriate self-assertion, discussed earlier in this chapter, is useful here. If an early childhood leader manages their time efficiently, the result should be more time available to work towards achieving set goals without feelings of stress or pressure.

Time management involves four major steps, according to Schiller and Dyke (1990):

1  Set your goals (in work, professional development, personal growth and material areas). It is useful to break these up into long- and short-term goals.
2  Analyse which task or project will help you to reach the particular goal.
3  Break the task or project down into small, achievable steps. Evidence of progress towards the goal is a good motivator.

4 Establish a priority rating. Which task needs to be completed first to move towards the goal?

There are some helpful tips in books dealing with time management and general organisational efficiency. Jorde-Bloom's (1982) classic text and MacDonald's (2004) book are written specifically for early childhood practitioners and there are publications such as those by Blanchard and Johnson (2004) and Covey (2004) that cover time management in generic organisational contexts.

Although this seems an obvious strategy, it is important to remember that lists are useful to help you plan each day, week and month. To avoid asking yourself the question 'Where did the time go', some people find making a list of general headings useful in establishing effective time management:

- things to do;
- people to see;
- phone calls to make;
- meetings to attend;
- deadlines to make.

Other headings can be based on priority:

- urgent and important—do it now;
- important but not urgent—do it some time today or tomorrow;
- this week—attend to it in the next few days;
- this month—remember any deadline and put it in the diary as a prompt for attention;
- term break/non-contact time—don't forget to make time to respond to these tasks.

Such headings can focus your attention on the demands on your time and can assist with establishing priorities for tasks. As you complete each task, cross it off the list. If a task remains unfinished, analyse why it has not been completed. Did you have enough time? Were there too many interruptions? Weren't you interested in it? Was it too difficult? Did you have all the information necessary? Is the morning better than the afternoon for complex report writing? Was this a task that could have been delegated?

Effective organisation of office space tends to be associated with efficient use of time. The early childhood leader's office space is a multi-purpose space which often doubles as a store room, staff room, resource library, parent room, interview room and time-out room. It may not be easy to keep it in perfect order. However, the more chaos and clutter in the office, the less accessible it is for efficient use of time. The creation of a workable filing system is essential to handle the amount of information that comes through to leaders of early childhood services. A computer is an essential item of equipment that can ease the administrative load. The time initially spent learning to use the computer will produce considerable savings later, particularly when compared with manual handling of paperwork. The impact of computer and information technology will be examined at the end of this chapter.

Telephone calls are reported to be a major source of stress in the lives of early childhood practitioners. The telephone is an important link between the setting and the outside world, especially in the current security-conscious environment. Parents also have the right to contact staff about their child at any time. It is not the telephone itself that is the problem; it is people's poor telephone skills. The most important strategies are to keep incoming and outgoing telephone calls short; to ensure that you have communicated the purpose of your call accurately; to make all necessary calls in one session; and to consider whether some calls can be handled by other staff. Finding a way of freeing yourself from answering the telephone and creating an uninterrupted period of time to complete an important task is essential.

Meetings can be another source of inefficient usage of time. Meetings seem to abound in the early childhood field and, because early childhood settings tend to be physically remote from the administrative offices in which many meetings are conducted, the time needed to attend a one-hour meeting can easily amount to two hours with associated travelling time. The early childhood leader who uses time efficiently will assess the need to hold or attend a meeting in terms of the goals of the setting. Only those people who are relevant to the purpose of the meeting should be invited and the person who chairs the meeting should ensure that the discussion focuses on the topic. Learning some techniques for chairing group meetings can be valuable if meetings make up a substantial part of your duties, and can assist enormously with the effective management of time.

It is evident that, with the increasing roles and responsibilities that early childhood practitioners are required to undertake, a change of mindset is necessary. Early childhood practitioners need to learn ways of working smarter, not harder.

## STRESS MANAGEMENT

The pressure of time is only one of a number of stressful factors associated with working in the early childhood field. Working with young children is physically, emotionally and intellectually demanding. Families appear to face considerable pressures associated with the demands of contemporary living, so the scope of the early childhood practitioner's job has broadened to include a wide range of responsibilities, such as:

- supporting parents in their parenting role;
- training staff;
- working with other professionals from a range of disciplines and agencies in relation to children's and families' needs; and
- acting as advocates for children, families and the profession.

Many of the recent changes in the roles and responsibilities of early childhood practitioners have not been supported by access to relevant training, with numerous early childhood staff having to 'learn on the job'. Given the staff-to-child ratio which is required by government regulations for early childhood services, it can be difficult for staff to gain time off or be relieved from duty in order to attend training courses, many of which are offered during the hours that early childhood settings are operational. It is therefore common for early childhood practitioners who do engage in further study and training to have to undertake pre-service, in-service and post-initial training in their own time. This demand can affect the quality of their personal lives and result in increased stress levels.

Stress in itself is neither good nor bad; whether a situation is deemed stressful by any individual depends on how it is perceived and experienced, and on individual coping abilities and resilience. When perceived as a challenge, stress is good for us. Human beings need a certain amount of stress to get going each day. Stress is part of modern life and work and, as such, it is unrealistic to expect that stress can or should be eliminated.

It is recognised that there are some individuals who, by the nature of their personalities, are more prone to stress than others. It is important for such individuals to examine closely their tendencies to perceive situations as stressful rather than in more optimistic terms and work towards reframing their perceptions and subsequently their reactions to such situations. Law and Glover (2000:50) note that 'our work should maximise our feelings of well-being or self-esteem'. They suggest that achieving a 'feel good' factor from our work—for example, by looking for the positives in our situation—can help alleviate stress. Emotionally intelligent early childhood practitioners appreciate the need to understand the links between thoughts, feelings and reactions. They understand that usually there are choices in how one perceives a situation, and that different consequences arise from different choices, and they use such insights in deciding how best to respond. Consequently, they understand that stress often can be managed by either changing the situation or changing ourselves.

Stress is somewhat self-induced in that it is a product of the balance between the number of demands in our lives and our individual perceptions regarding our capacity or resources to meet these demands. In the case of many early childhood practitioners, the demands often outweigh personal resources, with stress being the result of this imbalance. While time management and delegation can assist with the reduction of stress levels in the professional arena, a broader strategy for approaching stress in all aspects of our lives is more useful.

Stress levels determine our effectiveness in both our personal and professional lives. Too much stress or overstimulation tends to produce ineffective problem-solving, low self-esteem, physical exhaustion and illness, all of which result in low-quality performance in the workplace. This is termed burnout, which can develop from an imbalance between too many demands or high levels of tension and one's personal resources to respond appropriately. Lack of stress or understimulation can have an equally negative impact on coping strategies with boredom, fatigue, frustration and dissatisfaction reducing professional effectiveness. This is called rustout.

Neither of these extremes meets the needs of others or our own needs. With an optimum level of stimulation or challenge, early childhood practitioners can demonstrate their capacity for rational problem-solving and creativity, which produces a positive attitude to progress and change and enhances self-esteem and job satisfaction. With such a balance, it is possible to meet our own needs as well as be responsive to the needs of others. However, achieving this balance requires self-awareness, an understanding of work demands and continued effort to keep both of these in perspective.

The first step in managing stress in personal and professional arenas is to determine who and what is causing the stress. In other words, a stress inventory which lists all the people and situations that are associated with feeling stressed needs to be compiled. A stress inventory also permits reflection upon typical coping strategies and an evaluation of their effectiveness.

The following steps are helpful in analysing the main causes of stress:

- Briefly describe the stressful situation. For example, a conference with a parent concerning their child's unacceptable behaviour can be perceived as stressful.
- Identify who is involved in the situation.
- Establish how frequently this situation occurs. Conferences with parents occur frequently—on a weekly basis with some parents.
- Determine the degree of control you have over the situation and/or people involved. In such a case, you consider that you have some ability to influence parents' attitudes and behaviour.
- Identify typical ways of responding to or dealing with the situation. For example, when you encounter stressful situations, you tend to ignore them, hope the problem will resolve itself without your intervention or avoid direct confrontation by dropping hints around the parents.
- Evaluate how effective these strategies are for accomplishing your work and maintaining positive relationships. In your past experience, you have found such non-assertive strategies to be ineffective but you are too anxious to try anything new.
- Brainstorm possible alternative ways of dealing with the situation in a more constructive manner for your own needs. Assertiveness training to help you express your needs and practice in mutual problem-solving could be beneficial.

In meeting our need for a relatively stress-free working environment, there are two important aspects to consider: how frequently the situation occurs; and the degree of control we have over the situation. If a situation occurs frequently, it would seem that current coping strategies are not adequate and require reviewing. Where situations cannot be changed because of the lack of personal control, exploring strategies for changing personal perceptions and thinking can be more productive than trying to change the situation. In the above example, rather than thinking that your ability to deal with parent conferences is hopeless, try changing your thinking to: 'I don't like parent conferences but I can cope with them. I can learn skills to help me feel more confident.'

Stress-management strategies focus on changing the situation or changing yourself. Most people are reluctant to engage in personal change if another option is available. Therefore, strategies for changing the situation will be discussed first.

In the early childhood profession, stress at work can be reduced by analysing and making minor or more substantial changes to the job. If stress is related to the demands of the job, then the workload needs to be reorganised. The following techniques have been shown to be helpful:

- *Reduce the workload.* Delegate appropriate tasks to others. Other staff will benefit from and may even appreciate the opportunity to learn new skills. This provides another advantage in that additional backup is available if the leader is unable to be at work for any reason.
- *Establish priorities* for the demands placed upon you. Learn to be assertive, deal with only essential demands and avoid becoming involved in tasks that are peripheral to your role.
- Use and improve *time-management techniques* to ensure that you use time as efficiently as possible.
- *Assume control.* There are always options in any situation. Avoiding situations will not resolve any difficulties but can exacerbate them. Make choices and decisions rather than being at the mercy of events.
- *Finish any unfinished tasks* before starting new ones. The sense of completion can quickly neutralise anxiety about the amount of work that has to be done and promote the 'feel good' factor.
- If possible, *minimise change* and *keep to a routine*. Stress is often associated with uncertainty about change. If stress is a result of chronic change, such as has been occurring in the early childhood field in recent years, routine, predictability and stability can build up self-esteem and nurture feelings of security.
- *Seek or establish a support group.* Avoid withdrawing from and possibly alienating colleagues, peers and friends. Stress is a common

experience for early childhood practitioners, who therefore can empathise with each other when they feel overwhelmed by the demands and changes in the profession.

When early childhood practitioners have little personal control over a stressful situation and cannot change the situation to ameliorate stress levels, it is possible to manage stress by *changing the way the situation is perceived or viewed*. The following personal stress anti-dotes may be helpful in changing the way we think about stressful situations:

- Change the perception you hold about stress in general. Rather than seeing stressful situations as things to be avoided in life, view these situations as challenges and opportunities for growth and personal development. Accept that it is not the situation but how the situation is perceived which produces stress.
- Change your thinking to less catastrophic, less extreme, less polarised, less stressed and therefore more positive and rational thinking. Emotionally intelligent practitioners use self-talk to define situations. Self-talk is simply the ability to listen to the internal messages we give ourselves about any particular event. Instead of thinking, 'Isn't this dreadful! I just can't stand any more!', try something like, 'Well, I don't like this very much but I can deal with it! I could . . .' In this way, the tendency to irrational, over-emotional thinking is limited without denying the basic emotional response. An opportunity to perceive the situation more realistically and to adopt a rational, problem-solving approach is provided.
- Keep your sense of humour. Sometimes it is necessary to take a step back, get things into perspective and see the funny side of work. Laughter and humour produce good moods and enhance the ability to think flexibly and creatively, causing you to notice different aspects of a situation and find solutions to problems. According to Goleman (1996), bad moods 'foul' or undermine thinking. Having a laugh at yourself or the situation helps stimulate positive and pleasant feelings that move us in more positive directions.
- Learn to tolerate uncertainty in life. Not everything can be controlled, directed, planned or predicted. Learn to 'go with the flow' sometimes, particularly when you don't have the power to control events. Worrying will not improve or change the situation. It will only increase your sense of uncertainty and your stress level.

- Don't dwell on past mistakes as it's too late to change them now. Focus instead on how you can approach these situations more effectively in the future.
- Learn to anticipate change. Working in a 'people profession' means that constant change is inevitable, but there are usually numerous signs to alert you to the need for change or an imminent change. A perceptive professional will be attuned to signs of pending change, will plan for change and will facilitate the implementation of change in order to minimise stress in those affected by the change. Skills for managing change are discussed in Chapter 9.
- Develop the skills necessary to perform your job efficiently. Attend in-service courses and upgrade your qualifications to ensure that you possess the current technical expertise demanded in the profession.
- Improve the communication skills that are related to stress management, in particular assertion and conflict-resolution skills. Express your feelings appropriately and deal with incidents as they occur.

Early childhood leaders need to appreciate that it is important to create a positive emotional environment in which they communicate that they value each individual. Valuing helps those who are stressed to be more open about how they feel. While it does not eliminate stress, feeling valued by significant others in the workplace—for example, formal leaders, colleagues and parents—may help to compensate for perceived imbalance between the demands of the job and personal resources. Valuing also helps to promote motivation, collaboration and teamwork.

In addition to the techniques described above, there are two basic strategies for stress management in personal and professional life. The first one relates to personal health and the second relates to relaxation. Because stress has an underlying physiological component, susceptibility to stress can be reduced by ensuring that good health is maintained. Any practitioner who wishes to function effectively needs to have a balanced diet, avoid or minimise the use of drugs (including caffeine, nicotine and alcohol), take regular exercise and have adequate sleep. This is especially important in professions that require physical, emotional and intellectual stamina such as the early childhood profession. Learning to relax and developing recreational interests are also means of ensuring psychological health and stamina.

## ELECTRONIC COMMUNICATION

Communication and information technology, especially email and the internet, has brought many benefits to the workplace. This technology has freed many employees from the grind of repetitive and time-consuming administrative tasks, and has given staff access to different forms of communication and learning (Law and Glover, 2000). However, the growth of such technology is not without its problems. Cooper (2004) observes that effective relationships at work cannot be built purely with electronic communication, and points out that misunderstandings caused by email are common.

Many early childhood practitioners complain that they simply do not have access to the latest equipment in the workplace, that the equipment they do have is slow, especially when accessing the intranet or internet, and that they do not have the time to read and respond to increasing email communications. Some early childhood practitioners referred to this technology as 'electronic gobbledygook'—an indication of the negative attitudes held by some in the field.

Given that growing development in electronic communication will continue to impact on the working lives of early childhood practitioners, it is important that they become more confident and motivated to use it appropriately. Access to better equipment and training is essential, as is employee understanding of the personal benefits to be gained by appropriate engagement with the technology. The technology should empower people, not act as a barrier to communication, relationships and learning.

Email has become an important means of communication in the workplace, but it must be used in an appropriate and responsible manner. Information can be shared easily by email. However, firing an email to someone giving them work to do will not get the best out of them. Senders need to think about the impact of receiving information in the form of an email because certain barriers exist in this form of communication. The following factors should be considered:

- Is email the most appropriate form of communication? Would this message be delivered more appropriately in person? For example, it is entirely inappropriate to criticise staff performance in an email. This type of communication needs to be delivered in person. Any sensitive issue, such as appraisal, mentoring and any unpleasant message needs a face-to-face approach.
- Is the language used open to different interpretation and meaning

by different people? We all tend to hear and read what we want to hear and read. In emails, the message's intention is not clarified or highlighted by access to non-verbal communication. It is essential that the message's intention and meaning are clear, unambiguous, acceptable and understandable. For example, explaining a policy decision in an email to all staff may result in different staff members understanding what was meant in different ways. Very abbreviated messages can be perceived as curt and arrogant.

- If a response or action is required, can you be sure that the person actually received the email? Many emails still seem to vanish into the ether. Conflict can arise if the sender believes that the recipient did not respond to the message or if intended recipients argue that they did not receive the communication. Just because you sent someone an email does not mean that you have communicated with them.
- Is the distribution list of recipients inclusive? It is important to think about who needs to receive the message. Support and ancillary staff need to be included in some messages. Networking and teamwork can be enhanced or diminished by who is included in email communication.
- If an email is forwarded to a third party, it is essential to examine the chain of emails contained within the communication. There may be compromising or hurtful statements in earlier emails that are part of the chain.

As with verbal communication, good email communication is about sending messages in the most appropriate manner at the most appropriate time. Email is a tool for improving communication, but it also can be used as a weapon if the message shows lack of concern for the recipient. Inappropriate use of email can cause pressure on people that produces stress, overload and resentment.

Some early childhood practitioners, especially those in formal leadership positions, have identified the time needed to respond to emails as a source of stress. A number of practitioners reported being 'bombarded' with emails, many of which were not relevant to them. To minimise this difficulty, some people chose an hour—usually later in the day—to read and respond to emails, thereby preventing important time being swallowed by email correspondence. Others reported that, if possible, they dealt with email correspondence at home rather than at work. One disadvantage of this strategy is the inroad into personal time. Dealing with email is a time-management issue that requires strategies suited to individuals and their professional circumstances.

The intranet (within the organisation) and internet (beyond the organisation) are useful tools for accessing information, sharing information, learning and professional development. However, as with email, these need to be used legitimately for professional concerns. There have been instances where staff have tied up the technology for personal rather than professional agendas. In settings where access to equipment and time are limited, the technology needs to be used to meet professional needs and goals aimed at improving standards and quality. Looking up holidays, mortgage rates and new jobs at work is not appropriate or professional usage of the technology.

Mobile telephones and texting offer instantaneous communication with others anywhere and anytime. However, personal mobile phones need to be used appropriately and responsibly at work—that is, in your own time and never when on duty, especially where there is responsibility for the supervision of children. When used inappropriately, mobile phones are intrusive and impact negatively on quality of work.

The benefits of communication and information technology are many. However, there are numerous pitfalls which need to be avoided. Early childhood leaders must strive to ensure that communication and information technology is well managed in settings so that it saves time, frees staff from laborious tasks and improves inclusive communication.

## BRINGING IT TOGETHER

Effective early childhood practitioners have a balanced personal and professional life that enables them to meet others' needs while ensuring that their own needs are also met. This balance is a result of effective communication skills, the ability to delegate and to respond to conflict constructively, as well as the capacity to manage time and personal stress effectively.

# CHAPTER SIX
## WORKING TOGETHER TO FIND SOLUTIONS
## AND RESOLVE DIFFERENCES

*We have our differences about what to do but just because she is the leader does not mean she is always right . . .*

Childcare worker

**THIS CHAPTER EXPLORES**
- **sources of conflict within early childhood settings**
- **typical ways of managing conflict in early childhood settings**
- **constructive approaches to conflict management**

Conflict appears in many forms in early childhood settings, such as petty or major disputes, small or significant disagreements, minor to major differences of opinion, friction, irritation, clashes, aggressive confrontations, passive or active dissension, quarrels and mild to severe antagonism. Conflict in its various forms appears to be a constant feature of the psychological climate of early childhood services, given the frequency and intensity of disagreements, arguments, quarrels and disputes which are reported by practitioners, managers and leaders. What conflict signifies is the breakdown of communication and inter-personal relationships in the group. Where a workplace depends on social interaction, conflict is inevitable. This is a serious problem for early childhood services because the basis of service provision is social interaction and harmonious relationships. In any service where group relationships are related to the achievement of goals, or where the relationships need to be maintained in order to provide a service, skills for the management and resolution of conflict are essential. Early childhood practitioners need to learn to approach conflict in a positive manner and deal with it in ways that strengthen group relationships.

Quality care and early education depend on the ability of the staff to work productively together towards achieving the setting's goals. The leader of the group needs to develop skills to assist the staff in confronting the problems which are likely to arise as staff work towards their goals. Unfortunately, many early childhood practitioners still regard conflict as an abnormal occurrence that is not supposed to happen if people get on reasonably well with one another. 'Why are we having all of these problems?', 'What is wrong with our setting?', 'Why can't we stop fighting and get on with the job?' are questions typically asked by early childhood staff who also tend to believe that their setting is the only one having problems. What is not understood is that these sorts of questions are inappropriate for the work situation and illustrate that conflict is a misunderstood phenomenon. Rather, conflict needs to be considered as a natural part of work and life. The situation would be more of concern if conflict were not occurring. In fact, conflict can be positive and functional in that it can stimulate new ideas, growth and change. The real issue is not that conflict exists, but the way in which it is approached and managed. The type of question that needs to be asked by early childhood practitioners is: 'Given that conflict is a normal part of the work experience, how are we going to handle it?'

Conflict in early childhood settings is a form of interpersonal interaction in which two or more people struggle or compete over claims, beliefs, values, preferences, resources, power, status or any other desire. It is evident that the early childhood context provides a ripe arena for conflicts to emerge, given that individual philosophies about caring for and educating young children are derived from subjective beliefs, values and preferences supported by personal experience. In fact, many early childhood staff have reported that dealing with conflict over ethical dilemmas is a major source of tension in the workplace (Clyde and Rodd, 1989). All staff and parents will have their unique perspective on what is the best—and therefore, in their view, the only—way to care for and educate young children. The right to relate to children on the basis of one's subjective philosophy, regardless of the extent to which it complies with the setting's philosophy, is often defended by parents and staff with emotional, irrational and contradictory arguments.

It is obvious that uncontrolled or chronic conflict within work groups is harmful to both the quality of work and productivity, as well as to the quality of life and relationships in the setting. People spend their energy in dysfunctional ways, such as fighting, arguing, ridiculing each other, competing and using resources inappropriately when they need to be collaborating to provide a quality service for children and parents and a pleasant working environment for themselves. However, it must be remembered that it is not conflict itself which is the problem. Conflict only becomes unhealthy and unproductive when it is not dealt with effectively. In addition, conflicts which are not managed adequately may appear to be resolved but can re-emerge at the next point of tension in the group or in other forms. The fact that many early childhood leaders report continuous bickering, quarrels, minor conflicts and ongoing tension suggests that their attempts to deal with the difficulties are not getting to the source of the issue but are dealing with symptoms of other underlying, unrecognised problems.

Until recently, conflict in the workplace was regarded by workers and theorists alike to be negative, counterproductive and to be avoided if possible. Only negative outcomes were associated with conflict. It was considered to be a setback to the group, with statements such as 'It will take some time for us to get back on our feet!' signifying the negative outcome on work performance and 'Give her some time. She'll get over it!' illustrating the perceived negative impact on group relationships. Disharmony engendered by feelings of anger and competition was considered to stunt personal and professional development, weaken relationships, decrease flexibility and result in lowered levels of performance; consequently, it was regarded as unhealthy. However, disharmony, if handled sensitively and creatively, does not always need to have a negative outcome for work groups. It can give rise to a theoretical reconsideration and reconceptualisation of the role and function of conflict in the workplace.

Fortunately, organisational and human relations theorists now have a better understanding of the role of conflict and argue that, given the right situation and timing, conflict has functional, even positive, aspects for work groups. It is seen as an inevitable and necessary part of the group process because it provides an impetus for learning, growth, development and change. Conflict signifies that there is life and activity in the group and offers an opportunity for healthy learning. It can stimulate increased interest and curiosity, expose underlying tensions and unsatisfied needs, create new channels of communication and, if managed appropriately, result in the resolution of issues, increased flexibility in performance and strengthened relationships within the group. The way in which conflict is managed can turn it from a perceived setback into a positive learning experience for the group.

## SOURCES OF CONFLICT WITHIN EARLY CHILDHOOD SETTINGS

In order to approach conflict positively and manage it effectively, the early childhood practitioner needs an understanding of the origin of the conflict—where and how it arose. The source of the conflict can provide guidelines for dealing appropriately with the conflict. Communication skills usually form the basis of conflict management, but it is important to recognise that some conflicts in early childhood settings are a result of structural elements and therefore will be difficult to resolve.

### GROUP STRUCTURE

The physical environment of many early childhood settings contains certain structural constraints that can increase the likelihood of conflict occurring in comparison with other work settings. First, the staff are usually allocated to work in smaller groupings in separate rooms, which affects the ease of communication. The setting's team spirit can be decreased by staff forming allegiances to their sub-groupings—for example, the babies' room, the toddlers' room or the pre-schoolers' room. The fact that two or three staff members can be required to work closely together in relative isolation from other staff can lead to misperceptions of favouritism by the team leader, resentment about imagined benefits or privileges that staff in other rooms might receive and rumours about the team leader's attitude to performance in the various room teams.

Given that many early childhood settings operate for almost twelve hours every weekday and that consumer demand requires even more flexible hours of operation, early childhood staff are required to undertake shift work. This also affects the ease of communication between staff because there will be very few times when all staff are together (and free of responsibility) to discuss issues. Where information is passed on secondhand, there is a possibility of communication breakdown and misunderstanding which can lead to conflict. Staff breaks also need to be rostered to meet the minimum supervisory requirements for young children. Consequently, there is not even a common lunchtime in which to communicate as a group. Add rostered days off and holidays to these constraints and it becomes obvious that many factors exist which work against effective communication within the staff group and increase the likelihood of communication breakdown and conflict.

Time is an important issue in all early childhood services, and there is usually insufficient funding to employ relief workers to free individual staff members to attend meetings or to work in their small teams outside their allocated planning time. This means that anything extra such as staff meetings, in-service training or special curriculum planning meetings must be held in the evenings or during the weekend—that is, in the staff members' own time. Not all staff have developed a concept of professionalism where it is an accepted expectation that some of your own time will need to be devoted to work. Also, many staff have other responsibilities, such as their own family commitments. Consequently, not all staff are able to meet outside the opening hours of the setting in order to share information. Those who can are usually on a tight time schedule and want meetings to be held in as short a time as possible, which influences the depth of information-sharing and discussion that can be achieved.

Even within normal working hours, the potential for conflict due to communication failure is high. Staff have a responsibility for the safety and welfare of young children which entails constant and alert supervision at all times. Therefore, it is difficult to discuss an issue which arises during the day between two or three members of staff because they are not able to give it their full attention. Lack of attention to a staff member's comment may be interpreted as lack of interest, selfishness or some other negative explanation about why the comment was not taken up and acted upon. The need to focus attention on the children means that sometimes adult staff members will not have their own needs met and, instead of being appropriately assertive, staff members may become angry and initiate disharmony in the group.

The contact between parents and staff in the dropping off and picking up routines can also be conducive to conflict where neither parents nor staff stop to consider the needs of the other adult in the situation. Usually dropping off and picking up is a hurried process because the parent and staff have other responsibilities to meet. Staff may feel disregarded, unappreciated and exploited by parents who do not respond to their request to discuss a particular aspect of the child's progress and later respond to the parent in an off-hand or deprecatory manner. Staff may evaluate and label the parent in stereotyped terms and in future relate to the parent in terms of this stereotype. It may only take a few such experiences before a staff member may generalise this prejudice to all parents, which will result in very unsatisfactory relationships with parents who use the setting. Similarly, if a staff member does not immediately respond to a parent's request for attention, the parent may evaluate the staff member as insensitive, uncaring and unprofessional. These concerns may be discussed with other parents or the setting's leader, which is likely to leave the staff member feeling vulnerable, exposed and angry about the parent's reaction. The fact that neither parents nor staff have appropriate time or physical surroundings to discuss concerns at dropping off and picking up times can lead to misunderstanding and conflict. The problems with finding alternative times outside normal working hours have already been highlighted.

Early childhood practitioners need to be aware that the way in which early childhood settings are set up can provide communication difficulties which can very easily flare into situations of conflict if they are not dealt with immediately and effectively. There may be very little that can be done about the group structure and the physical setting, but staff and parents can be alerted to the potential difficulties that these factors can foster.

## GOALS AND POLICIES OF EARLY CHILDHOOD SETTINGS

Successful teams are characterised by a set of achievable goals that are understood and accepted by all. The same can be said of roles and responsibilities that need to be undertaken within a setting for its successful operation. Unfortunately, many early childhood staff teams have not had the opportunity to be involved in the development of goals, policies and job descriptions. Due to the uneven emergence of notions of professionalism, some early childhood teams do not consider this area to be part of their responsibility. However, all settings have some form of philosophy, statement of mission, aims and objectives, and policies that guide their operation. Given that these may have been imposed by the leader or a committee of management, not all staff will agree with and accept such goals and policies.

Conflict regarding goals and policies can be overt (where a staff member or parent openly disputes the validity of a certain policy) or covert (where the policy is superficially or tacitly accepted but is not supported or complied with in terms of action). Overt verbal or behavioural disagreement with goals or policies is easier to deal with because the conflict is obvious and there is a possibility for problem-solving. Covert disagreement can sabotage the implementation of goals and policies because people may verbally deny that there is a conflict and refuse to engage in discussion. The leader needs to be assertive about their concerns regarding the issue and encourage open problem-solving to help resolve the issue.

Unwritten laws that develop as part of the history of certain early childhood settings can also provide grounds for conflict. Given the high turnover of staff in many settings, it is likely that some of the staff will have had experience with different ways of dealing with issues and of meeting staff needs. Confusion about the acceptability of certain practices, such as 'mental health' days and unwritten laws which are so-called 'common knowledge' can provide a rich source of inequality, discrimination and conflict between leaders, staff and parents. The potential for conflict arising in such situations can be minimised if as many aspects of policy as possible are explained to staff and made accessible to public scrutiny.

The reason that conflict can spring from goals and policies is that they have a value basis. Part of the ethics of leadership requires that, in relation to conflict, the leader makes decisions about and acts on the basis of a clear personal and professional value system. The early childhood profession is dominated by individual beliefs, values and perspectives that can have a strong emotional component. Understanding that not all people are likely to accept or agree with the goals and policies of the setting is important. Providing opportunities for discussion, the sharing of perspectives and regular review is also necessary to minimise conflict in this area.

## VALUES

Many of the goals, policies and practice in the early childhood field are based on values. Value systems are individual and, although certain values may be held in common with other people, each of us develops a unique set of values which we use as guidelines or standards for decision-making and behaviour. Particularly when it comes to young children and families, each of us holds strong personal, emotionally laden values that are used to make decisions about what we believe to be in the best interests of children.

The personal ideas, values and beliefs of early childhood practitioners can be as influential on practice as professional value systems, particularly in the early stages of professional development (Vander Ven, 1988). It is not uncommon to find conflict between early childhood staff which is based on differing values systems and their relationship to practice in areas such as goals for children's behaviour, children's needs, group management, planning and organisation, materials, learning and development, children's characteristics, educational processes, educational play, evaluation and assessment and home and parents (Spodek, 1987). The leader in the early childhood setting will facilitate the clarification of value beliefs on practice and articulate the relevance of professional values while acknowledging the role of personal values in making decisions about children and families.

### REFLECTIONS ON LEADERSHIP IN PRACTICE

When I was a coordinator of an inner city childcare centre, I had two staff in the toddler room who just would not cooperate in their work. Their fighting and disagreements over work practices and values were affecting the children and the other staff. I had talked to them together and separately several times but could not get them to resolve their differences. So I decided to invite a mediator, someone outside the setting with skills in conflict resolution, to meet with them to see if she could help them resolve their differences. I was willing to invest funding in the mediation process because I didn't want to lose either of the staff members but I couldn't allow the fighting to go on. They met with the mediator a number of times and while I don't think there was complete resolution of their differences, they at least agreed to work more cooperatively together. I exercised leadership by recognising that I needed to get an expert in to help resolve this situation.

**Early childhood lecturer**

The values of the multicultural pluralist societies found in many countries around the world today demand as much respect as the more generally held community values. The early childhood profession recognises children's rights to have their culture and its value system affirmed in care and educational contexts, and acknowledges parents' desires to have their children interact with adults from their own culture while attending early childhood settings. However, this is another area where the potential for conflict is high. The values of specific cultures sometimes are quite different from those of the general community and of the profession—for example, the status and privileges which are given to young male children compared with young female children in some cultures, and the lack of respect accorded to female staff by fathers from particular backgrounds. These cultural differences can lead to conflict between staff from various cultural groups and to conflict between staff and parents. Appreciation of the ethics of leadership is important in guiding responses to conflicts that arise from different value systems.

## LEADERSHIP STYLE

Leadership and management style should not contribute to or exacerbate conflict (Said and Rolfe, 2001). Yet the level of conflict experienced in an early childhood setting may be related to the style of leadership displayed.

Leadership style is sometimes related to the level of maturity and experience of the staff where, for example, young and less experienced staff may be responsive to a more directive style which, if used with mature and experienced staff, could produce antagonism and conflict.

Leaders who have a tendency to be authoritarian may find that the level of conflict is higher in their settings than leaders who are more democratic and encourage staff participation in decision-making about operational matters. This is because most adults, particularly mature and experienced adults, resent being told what to do and think by someone else who does not recognise their expertise. Authoritarian leadership is likely to be most readily accepted by immature and inexperienced staff who are looking for direction and guidance in the workplace. However, as these people develop in confidence, they usually want to be more involved in matters that affect their work. Leaders who do not change their style to match staff needs for involvement may inadvertently stimulate resentment and rebellion on the part of staff.

Authoritarian leaders can tend to take on the responsibility of acting as mediators in conflicts between various staff, and between staff and parents, rather than facilitating the management of the conflict between the relevant parties. When the power hierarchy is invoked by either staff or parents to resolve disputes, one or both parties may be left feeling dissatisfied that their claims to justice were not given appropriate consideration and that resolution was imposed from outside. While the immediate issue may appear to be resolved, it is likely that any remaining underlying tension will re-emerge in another form or at another time. Early childhood practitioners need to understand that conflict has to be worked through by those parties immediately affected, with the leader demonstrating confidence that the parties themselves can reach a mutually acceptable solution. Support can be offered by modelling appropriate communication skills and discussion of alternatives in problem-solving sessions.

Permissive, 'anything goes' leadership does not avoid the problem of conflict. Leaders who do not provide direction and guidance, who accept poor quality performance from staff, who do not provide constructive feedback and who do not communicate high expectations of staff and parents will also find tension, resentment and disagreement among staff and parents. This type of leadership communicates a lack of respect and regard for children, parents, staff and the profession. Typically, lack of concern for the rights and needs of individuals, lack of tolerance and subjective prejudices cause conflict where there are few standards to act as guidelines for staff and parents.

A democratic leader understands that conflict is a symptom of a breakdown in communication and interpersonal relationships, and will involve relevant staff in an egalitarian process of problem-solving. This collaborative style of leadership is likely to result in issues being addressed by the relevant people before they develop into larger problems. In this way, fewer problems are likely to develop into full-blown conflicts because they are dealt with as they arise. It is not the case that settings who have leaders with democratic or collaborative styles of leadership are less conflict prone; rather, the conflicts are approached and managed differently. Techniques for effective management of conflict are discussed later in this chapter.

## JOB EXPECTATIONS AND DEMANDS

One important aspect of leadership style is the degree of definition provided by leaders concerning job expectations and demands. Over-definition and leader domination of job expectations and demands can diminish staff motivation and initiative. On the other hand, where roles and responsibilities have not been clearly defined and accepted as part of the team-building process, staff uncertainty and ambiguity about where responsibility lies can lead to disputes. Job expectations can be formed on the basis of previous experience, or can be derived from personal preference and presumption. Expectations derived from such sources may not be appropriate or relevant for the current situation. Therefore, it is essential that the leader provide opportunities for staff to clarify and negotiate who is responsible for what task or job.

Failure to articulate performance expectations for staff can also lead to tension and eventually conflict where staff can argue that 'I didn't know that you wanted it done that way!' or 'We didn't have to do it at the last place I worked! The coordinator always did it!' People can experience stress in situations where expectations and demands are not clear. Staff may deal with stress by becoming defensive and blaming the leader for not adequately informing them of what was required. Therefore, in order to avoid this source of conflict, the perceptive leader will ensure that all staff members (and parents if necessary) clearly understand what is expected from them.

## EMPLOYEE DISTRUST OF AUTHORITY

The leadership styles of some early childhood managers, coordinators or directors, such as the autocratic style, can suggest to employees that the leader does not have the best interest or the welfare of the group at heart. Uncertainty regarding the motivation of the leader for certain actions can arouse negative attitudes towards the leader and result in lack of cooperation by staff members. For example, the introduction of staff appraisal by a leader who is not trusted by the staff may be perceived in negative terms, such as the leader wanting to terminate the employment of one or more members, whereas the leader actually may want to introduce a program of staff development based upon mutually agreed goals.

Where staff distrust leaders and their motivation they are unlikely to support and participate in initiatives suggested by the leader. If conflict appears to stem from this source, the leader needs to work on developing basic trust between herself and the staff members, ensuring they have access to as much information as possible where policy and practical decision-making are involved. In addition, staff participation in decision-making and problem-solving can help overcome employee distrust of the leader.

## INABILITY TO ACCEPT FEEDBACK OR CRITICISM ON PERFORMANCE

One of the characteristics of effective communicators, and therefore of effective leaders, is their skill in delivering constructive feedback on staff performance. While many people understand feedback in terms of the negative aspect of criticism, the term 'feedback' also encompasses the positive aspect—that is, compliments and encouraging statements. The mistake many leaders make is to focus on the critical aspect and communicate personal blame to the individual for not accomplishing a desired or expected outcome.

Probably due to the demands on their time and attention, few leaders consistently encourage staff by commenting on the aspects of the day that have gone well, their strengths and assets, their contribution to the setting or the areas in which they have improved. For example, instead of saying 'You haven't included adequate information in your outdoor plans', the leader could say 'I can see that you've put a lot of effort into your planning this week. I'm a little concerned about the lack of detail for the outdoor experiences. Could we find a time to discuss the outdoor aspect?' Alternatively, the leader might make encouraging comments such as 'I notice that you've improved considerably in writing objectives for individual children', 'I really appreciated your contribution to the discussion on next week's plans at the staff meeting this morning' or 'Since you've been writing fuller plans, I've noticed that the day seems to be running more smoothly in your room'.

If leaders focus on the critical rather than the encouraging aspect of feedback, staff can learn only to expect a negative appraisal by leaders when the word 'feedback' is mentioned, and consequently, they will take a defensive attitude to any feedback. They may think that they need to defend themselves from the leader's supposed attack on their competence with a justification about why they did what they did. In some ways, staff inability to receive feedback is often a function of their previous negative experience with feedback and criticism from leaders.

However, if a leader can phrase feedback in a way that does not arouse staff defensiveness and opens channels for further communication, feedback can become a means of facilitating staff development rather than a point of contention. A practitioner would consider the following type of comment as helpful and acceptable: 'I noticed that you had set up a music experience which the children appeared to find very enjoyable. Can we get together to explore ways that you might extend Simon's participation? He seemed to be only peripherally involved.' Assisting staff to become familiar with constructive feedback which is phrased in an understanding and supportive style can avoid arguments in this area where staff believe that the leader has little understanding of and empathy for their position.

The introduction of regular staff appraisals for both leader and staff members in early childhood settings, where aspects of professional growth and development are acknowledged, and goals established for future improvement, is one way of assisting staff to learn the role of feedback and how to accept and use it constructively.

## INFORMATION AND MISINFORMATION

In terms of the effective running of an early childhood setting, the importance of accurate and unambiguous communication and the potential for communication breakdown have been highlighted. Another issue in the area of communication is the basis upon which information is shared—that is, who has access to what information. Practitioners need to be aware that information is power. Those who possess information relevant to a particular situation are in a better position to protect and provide for themselves, to make better decisions and to demonstrate competent performance. In other words, information empowers people, while a lack of information has the opposite effect.

Ethical considerations also affect what information is shared with whom. Early childhood practitioners come across many situations where ethical dilemmas arise in terms of whether information is made available or withheld—for example, requests for information from social workers or the Family Court counsellors, requests for information from access parents, requests for information from other parents about children who bite or hit and the issue of reporting suspected child abuse. The practitioner is required to bring sensitivity, discretion and professional expertise and ethics to such decisions. In human relationships, very few decisions are clear-cut and many decisions can result in conflict if they have not been fully thought out. The use of a code of ethics for guiding staff in ambiguous situations is an important professional strategy.

Effective and respected leaders collaborate with others. They are willing to share information openly and do not use the sharing and withholding of information as a means of wielding power in the setting. This is an important issue because much information comes directly to the setting's formal leader, who then has sole responsibility for making decisions about to whom and how that information will be disseminated. Staff who believe that they are being kept uninformed or denied access to information essential for them to perform their roles and responsibilities will be likely to lose confidence in the leader and perhaps ascribe negative motivation to such action.

Parents believe that they have the right to information available concerning their child and will quickly lose trust in an early childhood practitioner who does not provide them with what they regard as important information. The able leader uses discretion about the information which is provided to parents simply because the majority of parents are not trained to accurately interpret the kind of detailed observation that early childhood practitioners make. For example, a parent might comment on how other children's drawings look more sophisticated than those of her child. Rather than going into details of possible developmental delay, the sensitive practitioner might respond in terms of the factors that influence children's art and focus on the strengths of the child's drawing skills. Another common situation is meeting the parent's request to know who bit her child. Biting is a very difficult behaviour to prevent and staff may or may not know who the offender was. However, it may be in the best interests of all concerned to withhold that information so that children are not labelled and ostracised by other parents and to protect the biter's parents from the possible emotional backlash of the victim's and other children's parents. Reference to a professional code of ethics or standards of practice may help provide guidelines for the responsible management of information.

One sensitive issue in information-sharing is confidentiality. Within a setting meeting, the staff might discuss the progress of a child or problems that a parent has shared about her child. A staff member might be seeking assistance from the group to improve the learning opportunities designed for the child, and such professional discussions are beneficial for the staff members and the child. However, the information and opinions shared at a staff meeting must remain confidential and not be passed on to anyone else, particularly other parents. It is imperative that children and their families are not discussed with anyone outside the setting or in inappropriate venues, such as the supermarket or local shopping centre, because experience has shown that parents usually hear 'on the grapevine' and can justifiably be most upset at this breach of trust. The leader has the responsibility to ensure confidentiality to parents and, by the same token, to staff if for any reason staff performance needs to be discussed. Conflict about inappropriate information management can destroy basic trust between the leader, staff and parents, and diminish the quality of the service.

## PERSONALITY CLASHES

Conflict between members of early childhood settings has been explained and often dismissed by the use of the term 'personality clash', the implication being that the conflict was inevitable and cannot be resolved because of the fixed nature of the different personalities involved. While psychological research suggests that personality may be a largely inherited and stable trait (Berk, 2002), individual personality differences are not sufficient to explain why conflict occurs in the first place and is continued by two individuals. The more logical explanation is that the two individuals have chosen not to cooperate and not to meet the needs of the workplace by negotiating a mutually acceptable solution to their differences. In addition, the fact that the conflict is public in nature and is able to continue in the workplace suggests that the psychological climate in the setting accepts, and perhaps even subtly encourages, interpersonal friction as a way of responding to incidents which arise in early childhood settings.

Conflict which is continued by individuals in the workplace can be very destructive to general staff morale and parental confidence in the staff, as well as providing a poor model of human interaction and problem-solving for young children. The stereotype of 'personality clash' seems to be used by those who have no intention of working to resolve their differences or who wish to absolve individuals of responsibility for the conflict. The final outcome of the disruption caused to early childhood settings by individuals who choose not to cooperate and get on with the job is that inevitably one of the protagonists does not have a job. This outcome may occur either because one or both staff members choose to resign or because the leader or committee of management decides that the negative effects of continued conflict are affecting the quality of the service and terminate either one or both staff members' employment.

## RIGID MAINTENANCE OF PREJUDICES AND STEREOTYPED IDEAS

Some people—perhaps because of general personality tendencies—rigidly maintain their prejudices and stereotypes even when confronted with contrary evidence. In an area such as early childhood, where the knowledge base and understanding about young children and families is growing and increasing in complexity, staff need to be adaptable and flexible, willing to embrace new ideas and techniques as they become available. Professional relationships are grounded in communication and cannot function properly if some staff members are psychologically bound by outdated assumptions and stereotypes.

Attitudes to children and understanding of appropriate early childhood practice have changed dramatically over time, and some attitudes and practices that were once accepted have become outdated, irrelevant and inappropriate for today's society. For example, until the 1960s, physical punishment was believed to enhance obedience. Research now indicates that this is not true. In the same way, it used to be thought that tight authoritarian control over staff members was necessary to ensure that they met their work commitments. However, it is now accepted that this attitude has a negative effect on many employees' commitment to, motivation for and initiative at work. Children of single-parent families once were considered to be inherently disadvantaged. It is now accepted that the quality of children's experience depends on a range of factors.

Insensitivity to the need to consider new developments in the early childhood field can promote conflict between staff who want to maintain policy and practice derived from theories and ideas that are now outmoded and those who wish to incorporate current knowledge, understandings and skills into their work. Keeping up to date with research findings is now considered to be an ongoing professional responsibility.

## RESISTANCE TO CHANGE

The issue of change in early childhood is central to ongoing professionalism and will be discussed in detail in Chapter 10. However, it is important to recognise that employer and employee attitudes to change and subsequent resistance to change can be a source of conflict. Quality early childhood services are responsive to social, cultural, economic and political changes, among others. In the case where either the leader or the staff perceive change as a threat rather than an opportunity for growth, and where energy is misdirected into resisting rather than anticipating and easing the implementation of change, tension and frustration on the part of those who understand the need to be responsive to change can be a source of conflict.

The effective leader understands that change is threatening for many people, and that resistance to change is a normal human response. Nevertheless, leaders have to work to develop positive attitudes, in themselves and/or staff members, and towards overcoming areas of resistance in constructive ways rather than permitting any uncertainty about change to escalate into a situation of conflict.

There are many potential sources of conflict in early childhood settings and the preceding discussion has highlighted just a few. Among other potential sources of conflict, Ebbeck and Waniganayake (2003) list differing salary scales, high turnover of staff, staff appraisal, emergencies, the care/education dichotomy, an inability to implement polices and career progression. Effective early childhood leaders will analyse their settings in order to determine the likely sources of potential conflict and assess whether there are any structural modifications that could reduce the potential for conflict. However, conflict is inevitable and necessary for organisational growth. The next step is to manage conflict constructively.

## TYPICAL WAYS OF MANAGING CONFLICT

There are a number of commonly used approaches to dealing with conflict that vary in their outcome and degree of effectiveness. Unfortunately, the family appears to have been the training ground for many people; here, through observation and personal experience, ineffective and even destructive ways of dealing with conflict have been the norm. Unless people are particularly skilled in techniques for conflict management, the methods used by individuals in their personal relationships are usually inappropriate for the professional situation. Therefore, effective leaders will examine their own styles for responding to conflict and evaluate their outcomes in terms of the goals of the setting and staff morale.

The following typical ways of dealing with conflict can be observed in many early childhood settings, but tend to have unproductive or negative outcomes for the leader and the staff.

### DENIAL AND WITHDRAWAL

One common way of responding to conflict is to deny its existence. For example, the leader announces the new roster. Jane notices that she has another week of early shifts. Her tense body language and tone of voice communicate that she is unhappy with the new roster as she mutters to herself, 'How typical! I'm always given the worst shifts. The coordinator must really have it in for me!' Overhearing this complaint, the coordinator asks Jane if she has a problem with the new roster. Jane is non-assertive about her problem and replies, 'No, nothing's wrong. Everything is just fine' and walks away. This form of denial means that, even when an opportunity is presented to bring a potential problem up for discussion, there will be no movement towards acknowledging that there is a difference of opinion, defining what the difference is about or discussing possible alternatives. By denying that a problem exists, Jane has locked herself into a situation that she is unhappy with and she will experience the problems associated with being non-assertive which were discussed in Chapter 5.

In this example, Jane has also walked away. She has withdrawn from the situation and her behaviour indicates that she is not willing to participate in any discussion that may arise out of the posting of the new roster. It is almost impossible to resolve a conflict if one of the parties withdraws by turning silent or by physically removing themselves from the situation. Unless the other person is willing to be assertive and follow up the person who has withdrawn, it is unlikely that the issue will be resolved. The 'silent treatment' is manipulative and destructive to relationships as well as productivity, and the unresolved tension that is sure to build up will probably be released in an explosive outburst where the problem may be exaggerated and other past issues brought up to illustrate the injustice that has been suffered.

Denial and withdrawal do not resolve conflicts, but keep the dysfunctional tension buried just beneath the surface. The problem—which initially was small—is likely to re-emerge later in a different form or as a larger problem for the leader to deal with.

## SUPPRESSION AND SMOOTHING OVER

In this approach to conflict management, the parties acknowledge that a conflict exists but devalue its importance or significance to them. Using the above example of the new roster, Jane could acknowledge that she was not happy with the shift arrangement but would proceed to suppress her real feelings about the matter saying something like, 'Well, I don't really want to do those early shifts again but it doesn't matter. I guess I'm used to them by now.' The leader could attempt to smooth over the problem by commenting, 'It all works out in the long run, Jane. We all have to do our share of early shifts. I'll probably be on next time.'

Another way of suppressing and smoothing over conflicts is to minimise the degree of difference between the two parties. Staff members who disagree about a discipline practice might comment, 'I know it's pretty much the same thing but I would have done it differently' or 'Basically we're coming from the same point of view. It's just that I would do it a bit differently.'

The aim of suppression or smoothing over is to move away from the problem as quickly as possible and not to permit any real exploration of the different perspectives. The outcome is that the two parties are no closer to understanding one another's perspective or to negotiating a mutually accepted practice; however both are likely to feel that their position is really the right position and they will continue with the practice that initiated the feelings of tension. The problem is likely to re-emerge at a later time or in a different form and be more difficult to deal with because people have become entrenched in their positions. An opportunity for gaining a different perspective, learning and professional growth is lost when suppression is used.

## POWER AND DOMINANCE

The use of power in conflict situations demonstrates a basic lack of respect for the other parties. Power can be wielded from one's position in the hierarchy—for example, by the leader as the legitimate authority, by the deputy or second-in-charge with delegated authority, through group unity with the room staff standing against administration from the perspectives of longevity, seniority or possession of qualifications, or by essential staff such as the cook or cleaner, without whom it is impossible to meet minimum standards and requirements. Power can also be exerted by dominating conversations with a loud voice, by interrupting others and not letting them finish what they want to say, by crying and by using intimidating non-verbal communication.

Taking the example of Jane and the new roster, Jane could exert power and dominance over the other members of staff by behaving in an angry and aggressive way, by confronting the leader and demanding that the roster be changed, by pressuring non-assertive staff members to change shifts with her, by interrupting others and refusing to leave the coordinator's office until she got what she wanted, or by threatening to take the issue to a higher authority, such as the committee of management, chair of governors or the union. While Jane's behaviour might achieve a change in the roster, it will be at the expense of her respect from and relationships with others, and will also lower the quality of the service while staff deal with the other disruptions that accompany such aggressive outbursts.

The use of power to force others to submit or give way for peace and harmony can appear to result in the resolution of the problem, but creates resentment, anger, bitterness and eventually rebellion or subtler forms of sabotage from members of the group. Power is an aggressive means of responding to conflict and, rather than resolving conflict, power and dominance are more likely to escalate conflict in the long term. While other staff members might accept that one person can achieve their own ends in such a way, eventually they will feel exploited, perceive the leader as weak, and possibly interpret the organisational climate as one where power and dominance are accepted as the norm for moving towards one's goals. Instead of resolving one problem by permitting a display of power to be used to achieve certain ends, leaders may find that they have to deal with others who perceive this to be an effective form of conflict resolution.

## CONSTRUCTIVE APPROACHES TO CONFLICT RESOLUTION

There are a number of ways that conflict can be managed in early childhood settings which are more likely to produce positive outcomes for all involved. The basic premise of conflict resolution is to open and maintain channels of effective communication so that each party perceives themselves to be acknowledged and understood.

The following three-step framework of assertion, negotiation and problem-solving is simple and easy to implement for leaders in early childhood settings.

### ASSERTION

When an incident is perceived as having the potential to develop into a conflict, the first important step is to recognise it as problem that needs to be resolved. If the leader or any party involved in the incident can make an appropriately assertive statement which describes the behaviour, problem, performance, issue or action and associated feelings, this signals that one party has a different perception of the incident to that of other people. For example, when Jane had read the new roster, she could have made an assertive statement to the leader such as 'When I saw that I had been rostered on for another week of early shifts, I felt pretty upset because I have just finished doing a week of early shifts. I'd prefer to have a week of late shifts next week.'

The advantages of being assertive in this situation are that Jane has described the specific issue that her concern is related to, has vented her emotional reaction in an appropriate way and has indicated a preference for managing the situation in a way that will meet her needs. Other advantages are that Jane has directed her statement to the appropriate person—the leader who is responsible for the roster—and responded to the situation when it occurred, therefore avoiding a build-up of emotional tension and associated apprehension about confronting the leader. She has focused on the issue and not blamed or focused on the personality. The use of the 'I' statement indicates that she has taken responsibility for owning the problem. While being assertive cannot guarantee that Jane will be allocated the shifts that she wants, she has the satisfaction of having attempted to have her needs met in an appropriate manner.

This well-known assertive format can be useful in communicating a personal perspective:

When (description of the action, issue etc.)
I felt (description of the feeling or emotion)
because (explanation of importance or relevance)
I'd prefer (indication of an alternative)

Using one of these statements can assist in handling a range of disagreements and differences and prevent them from building up into more major disputes. If the assertion does not achieve the desired outcome, a further assertion can be valuable which lets the other person know that you empathise with their position but still require a modification of the issue. A comment such as 'I can see your point of view but I'd still prefer . . .' can communicate an intention to pursue the matter further. While it may be necessary to repeat the assertion a number of times, there comes a point where it is necessary to recognise that this technique for resolving the issue is not working. A different strategy needs to be selected.

## NEGOTIATION

If being assertive does not achieve a satisfactory resolution of the conflict, it is useful to move to a position of negotiation. In this step, the unsatisfactory nature of the situation is highlighted along with the motivation to achieve a mutually acceptable solution to the problem. This is important for situations where the aim is both to achieve goals and to maintain harmonious relationships. It is essential to communicate a cooperative intention, highlighting the costs of continuing the conflict and the benefits of resolving the conflict.

When negotiating a conflict, planning and timing are important. A meeting to discuss the issue needs to be set for a time when both parties are free and there is sufficient time to work through the issue. The first step is to obtain a joint definition of the conflict that is precise and does not exaggerate the problem. Both parties need to be fully aware of and communicate understanding of the other person's perspective and feelings about the conflict. Argumentative approaches and threats should be avoided. Concrete outcomes or alternatives should be emphasised. When moving towards an agreement, it is essential that the agreement be mutually acceptable and not the desired outcome of the dominant party. In situations where there has been difficulty in achieving a negotiated agreement, it can be useful to spell out the ways the two parties will behave differently in the future, the way in which any breach of the agreement will be dealt with and the way in which the two parties can check on how well the agreement is meeting both their needs.

Punctual return from tea break is an example of how a negotiated agreement can work. For example, Susan has been assertive with Pam who consistently returns late from morning tea. She has asserted, 'When you return late from morning tea, I feel angry because the children are late in packing up and getting ready for lunch. I'd prefer it if you came back by 11 o'clock.' But this has not resolved the problem. Susan then moves to a position of negotiation, saying, 'I'm really concerned with how we are coping with the transition from morning routine into lunchtime. I'd like us to discuss it in our planning time on Wednesday.' In the planning session, Susan empathises with Pam's position—for example, 'I know it's a real rush to get to the shop for a morning-tea cake. There's no time left to have a cup of coffee. But I'm having trouble coping with all the things that have to be done to get the children and the room ready for lunch when you are not back on time. I can see that my stress is having an effect on our work. If we can sort this out, we'll both be more relaxed for our own lunch and the afternoon with the children. Have you got any ideas about what we might do?' If a negotiated agreement is reached, Pam will agree to be back at a certain time and will understand the consequences of breaking the agreement. Susan and Pam will also discuss the smooth transition from morning to lunchtime in their planning meetings.

## PROBLEM-SOLVING

In cases where one party refuses to negotiate an agreement to a conflict, or where a negotiated agreement does not work or breaks down, it is essential to move quickly to a problem-solving strategy. It is possible that the three steps—assertion, negotiation and problem-solving—are employed in the same interaction. However, a number of attempts at assertion and negotiation are often employed before moving to a problem-solving approach. An assertive communication style is appropriate when using problem-solving strategies where conflicts are defined as mutual problems to be solved.

When employing a problem-solving approach, there are several steps that can be followed:

- Clarify the problem. What is the real issue? Where does each party stand on the issue?
- Gather the necessary facts and information.
- Generate or develop a number of alternatives by brainstorming.
- Evaluate and set priorities for the alternatives in order to determine the best solution. Create solutions by considering all alternatives.
- Plan the means of evaluating the most acceptable solution following a period of implementation.
- If the first solution chosen does not work (which can be a real possibility), return to the first step and begin the process again.

The problem-solving approach incorporates a collaborative perspective on conflicts. If one person has a problem, then we as a group have a problem. Blame is not apportioned. It acknowledges that all parties have the expertise to resolve problems that arise. It emphasises the intention to reach resolution rather than permitting the defence of particular positions. A problem-solving approach is a 'win–win' situation in which everyone's needs are respected and where people are invited to cooperate and contribute to the resolution of the issue. An attitude of 'we can work it out' communicated by the leader to the staff and parents can stimulate new levels of trust, more supportive relationships and greater commitment to the team and the job.

Leaders and those concerned with conflict resolution are advised to take Armstrong's (1994) recommendations:

- Use active listening.
- Look for and observe non-verbal cues and information.

- Help those involved to understand and define the problem.
- Allow feelings to be expressed.
- Look for alternative solutions.
- Encourage those involved in the conflict to work out how they will put an agreed solution in place.

## MEDIATION: TURNING CONFLICT INTO COOPERATION

Many leaders recognise the value of mediation in resolving conflict in early childhood settings. Mediation is not a new strategy for resolving disputes and it tends to be used when negotiation and problem-solving break down (Ebbeck and Waniganayake, 2003).

Mediation involves working towards settling difference by inviting a third party, who has no vested interest in the situation, to bring those who are entangled in a seemingly unresolvable exchange to the discussion table in the spirit of collaboration and creativity. However, the leader can assume the role of mediator in some circumstances. This can demonstrate to the team that working as a team is a high priority and a worthwhile investment of the leader's time and energy.

According to Noone (1996), the role of the mediator is to:

- facilitate communication;
- promote understanding;
- focus those involved on the specific matter being discussed;
- encourage creative problem-solving; and
- help those involved reach an agreed solution.

It is important that those in conflict are not pressured into mediation, but voluntarily agree to participate. Early childhood practitioners are more likely to agree to mediation if they understand its benefits, the difficulties associated with unresolved conflict, the role of the impartial facilitator, the importance of having the courage to communicate honestly, openly and respectfully and the centrality of confidentiality in the process. Effective mediators offer objective feedback, focus attention on progress with cooperation and facilitate empowerment and self-esteem of the individuals involved.

Successful mediation usually requires a number of meetings, including an introductory session to determine the nature and depth of the problem and a number of follow-up meetings that focus on listening to and appreciating different perspectives, identifying common ground and working towards an agreed settlement.

When early childhood leaders accept a role in mediation, it is important to do so when team morale and work productivity appear to be threatened. Leaders can set an example to others regarding ways of cooperative conflict resolution.

Because it often necessitates the involvement of a skilled, impartial and paid facilitator, mediation tends to be used as a last resort when other approaches to conflict resolution have not been successful. However, it is an important tool in early childhood settings which are recognised as being prone to conflict situations. Conflict which is handled well builds cohesiveness and creates the problem-solving atmosphere which is so important to raising quality in these settings.

## BRINGING IT TOGETHER

Effective leaders in early childhood settings will place great emphasis on developing their own skills for managing conflict and on teaching staff to view conflict as normal and as an impetus for personal and professional growth. They will implement recognised management practices for handling disputes and encourage staff to assume responsibility for handling their own problems. In addition, they will encourage a professional climate where colleagues are aware of and understand one another's expertise and where individual differences are valued. The leader will appreciate their ethical responsibility for managing conflicts constructively and, together with the staff, will be aware of the role of conflict in team development (see Chapter 8), and will take responsibility for assisting the team's progress to more productive working relationships.

# CHAPTER SEVEN
## DECISION-MAKING

*Leaders are good decision-makers and feel empowered to speak out . . .*
Director, early learning centre

**THIS CHAPTER EXPLORES**
- **decision-making as a critical leadership skill**
- **types of decisions**
- **methods of decision-making**
- **problem-solving**
- **professional ethics and decision-making**
- **guidelines for decision-making**

Decision-making is the crux of the leadership process and is the means by which leaders plan, organise and guide members of early childhood settings towards accomplishing their goals. This skill seems to be difficult for many leaders, particularly those who are new to the position. However, it is an extremely important skill for early childhood leaders because the decisions taken will affect the lives of children, parents, staff, the community and the overall profession.

Decision-making involves a choice, guided by professional standards, between two or more alternatives, and can be regarded as a step in the larger process of problem-solving in goal-directed groups (Robbins, 2004). The quality of the decisions made will impinge upon the quality of the service provided because both the quality of work (i.e. task performance) and the quality of life (i.e. group morale) are affected by this ethical aspect of leadership.

What separates a mediocre leader from an able leader is usually the quality of decisions. Decisions are effective to the extent that they meet the following criteria:

- The resources of the group are fully utilised.
- Time is well-used.
- The decision is correct or of high quality.
- All the required group members fully implement the decision.
- The problem-solving ability of the group is enhanced.

In organisations that are focused primarily upon meeting the needs of human beings, such as early childhood settings, decisions are a focus of daily activity. While many day-to-day decisions are about trivial things—for example, arrangements for a social function—others are challenging (Rand, 2000), and involve complex decisions about programming and curriculum, menu, what information is publicised in the newsletter, staffing, parent involvement and financial, policy and ethical issues.

The leader is usually responsible and accountable for the majority of the decisions required for the efficient operation of an early childhood setting, but decisions can be made in a variety of ways. The decisions may be routine, problem-solving or innovative in nature. The method of decision-making chosen by the leader will be influenced by the nature of the decision to be made, who is included in the decision-making process, the desired quality of the decision, the extent to which those affected by the decision accept it, and the level of support given to implementing the decision.

Decision-making style is linked to:

- the personal characteristics and style of the early childhood leader;
- the characteristics of the group;
- the nature of the decision to be made; and
- the context of the decision.

In recent times, the focus has been upon assisting leaders to make rational, cognitive and objective decisions. The use of sophisticated computer simulations and mathematical models which are based on information management and its systematic analysis are examples of decision-making techniques which have attempted to bypass the human, emotional and subjective element of the decision-making process. However, the human input into decision-making cannot be ignored because good decisions often involve a combination of reason and emotion, fact and feeling, objectivity and intuition. Emerging information about the brain, particularly in relation to the influence of emotions on perception, thinking, memory and problem-solving, provides insight into the essence of leadership and decision-making (Dickman and Stanford-Blair, 2000).

Hasenfeld (1983:29) suggests that, in decision-making, leaders search 'for a satisfying solution by constructing a simplified model of reality that is based on past experiences, selective perception of existing stimuli, and familiar alternatives'.

Some newer approaches to problem-solving—for example, 'blue skies thinking' and 'thinking out of the box'—have contributed to more imaginative, novel and original solutions to problems (de Bono, 2004a, 2004b; Turner, 2003). Essentially, these strategies challenge leaders to engage in lateral, creative and imaginative thinking in order to come up with a host of new ideas, unusual or unexpected possibilities, connections and solutions. Such thinking skills can allow a leader to see 'the big picture', to experiment, take informed risks and to try out new strategies. If leaders have the courage to use these thinking tools and to encourage staff to do likewise, they may profit from the team's ideas and innovations. These combinations and strategies may stimulate the creative aspect of decision-making that differentiates good and poor decision-makers (Robbins, 2004).

Although many leaders would argue that they use a rational approach to decision-making that involves gathering the relevant information and making an informed choice, some problems in early childhood services do not lend themselves easily to rational decision-making—for example, behaviour management, ethical dilemmas and staffing decisions. Factors such as lack of knowledge, time pressures, organisational structure or emotions will affect the ability to be rational.

Goleman (1996) argues that decision-making is easily flawed when emotions are not used intelligently. He points out that emotions can disrupt thinking—for example, in stressful situations we sometimes say that 'we can't think straight'. The inability to deal with strong emotions can impair decision-making about even mundane matters.

Faulty logic, a lack of analytical skills and abilities, and permitting emotional issues to cloud the situation can result in poor-quality decisions. A number of national early childhood professional bodies, among them the National Association for the Education of Young Children and the Australian Early Childhood Association, have developed codes of ethics that are designed as reference points to assist staff with making some of the more difficult decisions. The value of such tools has not been fully recognised and many early childhood practitioners under-utilise this valuable resource for rational decision-making.

## TYPES OF DECISIONS

Decisions can be classified into two general categories: programmed decisions and non-programmed decisions.

Programmed decisions are appropriate for routine, regularly occurring incidents and previously encountered situations, and minimise the need for the decision-maker to exercise discretion. In programmed decision-making, an approach that has been found to be successful in previous situations is applied. It is very much a case of 'if this happens, do that'. For example, if a parent does not arrive to collect their child on time, the situation calls for a programmed decision because the decision-maker will follow policy and do what others would have done in the same situation. All staff in early childhood settings make programmed decisions every day. Pre-service and post-initial training provides practitioners with a repertoire of programmed responses that can be applied to frequently occurring situations. These manifest as goals and objectives, standards, policies and procedures.

Non-programmed decision-making is used in relatively novel, ambiguous, unstructured and spontaneous situations for which the organisation has not developed policies and procedures. A more general problem-solving approach is required to customise the solution for the specific situation. For example, the selection of a deputy or room leader is a non-programmed decision, as is the development of a program or curriculum. Non-programmed decisions are based on the judgment, intuition and creativity of the leader, and consequently necessitate a more competent decision-maker. It is more likely that the leader of an early childhood setting will have specific responsibility for making non-programmed decisions. In these services, where administrative responsibility for children, staff and parents is becoming less routine, more ambiguous and less amenable to programmed decisions, leaders will need to gain skills in effective decision-making.

According to Carlisle (1979), there are three types of decisions:

- intuitive;
- judgmental; and
- problem-solving.

Intuitive decisions are based on feelings and emotions rather than rationality or pure logic. Although some objective information is used to guide the decision, hunches, intuition and feelings are uppermost in influencing the leader to 'feel right' about the decision, regardless of information or advice to the contrary. Experienced leaders might come to high-quality decisions using the intuitive approach, but the disadvantages of being swayed by one's ego, lack of perspective and devaluing important information may lead to inappropriate decisions which the leader is unable to explain or defend. Intuitive decision-making might be employed in the hiring of a staff member where, qualifications and experience being equal among applicants, the leader simply has 'a gut feeling' that a particular applicant would fit in better with the existing staff team. In dealing with a particularly vulnerable parent, the leader might intuitively feel that sharing information about her child's lack of progress would be detrimental to the parent's well-being and decide to withhold the information for the time being.

**REFLECTIONS ON LEADERSHIP IN PRACTICE**

In my experience, leadership was displayed when a new manager was employed and quickly redecorated the nursery, changing it from how it had been for many years into a brighter place to work. She made the decision, told us what was going to happen and then followed through. That decision totally changed the atmosphere into one that seemed lighter and more energetic. We loved coming to work because it felt like a good place to be.

**Childcare worker**

Judgmental decisions are based upon expert knowledge and experience, where the leader is able to predict accurately the outcome of a particular course of action or decision. The leader's technical expertise means that little time is needed to reflect upon the decision because the problem has been encountered and successfully handled before. Quick judgments may be accurate, but there will always be a situation in which the basic assumptions or underlying conditions have changed and are no longer relevant to the decision. Judgmental decisions might be appropriate for ensuring that the setting complies with the local regulations, which staff will be allocated to a particular group of children or decisions concerning the medical treatment of a child whose parents cannot be contacted.

The problem-solving approach is a rational method where systematic, objective steps are undertaken in order to solve complex or previously unencountered problems for which there may be several possible solutions. It is useful for situations where more information is needed and where time is required to study, analyse and reflect upon the problem. Preventative decision-making is also included under the problem-solving approach where the leader looks ahead and, on the basis of existing information and conditions, anticipates what might occur. However, the quantity of information available to the leader is not the central issue. Being flooded with information can delay the problem-solving process. Poor-quality or irrelevant information will produce low-quality decisions. It may not be the amount of information that is accessed by the leader that is relevant, but how key the information is to the decision to be made. Problem-solving as an approach for decision-making would be appropriate for any major change to the setting, such as enrolment policy, program management or hours of operation, staff changes or the response to complaints from parents regarding program or curriculum focus.

These three types of decisions highlight another aspect of decision-making: the relative effectiveness of the individual versus the group. While shared decision-making may promote a sense of ownership, it can be detrimental if it is inappropriate for the nature of the decision (Law and Glover, 2000)—for example, the time involved. Also, the quality of the outcome of individual leader-led decisions depends on their acceptability to the team—that is, the extent to which others will implement them.

Both the intuitive and judgmental approaches may be used by individuals and accepted by staff and parents on the basis of the leader's expertise. However, if the decision proves to be inappropriate or poor, the leader is likely to bear the brunt of the group's dissatisfaction, resentment and diminished morale. The problem-solving approach may be undertaken by one individual but, given the nature of the situation and the time required to gather, analyse and evaluate information and develop possible solutions, the sharing of the responsibility for this process among group members is likely to result in higher quality and faster decision-making. Early childhood practitioners are cautioned about the over-use of intuitive and judgmental approaches because of certain limitations that are inherent in such approaches. These limitations are discussed in Chapter 10 as part of a fuller discussion about sources of information for decision-making. Awareness of the range of available sources of information, other than intuition and judgment, is essential because it provides early childhood practitioners with an opportunity to create a better match between the problem to be solved and the method employed in order to come up with the most appropriate solution.

## METHODS OF DECISION-MAKING

Johnson and Johnson (2003) have outlined a number of decision-making methods which vary according to individual and group input. A review of the literature on group decision-making reveals that, in some situations, decisions made by groups can be superior to those made by individuals. However, Robbins (2004) points out that:

- group decisions are rarely better than the best performer in the group;
- groups consume more resources so any improved effectiveness in group decision-making must be counterbalanced against poorer efficiency; and
- the type of situation, as well as the interpersonal relationships in the group, can impact on the quality of group decision-making.

The following section examines several decision-making methods that involve individual and group input.

### INDIVIDUAL DECISION-MAKING BY THE DESIGNATED LEADER

This is a method where the leader makes the decision independently of the group. This style may not be the preferred style of the leader, but she or he may be placed in this position because of group apathy or group members' stereotyped beliefs about the degree of expertise, power and responsibility of the leader. Many leaders in early childhood settings have complained that group norms operate where they are expected to make most of the decisions because they are the designated leaders, regardless of whether the decision would be handled better by the group. The other staff members do not see it as their role or responsibility to participate in decision-making, and instead rely on the leader to perform this role. The disadvantages of this approach include:

- a lack of commitment of the group to the implementation of the decision;
- possible staff disagreement;
- resentment and hostility about lack of involvement in the decision-making process; and
- under-utilisation of the resources of the group.

It is not uncommon for staff and/or parents to go along with the leader's decisions until the leader makes an unpopular decision that results in an overt or subtle conflict between the staff and/or parents and the leader. This method of individual decision-making is appropriate in circumstances where the group may lack the skill to make the decision and where there is insufficient time to involve group members.

## INDIVIDUAL DECISION-MAKING BY THE DESIGNATED EXPERT

This method is similar to that outlined above, but an individual member of the group is acknowledged as having expertise in a particular area and given the authority to make the decision. An example of appropriate use of this method would be delegating the purchase of musical equipment to the staff member who is most qualified and experienced in the music area. The research on decision-making supports the notion that high-quality expertise can result in high-quality decisions by individuals. However, if it is essential for group members to accept the decision, then having group members participate in the decision-making process is logical. Apart from having the advantage of using the resources of the group, the advantages and disadvantages of this method are the same as in the first method described above.

## DECISION BY AVERAGING THE OPINIONS OF INDIVIDUALS

With this method, group members may be consulted individually or at a meeting to find out what each person thinks. The final decision is based on the most popular choice or alternative identified by the members. For example, determining the most popular topic for the speaker at the annual general meeting could be undertaken using this method. The difficulties associated with this approach include:

- lack of group discussion and interaction;
- unresolved conflict which may impact on future group decision-making; and
- the possibility that non-assertive members will voice what they believe the leader wants to hear or what they believe will obtain personal approval from the leader in a personal, one-to-one interview, rather than what they really think.

However, this approach is useful when an urgent decision has to be made, when it is difficult to get group members together for a meeting (as with shift work and rosters in early childhood settings or distances between staff in different settings), when staff or parent commitment is necessary to effectively implement a decision, or when the group lacks the harmony, motivation or skills to make the decision in any other way.

## DECISION BY THE LEADER FOLLOWING GROUP DISCUSSION

With this method, the group has the opportunity to discuss the situation, but the leader reserves the right to make the final decision. In this method, the group is consulted by the leader and has the opportunity to provide input, but has no responsibility for the final decision. Consulting with the group about the funding submission or details to be included in the annual report would be appropriate for this method.

The level of discussion will be an important factor in this method, with the leader needing to employ sophisticated communication skills to ensure that open, honest discussion is facilitated. With this method, there is benefit from group discussion, but the disadvantages associated with decisions by averaging individuals' opinions can influence the quality of the decision finally taken.

## DECISION BY MINORITY

Here, the leader delegates the decision to the group or to a small committee comprised of individuals with appropriate knowledge and skills who will consider the issue, take a decision and report back to the larger group. This method can be useful for:

- a routine decision;
- a problem-solving decision where not everybody needs to be involved in the process; or

- a decision where only a few members have the relevant resources.

The organisation of a setting-based in-service program or the end-of-year function could be handled appropriately by a small group of staff and/or parents. The production of a parent handbook also lends itself to this method. Again because of the lack of involvement of the wider group, the disadvantages inherent in the previous methods of decision-making also apply to this method.

## DECISION BY MAJORITY VOTE

Following a period of group discussion, a vote is taken either publicly or anonymously, and the alternative favoured by the majority of the group members is accepted. This is a common decision-making method in early childhood settings and has the advantages of permitting group discussion and interaction as well as using the resources of the group. Many routine decisions—for example, the purchase of food and cleaning materials, the choice of a particular speaker for an in-service afternoon, and problem-solving decisions, such as the establishment of dispute and grievance procedures—can be handled by majority vote following discussion. Again, the productivity of the discussion will be dependent on the communication skills of the person chairing or facilitating the discussion. Indeed, the end result could be achieved without full participation of all group members, with those who are non-assertive being overpowered by the more vocal members. It is also possible to alienate the minority whose needs and interests may be denied in the final decision, with the result being lack of commitment to implementing the decision. Decision by majority vote can be subject to lobbying by those individuals with vested interests in certain decisions that may not be in the best interest of the group.

## DECISION BY CONSENSUS

This method is considered by many to be the most effective means of decision-making, producing innovative, creative and high-quality decisions. In this method, the issues are thoroughly discussed, with each group member participating fully until a basic agreement that is acceptable to everyone involved is reached. The decision has been the responsibility of each member, who is then partially accountable for its effective implementation. The development of a discipline statement, setting goals, philosophy and general curriculum issues can be handled using this method. The advantages of the consensus method include:

- the use of the full resources of the group;
- gaining full commitment to the implementation of solutions to serious and complex problems; and
- enhancing confidence in future decision-making by the group.

The disadvantages of this method are that it can be very time-consuming for a group to arrive at consensus, it requires a high level of motivation and psychological energy, and it is inappropriate for emergency, pressure or high stress contexts.

## GROUPTHINK: CONSENSUS THROUGH CONFORMITY

A phenomenon called 'groupthink' (West, 2004) has been found to affect the quality of decisions made by consensus. Groupthink refers to a mode of reasoning that individual group members engage in when their desire for consensus overrides their ability to assess a problem realistically or to consider a wide range of possible alternative courses of action. Critical thinking is sacrificed for consensus and a sense of unanimity. People refrain from offering opinions that do not appear to favour the thinking of the majority of the group and articulate views that are perceived to be in line with the group's direction. The result is a low-quality decision that will diminish the group's confidence in its ability to produce innovative, creative, problem-solving decisions.

West (2004:120) observes that leaders who use a directive style tend to inhibit exploration and expression of opposing opinion. In addition, leaders who push their own views strongly tend to diminish the quality of decision-making. However, leaders who directly encourage participation by team members who are reserved and reticent, and who also curb the contribution of more dominant team members, appear to empower higher quality decision-making. Effective leaders are aware that leadership style can impact on quality decision-making.

Leaders need to become familiar with the phenomenon of groupthink, and take steps to avoid the ramifications of it, such as adopting an initial stand of impartiality, assigning someone to act as devil's advocate, developing alternative scenarios, re-examining previously discarded alternatives, and holding second-chance meetings for everyone to express residual doubts and concerns. In this way, decision by consensus is more likely to reflect real consensus rather than the pressures of groupthink.

## LIMITATIONS OF INDIVIDUAL DECISION-MAKING

While the disadvantages of group decision-making have been outlined, there are a number of limitations to individual decision-making which need to be considered by leaders in early childhood settings.

First, some leaders have the tendency to put off decision-making until it is too late for effective action. Hence, the opportunity is lost or the problem has become so big that it is not easily solved.

Second, some leaders time decision-making so that, while not acting too late, they ensure that no significant progress can be achieved. Equilibrium is maintained and the organisation is kept on track, but change and innovation are discouraged. These types of leaders do not demonstrate skill in three important factors related to decision-making:

- judgment;
- the risk to be taken; and
- the information needed to make better decisions.

Leaders who are 'considered risk takers' are likely to make the most effective decisions because they tend to:

- examine the prevailing circumstances at the time the decision has to be taken;
- assess the degree of urgency or the risk factor necessitating the decision; and
- use the amount, type and quality of the information available at the time.

Early childhood leaders need to assess their personal tendencies and gain training and experience in decision-making so their judgment, timeliness and skills of critical analysis can be nurtured. Confidence to make decisions and take acceptable risks is enhanced with training (Hill and Ragland, 1995). Until a degree of skill is obtained in decision-making, early childhood leaders should consider the benefits of the group decision-making process.

Another problem which may affect the quality of decisions that early childhood practitioners make relates to field-dependent versus field-independent cognitive processing styles. Field-independent individuals tend to employ their own internal standards and values as sources to guide them in processing information—that is, they can separate and abstract objects from the surrounding field and use analytical skills to solve problems that are presented in reorganised or different contexts. Field-dependent individuals, on the other hand, focus on external points of reference and rely on authority to provide guidelines for information processing. The attributes of field dependence are related to the formation of empathetic relationships with others—the focus of direct care with children and interaction with parents and staff. However, the more analytical attributes of field independence are related to the cognitive flexibility necessary for quality decision-making and problem-solving. While most human beings possess some of the characteristics of both styles of information processing, leaders of early childhood services need to develop significant attributes of field independence to enhance their professional performance in the leadership role.

## PROFESSIONAL ETHICS AND DECISION-MAKING

Leadership involves making decisions that are sound because they are grounded in ethics as well as practice. Early childhood practitioners are continually confronted by choices about purpose, meaning, practices and relationships, which means that they make decisions that are ethical in nature (Moss, 2001). Effective leaders explicitly apply ethical principles in decision-making and encourage team members to do likewise (Newman, 2000). Being an ethical leader is discussed more fully in Chapter 12. However, the relevance of a code of ethics to guide professional decision-making needs to be highlighted for members of those professional groups, such as early childhood practitioners, who have the autonomy to exercise considerable discretion in terms of how they interact with consumers of their service, as well as how they operate and conduct their service.

A professional code of ethics offers a protocol for critical reflection by practitioners about their practice and relationships, a reference point for professional behaviour, and guidance for making appropriate and valid decisions when ethical concerns are present that can enhance professional confidence and ability. A code of ethics can provide guiding principles for decision-making about obligations and responsibilities in daily practice (Stonehouse and Creaser, 1991), can make decision-making easier because it provides a basis for action which is less likely to be challenged by those inside and outside the profession (Feeney and Kipnis, 1991), and can play an important role in professionalisation—that is, the establishment and maintenance of standards within a profession (Coady, 1991).

A code of ethics provides guidelines concerning what early childhood practitioners are committed to provide in terms of quality services for young children and their parents. While existing codes of ethics do not attempt to provide prescriptive or 'right' answers to the complex questions and ethical dilemmas faced by early childhood practitioners, they do help practitioners to work out what is right and good, rather than expedient and simply practical, and point to attitudes and behaviours which practitioners should never engage in or condone (Stonehouse and Creaser, 1991). As such, reference to a code of ethics can help expedite both day-to-day and long-term decision-making regarding what responsible early childhood practitioners should and should not do (Rodd and Clyde, 1991).

## GUIDELINES FOR DECISION-MAKING

Many authors have constructed a set of guidelines that can be used by novice and experienced decision-makers alike, whether leaders or groups, to improve the quality of their decisions:

1  Ascertain the need for a decision by defining the situation, problem or goal. Does an unsatisfactory situation exist? Is there some disparity between what is and what should be? For whom is the situation unacceptable? Is the situation a symptom of another underlying problem? What are the hidden agendas, if any? In defining the situation, the effective leader will attempt to gather the facts and feelings as close to the reality of the situation as possible.
2  Establish the decision criteria. This means indentifying the characteristics that appear important in making the decision, collecting and studying the relevant opinions, facts and information, allocating weight to the criteria in order to develop priorities in the decision criteria and knowing which criteria are central and which are peripheral to the decision.
3  Develop alternative solutions and formulate choices. It is important to identify all of the different alternatives that are available and avoid evaluation at this stage. It is the leader's responsibility to explore all existing possibilities to ensure a fair and intelligent

decision, and to refrain from formulating preferences and expectations as alternatives are uncovered.

4 Evaluate the alternatives in terms of the likely results of choosing that direction. The strengths and limitations of each alternative should be compared with the relative weightings established in step 2. Questions such as when, where, how, with whom and what the likely results may be need to be answered for each alternative. Feelings about each alternative need to be considered at this stage because they can bias and alter rational reasons for particular alternatives.

5 Select the best alternative. This means choosing the solution that appears to be the most appropriate and makes the most sense. Avoid procrastinating and postponing the decision. Note that the 'best' alternative at the time is still a subjective choice and might turn out to be inappropriate later because, despite the systematic and objective efforts of the leader and group, a wrong choice can be made.

6 Follow through to support the implementation of the decision. This translates to providing personal support to those who will implement and maintain the decision. It also includes stimulating interest and enthusiasm in the process, ensuring backup and sufficient time for implementation, and communicating shared responsibility and accountability for the success of the decision.

7 Evaluate the effectiveness of the decision in resolving the initial problem. It's crucial to be flexible and keep an open mind in case the first choice was inappropriate. Be willing to modify the initial decision or engage in the decision-making process again using the present information to reach a new alternative.

## PROBLEM-SOLVING

In the more general process of problem-solving, the same steps are employed. Problem-solving is useful when an element of conflict exists in the situation. The situation can be defined as a mutual problem to be solved rather than a win–lose circumstance. Because conflict triggers emotional responses, it is important to channel the emotional energy towards constructive ends by adopting appropriate win–win attitudes. In problem-solving, it is beneficial for the participants to focus on the positive results associated with the process of arriving at a solution. The group members need to have developed a certain attitude to conflict so that it is regarded as a healthy and normal part of group process, and they need to be willing to communicate honestly and openly with each other concerning the issue. Conflict resolution is discussed in detail in Chapter 6.

## BRINGING IT TOGETHER

The challenge of leadership is for early childhood practitioners to develop vision and assertiveness in order to make effective and ethical decisions that will move the organisation towards achieving its goals while maintaining a sense of cooperation, loyalty and harmony in group members. The leader should focus attention on the big picture and not become preoccupied with day-to-day details. Skill needs to be developed in non-programmed decision-making where judgment, intuition and calculated risk-taking produce creative approaches by the leader to goal attainment and to the situations and problems which emerge in any setting.

# CHAPTER EIGHT

# BUILDING AND LEADING
# A TEAM

*Good leaders build teams by making everyone feel that their contribution matters . . .*

Early education team leader

**THIS CHAPTER EXPLORES**
- **the advantages of joining together to achieve quality**
- **what constitutes a team in early childhood**
- **working in a multi-disciplinary team**
- **the stages of team development**
- **team leadership**
- **a framework for team-building**

In the administration of early childhood settings, considerable emphasis has been placed upon the significance of effective leadership. The quality and qualifications of leaders in these settings helps ensure high-quality provision (Sylva and Siraj-Blatchford, 2003) and helps raise standards and expectations for the other staff to follow. However, numerous studies of work groups suggest that, in groups which successfully meet the demands of goal attainment and harmonious relationships, leadership responsibilities are not placed upon one person, but are shared widely.

The reality is that, in any human service organisation, all members of staff contribute to the operation and administration of the service—

for example, by answering the telephone, dealing with inquiries, making programmed decisions, managing their own problems and responding to the needs of any situation which may arise. Teamwork, in which individual interests and needs are subordinated in order to engage in joint, coordinated activity to achieve the common goals and purposes of a united group, is equally important, particularly in early childhood services which involve people, their relationships and feelings.

## JOINING TOGETHER TO ACHIEVE QUALITY

The team approach is considered by many to be the most appropriate way of meeting the demands of the complex network of early childhood provision—for example, for the development of organisational vision, policy, plans and operational procedures, as well as for effective day-to-day running of the range of early childhood services presently offered. Ebbeck and Waniganayake (2003:195) comment that 'building effective teams is fundamental to early childhood practice'. A cohesive team is a key resource for the provision of quality child care and education for young children. According to Whalley (2001:140), 'working as a team is a process not a technique. It is rooted in an ideology of empowerment, encouraging adults . . . to take control of their own lives and giving children the permission to do the same . . .'

Many early childhood practitioners think that leaders should be community-minded because early childhood settings are essentially communities of learners where 'children . . . discover and adults rediscover the joys, difficulties and satisfactions of learning' (Law and Glover, 2000:149). Teams are like small communities, and to do their job effectively they need to be nurtured by the leader. Effective leaders assume an enabling role to build a strong team.

*A leader needs to build the self-esteem of the community . . .*
**Early years/primary adviser**

Effective leadership and collective responsibility—that is, teamwork—can have a major impact on the quality of the service offered. Considerable research evidence reveals a connection between young children's development and the stability of care in early childhood settings. Instability of care, be it a result of frequent changes in a setting or frequent changes of staff within the setting, can have negative effects on children's development (Hennessy et al., 1992). The tone of the working environment can produce a lack of responsiveness and sensitivity among some staff that can lead to high staff turnover rates. Effective leadership and teamwork are considered to be factors which contribute to increased self-esteem, high job satisfaction and staff morale, reduced stress and a decreased likelihood of staff burnout (Schiller, 1987). The end-product of teamwork is an improvement in the quality of care and education for children.

While some people still enter the early childhood field with the assumption that the focus of the job is on autonomous work with children, the reality of these settings today is that the increasingly multifaceted work of the early childhood practitioner requires effective interaction with other adults as members of a multi-disciplinary team. When practitioners talk about the staff at their settings, the word 'team' is often used.

*Sharing distributed leadership throughout the setting and emphasis on teamwork are key leadership attributes . . .*
**Early years/primary adviser**

Most early childhood leaders and staff appreciate that teamwork is important for the working conditions of their settings, and understand that what constitutes a team can vary. For example, in pre-schools, the team may consist of two adults: the director or leader and an assistant. In long day or occasional childcare settings, the team may consist of the entire staff group or of the staff who work together in a room or with a particular group of children. In family day care and childminding, the team may mean the coordinator, field workers, office staff and a large group of independent providers who are physically isolated from the centralised administration. Depending on the meaning given to the concept of team, parents may or may not be included in the broader definition. Regardless of its definition, the essence of a team is that all participants work together effectively to achieve a common goal.

The size of the team has been shown to be important. It appears that in small teams—for example, two or three people—it is more difficult to access the range of knowledge, skills and experience that contribute to creative problem-solving than with larger teams of five to seven people (Law and Glover, 2000). As early childhood services become more complex and multi-disciplinary, and are centralised under organisational umbrellas such as the Sure Start Partnerships and Children's Centres in England, early childhood teams will grow larger and offer greater resources for effectiveness and efficiency.

It seems that the more women there are in a team (but not women-only teams), the more positive team members are about working in a team (West, 2004). Women tend to focus on social inclusion whereas men tend to focus on the job to be done. Early childhood teams that are composed of both men and women are likely to be more effective.

Teamwork is considered to be such an important issue for working in early childhood services that ability to operate as a member of a team is an employment criterion specified in job descriptions. Teamwork is also related to the current belief in the value of participatory management and distributed leadership.

Teams are considered to incorporate opportunities to make things happen and offer additional benefits (Woodcock, 1979). These include:

- help and support;
- coordination of individual activities;
- increased commitment;
- a sense of belonging;
- identification of professional development needs;
- learning opportunities;
- better communication; and
- a satisfying, stimulating, pleasant work environment.

Teams can provide social support to members that lessens the strain, stress and tension present in day-to-day activities in early childhood services, and which ultimately can lead to burnout. Interpersonal relationships can become a source of support, satisfaction and stimulation, thereby enhancing general group morale. By using the unique expertise and resources that each member contributes to the team, motivation and job satisfaction are enhanced, which in turn will result in effective accomplishment of the task.

While many early childhood practitioners around the world recognise certain advantages of teamwork, it appears that some members of these services (the staff and the leader) too often assume that it is the leader's job to keep the team on track, to make decisions and to solve problems. Apparently, early childhood practitioners have yet to appreciate fully the notion of teamwork and how it can be applied in their setting.

## WHAT IS A TEAM IN EARLY CHILDHOOD?

In the second edition of this book, research findings (Rodd, 1998:100–4) reported Australian and English early childhood practitioners' understanding about teamwork. The data showed that practitioners had a good appreciation of teams and teamwork. A team was defined generally as:

> a group of people cooperating with each other to work towards achieving an agreed set of aims, objectives or goals while simultaneously considering the personal needs and interests of individuals.

Research indicates that practitioners continue to associate the following concepts with teams:

- the pursuit of a common philosophy, ideals and values;
- commitment to working through the issues;
- shared responsibility;
- open and honest communication; and
- access to a support system.

Whalley (1994) comments that early childhood practitioners learnt to be strong—that is, became empowered—through working in a team. Practitioners consistently acknowledge the advantages of working in a team and they believe that an autocratic leadership style stifles effective teamwork by fostering competition, lack of respect, resentment, isolation and reduced commitment.

> I was told that I was responsible for organising a training day but the manager would not even let me send a letter out without seeing it first. I couldn't make one decision without referring it to her—she might as well have saved me the trouble and done it herself . . .
>
> Nursery officer

These factors are thought to diminish early childhood practitioners' ability to get the job done and maintain positive relationships at work.

The concept of teamwork is usually portrayed as positive and optimistic, and many practitioners describe their expectations regarding participation in a team in such a light. However, as Law and Glover (2000:71) observe, the reality does not always match the rhetoric. Unfortunately, the experience of working in teams is not always consistent with expectations.

> *The staff say they like working in a team and they seem to get a lot of positives out of it when it works well . . . but often there are difficulties and differences that are not resolved . . .*
>
> **Nursery manager**

Teams are more than groups of people in a workplace, and not all work groups are teams. Effective teamwork grows out of work groups that are transformed into teams by appropriate leadership. Teamwork in practice can be quite a different proposition from teamwork in theory, with a range of negative experiences reported by early childhood practitioners.

It appears that, although many practitioners value the teamwork approach to the administration of settings, some problems exist in turning groups of individual staff members into team members (that is, team-building) and maintaining team spirit once this energy has been fired up.

Leadership style is perceived as having a major impact on the development of a team approach in early childhood settings. However, the leader generally is not held totally accountable for achieving the goals. Team members are considered to hold particular roles and responsibilities in relation to the team's viability and the achievement of its goals.

> *Leadership is exercised by the manager when getting the team to complete tasks.*
>
> **Pre-school development worker**

Most early childhood practitioners understand that teamwork is more than just turning up for work each day. It involves a special understanding of the roles and responsibilities of both the leader and each team member.

> **REFLECTIONS ON LEADERSHIP IN PRACTICE**
> My head teacher calls meetings to 'brief' the staff on what he expects at the beginning of each school year. He raises morale because he encourages us to share ideas and he guides us through group activities. He shares leadership with us because he focuses on the group not the hierarchy.
>
> **Teaching assistant**

For leaders, teamwork means acting more as a facilitator than a superior. For staff members, it means taking an active role in the work situation rather than being a passive follower of instructions and directions. Benefits from teamwork are perceived as accruing for both leader and team members. The inconsistency between expectations and reality in teamwork suggests that early childhood leaders have not developed skill in building and leading teams. An exploration of the stages of team development and team leadership can clarify some of the issues relevant to effective teamwork.

## WORKING IN MULTI-DISCIPLINARY TEAMS

According to Edgington (2000:2), early childhood practitioners have always worked within a multi-disciplinary context, given that 'services for children and families have been developed by professionals holding a range of qualifications within the disciplines of education, social work and health, and are funded by and organised by the local authority, by private enterprise or by the voluntary sector'. However, the professionals from the various disciplines have brought their own values, philosophies, agendas, jargon and ways of approaching the needs of young children and their families. These differences have prevented the development of a partnership approach and it is only recently that any move has been made towards developing collaborative or team approaches. Whalley (1994) calls for a holistic approach to the profession, created from consensus derived from shared values about working with children and families.

Because many governments and service providers now see the benefits of, and look towards offering, more integrated services in early childhood, practitioners will find themselves working more closely with professionals and paraprofessionals from other disciplines, such as community health workers, social workers, educational psychologists, family workers, community police officers, special education teachers, speech therapists, play therapists, learning support assistants, doctors, physiotherapists, community psychiatric nurses, trainers and researchers.

> . . . we realised that to provide an effective service it was inappropriate for us to separate the health, education and social needs of children and that working co-operatively was cost effective . . . (Whalley, 1994:12)

Given that there is increasing inter-agency and multi-disciplinary collaboration, many practitioners will find themselves working in a multi-disciplinary team in the early childhood field. Members of such teams will need to overcome a range of barriers to effective inter-professional collaboration, and work together cooperatively to develop shared vision, values and philosophy, goals and objectives, and quality assurance and evaluation protocols. Rather than defending the approach of individual disciplines, they need to work on understanding and reconciling any differences to create what Abbott and Hevey (2001) call 'a multi-disciplinary ethos'. Staff in such teams need to work participatively in an integrated way with a range of people and agencies to establish mutually agreed principles and priorities. Abbott and Moylett (1997) suggest that multi-disciplinary teamwork is the answer to developing a shared understanding and continuity in early childhood.

## THE STAGES OF TEAM DEVELOPMENT

Team development is not an easy task. It requires concerted, ongoing effort on behalf of each member and an even greater effort from the leader who is to move the team from birth to maturity. A number of writers have identified sequences of team development that a group of co-workers will move through over differing periods of time (Adair, 1986; Woodcock, 1979; Woodcock and Francis, 1981). The speed with which each group will accomplish the demands of a particular stage and move on to the next stage is related to the skill possessed by the leader. Consequently, leaders in early childhood settings need to be informed about the stage of team development at which the group currently functions, and they need to possess the skills to assist the group to move as quickly as possible to a higher stage of development (Walker, 1995).

In many ways, the stages of team development are similar to those commonly described for general group development—forming, storming, norming, performing and adjourning (Curran, 1989). The following stages are outlined in terms of the task and relationship requirements for early childhood settings.

## STAGE 1: CONNECTING—GETTING TOGETHER AS A TEAM

The first stage in the development of a team is when a group of people become aware that they are going to be working together. This may be when a new setting is established and a completely new group of staff is employed to work together. More likely, a new person or persons will join an existing group of staff or a person may resign and not be replaced, as long as this does not violate the staff-to-child ratio. Whenever there is a different group composition, the start of a new team has been signalled. This will require assimilation of the new person into the team and accommodation by the existing staff to the new conditions. The leader must address the demands of the task and relationships in order to assist staff to be productive and feel comfortable in this initial stage of team development.

In terms of the task, the major concern is with orientation to the work where structured activities such as information-sharing, organising roles and responsibilities and goal-setting are important because they act to alleviate staff members' apprehension about change and anxiety about competence to undertake the job. Staff will focus on the designated figure of authority to provide a blueprint for the direction of the setting and may ask a variety of questions—for example, 'What are we supposed to do?', 'What happens next?' and 'What are our goals?' Conformity to the leader's approach will be high and few challenges can be expected. The leader needs to provide clear directions and guidelines for staff at this point, which communicate vision and values, general objectives and expectations about staff participation, and confidence in the team to increase staff commitment to the setting's goals. Staff should be encouraged to set personal goals as a means of ongoing self-evaluation.

The relationship and group morale aspect can be difficult to manage at this initial stage because many staff are concerned about belonging, inclusion and rejection, and some may be unwilling to disclose their personal concerns and weaknesses. They are likely to be concerned with self-protection in what is perceived as an unknown situation, so may keep feelings hidden, display little concern for others and be unlikely to listen effectively because their own needs will dominate their attention. The climate of the setting may be characterised by politeness and a wish to avoid contentious issues or anything that might result in conflict. Woodcock and Francis (1981) call this 'ritual sniffing' because the staff are focused upon getting acquainted with the others in the group, assessing others' strengths and weaknesses, and generally testing out the situation in order to determine the written and unwritten ground rules which operate in the group. The leader needs to provide opportunities for staff to get to know one another professionally and personally. Introducing some kind of informal social function such as coffee after work or a shared meal before a staff meeting can help facilitate understanding and acceptance of others in the group and the formation of initial relationships. The leader needs to be available and accessible, non-threatening and observant of the interaction patterns and styles.

When the group members feel moderately comfortable with one another because a certain level of trust and security in the people and the task has been achieved, a degree of risk-taking in terms of challenging aspects of the task and the expertise of others to undertake the task may emerge. Small indications of conflict may be noticed. The group is now in transition to the next stage of team development.

## STAGE 2: CONFRONTING CONFLICT IN THE TEAM

It generally comes as some surprise, both to the leader and the team members, when the group which initially appeared to get along so well disintegrates into one which is marked by open and covert displays of antagonism to one another, dispute, dissension and discord. In terms of team development, the honeymoon period is over. The challenges for the team members at this second stage are establishing a niche in the pecking order and negotiation of roles and responsibilities. The direction and activities of the leader are likely to be evaluated and possibly challenged by team members who are feeling more confident about their position in the group.

With regard to the task performance aspect of the team, staff become concerned with aspects of the administrative organisation of the setting. Rules, procedures, policies and agendas become the focus of attention, with queries raised about who has the power to direct, control and change the administrative structure. Commitment to the group goals may appear to be reduced as staff debate the overall direction and goals. As group members get to know each other better, they also can identify one another's strengths and limitations. This can bring about confrontation regarding values, beliefs and appropriate practice which can produce an organisational climate that is characterised by criticism. Questions and statements such as 'What authority have you got to make that decision?', 'Who makes the rules here, the staff or the Coordinator?', 'Who are you to tell me what to do? I only take directions from the manager!', 'How is my performance going to be appraised?' and 'The committee can't tell us to do that!' may be heard from staff as they attempt to clarify where the power lies in the setting.

In this second stage, relationships between members of the team become more significant and can be influential in the ways emerging group differences are dealt with. Staff needs for recognition of their unique contribution can be met only in an atmosphere of mutual support and respect. These individual needs, and subsequently overall group morale, can be undermined by a climate which is marked by criticism. In order to bolster self-esteem, staff may form cliques and alliances to pressure the leader and other staff members to meet their demands. Increased stress is likely to be experienced by all those connected with the setting, including children and parents, if the infighting, power struggles, disputes and destructive criticism are not managed appropriately.

Early childhood leaders need to have a thorough understanding of conflict and its role in organisations. This was addressed in Chapter 6. In the process of galvanising a group of disparate individuals into a cohesive team, conflict is inevitable, normal and healthy. It is a sign that the group is growing. The constructive resolution of differences can clear the way for more cooperative and productive endeavour on the part of the team. Ignoring or avoiding conflict in this stage will hinder the team's progress to a more advanced and harmonious stage of development. In groups where conflict and confrontation are not resolved, decision-making and problem-solving ability is poor, commitment is low and the group members do not enjoy being part of the group. Psychological and/or physical withdrawal may occur, which will diminish the team's productivity.

The effective leader whose team is in this second stage of development will need to employ sophisticated communication skills to manage the conflict in order to move people towards greater acceptance, increased trust and commitment to the task. Active listening, assertion and conflict-management skills are essential, and the leader may need to provide guidelines for handling differences between staff in a professional manner. In addition, leaders need to be confident about their ability to manage the situation constructively and communicate confidence in the staff regarding their ability to clarify any issues of concern while maintaining respect for others in the group. Holding individual, small and large group meetings, where information, standards and expectations are clarified and established goals are focused upon, can be useful at this point.

Many leaders of early childhood settings have reported that their team appears to be 'stuck' in a cycle of conflict resulting in high levels of stress for all involved, decreased morale and commitment and high staff turnover. As well as the extra energy required to work in a conflict-prone environment, leaders may need to respond to other issues such as staff resignations and staff replacements. In such circumstances, the leader will need to facilitate a sense of closure and reorient the team to the fact that they will be re-forming. The team will return to the first stage of development and begin the process of getting together as a team again. If the leader does not possess the confidence and skills to deal with conflict, the same scenario will probably be repeated when the new team moves into the second stage of confronting conflict. Without competent intervention, the cycle is repeated with the resultant perception that the team is conflict-prone, or 'stuck' in a destructive cycle of discord.

A major disadvantage of extended periods in the second stage is that early childhood settings that experience high staff turnover as a result of unresolved conflict do not capitalise on the training and experience that staff members have gained. The level of service quality that is expected by staff and parents is more difficult to achieve with a high staff turnover. Individual staff develop expertise over time that is not easy to replace. This places an added burden on leaders because they are continually involved in staff orientation, initiation and supervision until the new staff attain competence levels to work more independently. The leader therefore has less time to devote to other important aspects of administering a high-quality service. In addition, continuous staff turnover keeps the level of team development at lower levels, requiring more input from the leader to ensure that the team grows and advances.

If the leader manages the challenges of this second stage, the team will begin to resolve personal animosities and to focus back on improving activities and performance related to achieving the setting's goals. The team now is advancing to the third stage.

## STAGE 3: COOPERATING AS A TEAM

The assumption that a group that starts to evidence consensus and cooperation is now working as a team is generally accurate. While the group may appear to be operating in a more dynamic manner, some members are not yet performing in a unified or methodical way. However, having worked through some of the important issues in the previous stage, the team is now willing to take some risks and experiment with new practices, debate values and assumptions, review methods of operation and discuss issues of management and leadership. New confidence gained from resolving the earlier conflicts produces a receptiveness in team members to new ideas and risk-taking. If a leader has skilfully handled the first two stages, the team will move quickly through this third stage.

The challenges surrounding task performance issues focus on information-sharing, win–win attitudes to problem-solving, and a willingness to take calculated risks and change. These task-related activities are anchored in the new level of trust that has developed through the management of conflict. Individuals trust both themselves in the job and the other group members. This may motivate previously inactive members of staff to become more involved with a broader range of responsibilities. Change has begun. A breach of trust at this stage will reverse the team's progress, however, and it is possible that the team will regress to the previous stage. Skill in decision-making and problem-solving is needed by the leader and by team members in order to capitalise on the team's potential at this point. The leadership style exhibited by the designated leader is important. The group is interested in contribution and participation at this stage; therefore, the participatory, democratic style is appropriate for meeting staff members' needs. Some members of the team will be interested in sharing responsibility with the leader, so effective delegation also will become an important skill.

The focus of the team at the third stage of development continues to be on group relationships. Having been fragmented by conflict, staff members now are interested in achieving cohesion. The beginning of a 'team spirit' is evident, with staff spontaneously referring to themselves and their colleagues as 'the team'. Team members are more open-minded, more willing to listen to and support one another, and able to focus on the needs of the group rather than their own needs. Mutually accepted group norms begin to guide the work and relationships. The word 'we' is heard more often than 'I' or 'you' when the activities of the setting are discussed. The climate of the setting includes a lighthearted aspect where joking and humour illustrate good-natured attitudes in the staff.

Although conflict and disagreements may still occur, they are perceived as less threatening by the staff and handled differently. The problem-solving approach to conflict and decision-making is evident because the team wishes to protect group cohesion and positive relationships.

At this third stage, the role of the leader is to promote consensus and cooperation. Staff involvement and participation in goal-setting, the development of policies and their implementation in practice needs to be supported by the leader. A willingness to identify and address potential problems is essential. Open communication, constructive feedback and acknowledgment of contributions to the group will facilitate consensus and cooperation in the team. As the group begins to take pride in its achievements, it is truly becoming a team and is advancing into the fourth stage.

## STAGE 4: COLLABORATING AS AN EFFECTIVE TEAM

The rate at which a group of individuals will proceed to this fourth stage depends on the effectiveness of the leader in facilitating the transition through the previous stages. It is not until this fourth stage that the group of individuals who committed themselves to working together in the first stage can be said to be operating as an effective team.

At this stage, all members of the team are making a unique but equal contribution to the task. The team shares responsibility for the efficient operation of a quality service with the leader. Leadership style is decided according to the situation. Regular review and evaluation of goals, policies and practice are undertaken with a view to constant improvement of the service. Staff appraisal, either with the leader or by self-appraisal, is accepted as a means of professional staff development. The team adopts a creative problem-solving approach to its operation and engages in preventive decision-making. Change is anticipated, planned for and the team is prepared for and included in phased implementation. The team rewards its performance by articulating a sense of pride concerning its achievements.

The relationship aspect of the team is based on mutual respect and support. Team members recognise their interdependence as well as their independence. Individual differences and successes are valued. People are now able to 'agree to disagree' if mutually acceptable solutions to problems are not forthcoming. The climate is marked by concern for other team members, warmth and friendliness.

The team is working efficiently and members are enjoying their work. The leader is able to relax and enjoy the fruits of previous efforts. However, leaders need to keep close contact with the various teams and ensure that any small quality control adjustments are made and shared. Opportunities for contact and relationships with outside groups are pursued, and assistance from outside sources is welcomed by team members. The team is willing to extend its energies beyond the confines of the setting. Leaders have opportunities to facilitate the development of appropriate staff members through the mentoring process, thereby contributing to the development of another future leader. This is discussed in Chapter 9.

A team that reaches this stage of mature development can operate productively for a long period of time, as long as attention is given to ensuring effective working methods and the maintenance of relationships. While self-evaluation should be encouraged in all staff members from the time they join the group, formal evaluation of the team and its performance needs to be introduced at this point. This will ensure that questions such as 'How are we going?', 'Where do we want to go next?' and 'What are our needs now?' are addressed in order to keep the team at its maximum operational efficiency. However, if any of the conditions change, such as a staff member leaving or the dissolution of the group because its purpose no longer exists, the team enters the final stage in its development: that of separation and closure.

## STAGE 5: CLOSURE

This final stage tends to be ignored by many team leaders who, in their haste to move the team back to a more productive and positive stage, fail to acknowledge the team's need to celebrate or mourn its existence and track record. A change in or the disbanding of a team can occur at any stage in a team's development. The sensitive leader will ensure that the team has an opportunity to experience some form of closure so that staff members can deal with any unfinished business that might prevent them from approaching their future working situation positively.

When a team ceases to be operational, the members have to come to terms with two issues: disengagement from the task and separation from and/or closure of relationships. Usually there is a period of time for the team to work these issues through. It is the leader's responsibility to ensure that the team has access to a means of debriefing and bringing closure to the experience. Comments such as 'Remember when Jenny was here? She would have known what to do' or 'Didn't we work well together before all the changes!' suggest that the staff have not had sufficient time to come to terms with the demise of the previous team. These nostalgic memories may interfere with commitment to the new team and acceptance of any new staff members.

If the team has worked well and it has been a satisfying experience for those involved, the staff will be able to celebrate the end of the team by reviewing and evaluating individual development, task performance and work relationships. The team should recognise and celebrate its accomplishments and express its satisfaction with the process. The emotional responses of the team members to the closure of the group need to be acknowledged and dealt with. Some frustration and anger may be expressed to the leader who understands that this is part of the normal process of separation. There may also be some confusion about emotional responses, with individuals vacillating between feeling happy and satisfied about the team's achievements and sad and angry about the team's breakup. The stress associated with the closure of the team may produce lower quality performance. However, leaders need to de-emphasise task-related aspects at this point and focus upon meeting the staff members' social and emotional needs in preparation for establishing a new team.

If the ending of the team is marked by a lack of achievement and/or poor relationships, it is more difficult—but even more important—to engage in a process of closure. Each team member's contribution should be reviewed and evaluated as well as the overall group dynamic in order to identify the problems that prevented the team from operating effectively. In this way, the leader and the group members should gain a basis for planning for the next team experience.

## TEAM LEADERSHIP

Becoming an effective leader in early childhood has an inherent difficulty that few leaders in other professions have to deal with. In some services—for example, child care—leaders have to adapt on a daily basis to moving from the position of administrative leader to being a member of a room team responsible for the direct care of children. The way in which the leader's time is allocated officially to combine administration, direct care and teaching ensures that both the leader and the team members have to adapt to the constant changes in the leader's position in the team. This can place a great strain on the resources of the leader, who is required to relinquish the authority of leadership when working as an equal member of a direct care or teaching team and to resume and command that same authority when undertaking administrative functions. Team members can become confused about the appropriate way to interact with the leader when in the direct care and teaching team role. This constant fluctuation between leader and team member requires sensitive management by the leader. Team leadership has some advantages for early childhood leaders who find themselves in this position.

To review the leader's role in relation to the team, the key functions are to provide and communicate a vision to the group, develop the team culture, set goals, monitor and communicate the team's achievements to the team and relevant others, and facilitate and encourage the development of individuals. These functions can be fulfilled using the various styles of leadership that are outlined in Chapter 2. However, in order to engage in the process of 'team leadership' where special effort is devoted to enhancing the team culture in order to achieve better results, the leader also needs to exhibit the following features that differentiate team leadership from other styles of leadership. An effective team leader:

- uses personality to lead by example, thereby stimulating a particular team culture;
- is innovative and is perceived to be making things better by improving team morale and productivity;
- ensures that constructive relationships are established and maintained with the staff and peers;
- focuses attention on behaviour or the situation, not on the person;
- fosters the self-esteem and confidence of team members; and
- coaches team members to improve their performance.

Certain values and approaches have been found to be associated with developing this team leadership orientation. They can assist in matching the leadership style to follower needs and situational demands. Early childhood practitioners will find that the following attributes may be useful in meeting the demands of team leadership:

- adaptable (the capacity to be responsive and innovative);
- energetic (action-oriented and committed to work);
- people-oriented (values people and communicates openly);
- quality-conscious (pays attention to standards of excellence and consumer needs and expectations);
- uniting (clarifies the common purpose and promotes the value of cooperation);
- entrepreneurial (autonomous and able to articulate the uniqueness of the service);
- focused (self-disciplined and predictable);
- informal (a relaxed, straightforward approach to people and situations).

These features, values and approaches of team leadership are fundamental to the early childhood leader making things happen in ways which can increase staff and parent participation. When attempting to build and lead a team, leaders need to be conscious of the positive impact that team leadership can have on a group of individuals who are working together, and incorporate appropriate aspects of the team leadership approach into their style. In addition to the leader's individual style, a systematic, step-by-step approach to team-building and maintenance can be followed to assist the team's advancement in productivity.

## A FRAMEWORK FOR TEAM-BUILDING

As discussed previously in the stages of team development, the process of galvanising a group of individuals into a cohesive team is not a quick and painless one. Becoming a team demands effort from every member of the group, and requires that the leader relate to the group in a certain way. However, helping a group of individuals develop into a staff team can be a very rewarding experience for a leader. Although numerous obstacles to team-building exist in early childhood settings, such as heterogeneous skills, interests and values, and the fragmentation of staff through the physical setting and shift work, the process can be implemented gradually, with staff encouraged to provide feedback about their satisfaction or otherwise with the process.

The team-building process basically focuses on the two dimensions of any team: staff morale and task demands. In order to build team morale, the group needs to be able to provide social support for the interpersonal demands that evolve in any work group. This support may consist of emotional, informational, instrumental or appraisal support. The leader may need to help the group identify how members may be able to assist and support one another. The accomplishment of the task requires an analysis of work demands and the development of role profiles based on the expectations of the leader and peers. The leader will need to respond to the staff's increasing participation in decision-making and increasing personal control over how the job is performed. Attention to these two dimensions will produce a cohesive group that works to accomplish specific tasks in a supportive environment (West, 2004).

Leaders who want to encourage a team approach in settings can be guided by the following five-step framework for team-building in early childhood settings (Neugebauer and Neugebauer, 1998).

1 *Set achievable goals* which have been mutually agreed upon by members of the team. Ensure that the assertive staff members do not dominate the process, especially during discussion at staff meetings.

2 *Clarify roles.* Team members work most effectively when their roles are clear to all and free of conflict. Each staff member should be aware of who is responsible for what. While it will be easier to clarify the formal roles that need to be fulfilled, the informal roles that relate to the internal functioning of the group should not be forgotten (Johnson and Johnson, 2003). The leader needs to analyse the group to make sure that someone is taking responsibility for the team task roles (initiating, information-gathering, opinion-seeking and giving, clarifying, elaborating, energising, summarising and consensus-testing) and team maintenance roles (encouraging, harmonising, compromising, gatekeeping, observing and standard setting).

3 *Build supportive relationships*—that is, build in opportunities for feedback, develop trust and provide resources to stimulate a co-operative team spirit. Teams where members feel supported are more likely to deal with (rather than ignore) common team problems such as role ambiguity, role conflict and group conflict.

4 *Encourage active participation* to capitalise on the knowledge and skills of individual team members. In an atmosphere of acceptance, team members will be encouraged to contribute their ideas, opinions and energies. Being part of a cooperative venture can be extremely motivating for team members, and this will increase productivity.

5 *Monitor team effectiveness.* There is little point in putting time and energy into team leadership and the team-building process if the team is not achieving the goals effectively or if the team is unhappy with the process. Regular opportunities need to be provided by the leader to assess the extent of goal achievement and how well members are working together as a team. This review process can help identify any problems and establish their cause, as well as assisting with future planning.

The success of the team approach relies on open communication, democratic organisation and effective problem-solving skills. An effective team should fulfil staff needs for participation and support and result in efficient and effective approaches to the task.

## BRINGING IT TOGETHER

Team-building and effective team leadership usually result in high-quality interaction between team members and the leader, which increases trust and openness, the development of interpersonal relationships, joint goal-setting, clarification of roles and responsibilities, and analysis of the appropriate processes related to the team's purpose. The team approach to work in early childhood settings can also assist in staff development and in meeting the challenge of change because it provides the backdrop of support for and commitment to quality service delivery.

# CHAPTER NINE

# SUPPORTING PROFESSIONAL DEVELOPMENT: SUPERVISION, MENTORING AND COACHING

*It is essential that leadership development programs are set up but that doesn't necessarily mean training courses. Leadership potential can be nurtured through putting the right people together in supervisory and mentoring meetings.*

Head teacher, early excellence centre

**THIS CHAPTER EXPLORES**
- **the leader's role in supervision**
- **guidelines for supporting adults as learners**
- **the leader's role as a mentor**
- **the leader's role as a coach**
- **the deputy: a special opportunity for leadership in an early childhood team**

The quality of early childhood services is directly related to the quality of the personnel who operate them, from the designated leader to the staff who work with children, whether they are trained or untrained, experienced or inexperienced. Given that early childhood services operate under continuing financial constraints, and with the added issues of low salaries for childcare personnel, staff turnover and shortages, early childhood leaders face an ignominious situation. How can they fulfil professional support responsibilities to move practice forward in ways that maintain staff morale and achieve the goals of the setting?

A number of options for fulfilling this responsibility are open to leaders: supervision, mentoring and coaching. As many practitioners have commented that they learn better from others in the field than from more formal training opportunities, effective implementation of these strategies for professional development is increasingly important.

The shift towards distributed leadership in early childhood settings means that many practitioners will be encouraged to take on responsibilities that are outside their normal roles. These practitioners will need focused support, guidance and development opportunities to enable them to successfully meet the challenge of leadership.

The specific approach employed by leaders can help staff to become self-evaluative and reflective about their performance and also help to develop confident, early childhood practitioners who are motivated to provide quality care and early education for young children.

## SUPERVISION

Supervision is a professional responsibility of the early childhood leader in which the leader helps staff members to use their knowledge and skills effectively in the performance of their daily work, and to deepen their understanding of professional philosophies and values. The range of supervisory responsibilities for leaders is complex and needs to address both personal and self-development issues as well as professional and team-building issues (Whalley, 2001). The professional support provided through effective supervision helps staff listen to and accept constructive feedback and learn to reflect upon and critically evaluate their own performance.

Supervision involves offering staff positive feedback, constructive criticism about performance, information on training needs and options and advice regarding professional development matters. Supervision needs to be undertaken in such a way that difficult issues—for example, inappropriate dress, levels of personal hygiene, inappropriate interaction with parents or unacceptable performance—are able to be discussed openly and in confidence. Whalley (2001:139) observes that supervision 'becomes a mechanism of quality control because it involves target-setting, goals and reviews'.

Effective supervision is characterised by reflective dialogue, a process in which early childhood practitioners collect evidence through observation, and illustrate and evaluate their practice in collaborative conversations (Anning and Edwards, 1999). These conversations facilitate professional learning, understanding and practice because they offer opportunities for sharing insights, exchanging information, constructing knowledge, gaining understanding and exploring roles and responsibilities.

Effective supervision reduces the isolation of early childhood practitioners by connecting them to the leader and team through talking about and scrutinising the what, why and how of practice, and reflecting about new possibilities.

### REFLECTIONS ON LEADERSHIP IN PRACTICE

Early childhood practitioners benefit from having the opportunity to take on leadership roles, especially where supervisors help them to understand what is involved and recognise when they are displaying leadership qualities and action.

**Deputy supervisor**

Some leaders are required to engage in supervision when they are in the early stages of professional development, and they themselves are in need of supervisory support. To date, early childhood practitioners already have assumed a large proportion of the responsibility for supervising the training of future practitioners in student experience and are responsible for guiding untrained staff, paraprofessionals and professionals from other disciplines in the philosophy and practices of early childhood. Many of those who are presently engaged in supervision at these levels usually have had little or no training, and have limited access to support and backup if problems arise during the process. In addition, the introduction of accreditation and quality assurance schemes means that early childhood leaders will assume greater responsibility for on-the-job training, development and supervision of their staff, as well as greater input into the support and education of parents in their parenting role. It is evident that the supervisory responsibility is growing.

Perceptive leaders will need to reflect upon their attitudes to and capabilities for the supervisory responsibility. Many people regard the process of supervision with suspicion. This can be an obstacle for those leaders who are responsible for quality early childhood services. Reluctance by either leader or staff members to participate in a supervision program may reflect the traditional view of supervision which is related to control and surveillance. Today, supervision is viewed more commonly as a form of continuing staff development in which staff competence is the overriding objective. Given the increasing participation of staff in the operation and administration of early childhood settings, supervision is no longer considered to be the sole responsibility of one individual—that is, the leader—but more appropriately is regarded as a collaborative process between leader and staff member. Moreover, supervision can be conducted formally and informally, and on a group or team basis as well as on the traditional one-to-one basis. Supervision can be the means of communicating to staff that they are important assets and that they are valued for their special contribution.

## REFLECTIONS ON LEADERSHIP IN PRACTICE

My supervisor displayed leadership when she encouraged me to apply for this position. She gave me fair and open feedback about my strengths and limitations and that helped me succeed. Her leadership was about creating an enriching environment that valued each person, their contribution and not being threatened by people's ambitions.

**Deputy supervisor**

The diversity of policies, settings, staff and services within early childhood makes the creation of a supervisory profile for early childhood leaders difficult. However, training and experience are important variables in improving this aspect of professional practice. Effective supervisors possess a range of attributes which are regarded as desirable rather than prescriptive, offering direction for further professional development. They include:

- expertise in the knowledge and skills and possession of professional values and attitudes relevant for the early childhood profession;
- the ability to transmit knowledge and skills in a manner conducive to adult learning;
- sophisticated communication skills, including listening skills, response skills for appropriate feedback (especially showing appreciation and giving recognition), conflict-resolution skills and decision-making skills;

- the ability to anticipate and prepare staff for impending change;
- the ability to involve staff in setting team and individual objectives for short- and long-term achievement;
- the ability to monitor progress on a regular basis;
- confidentiality; and
- openness and receptivity to new ideas, flexibility and accessibility to staff.

## SUPPORTING ADULTS AS LEARNERS

One of the most important aspects of supervision is the leader's ability to work with staff in ways that optimise adult learning styles. Early childhood leaders need to understand that adults possess unique traits which differentiate them from children as learners. Examples of these characteristics are readiness, attitude, motivation, previous experiences and autonomy. Adult learning is grounded in experience—that is, it is focused on problem-solving and on the relevance of process. Adopting specific adult learning approaches helps adults to become better learners by encouraging them to be self-directed and think critically (Thomson and Calder, 1998).

Supervisory styles that emphasise the links between theory, research and practice, and encourage immediate application of new learning, will help reduce the frustration that many adult learners experience while acquiring new knowledge and skills. Adult learners appear to experience less frustration when mastering new knowledge and skills if they are intrinsically motivated, appreciate the need to learn something specific and understand its pertinence to their work (Law and Glover, 2000). Leaders who are open, respectful and collaborative will encourage staff to move beyond basic understanding of concepts and practices to more sophisticated approaches to information-processing, such as analysis, synthesis and evaluation of ideas and practices—in other words, to become a reflective practitioner.

The following principles have been suggested as central to the consideration of teaching and learning techniques and processes when working with adults in a situation of learning (Albert and Einstein, 1986). Adults learn more effectively when:

- they are involved in the learning process, responsible for getting their own needs met, having the opportunity to build on existing skills in self-direction and decision-making;

- their previous knowledge, skills and experience are used, with the leader encouraging other staff to help members within the team;
- their immediate concerns and problems are focused upon in ways which result in new information, skills, insights and solutions that can be applied to their current situation;
- appropriate and varied teaching methods are used as effective training strategies, such as group discussions, brainstorming, role-playing, problem-solving and providing feedback;
- a democratic atmosphere is established and maintained through the leader's emphasis on equality, shared responsibility, cooperation and mutual respect; and
- staff are actively involved in the learning process and learn by doing as well as by reflective thinking.

Effective leaders capitalise on adult learning styles in their supervisory role by understanding the principles underpinning adult learning and by developing the necessary skills for working with adults in order to improve professional performance.

Capable supervisors will match the model of supervision to the needs and the stage of professional development of the team members, as described in Chapter 2. Katz (1995a) argues that the training and supervisory needs of early childhood staff change with experience. New and inexperienced staff will require more concrete support and technical assistance than more experienced staff. Those who have gained a degree of experience are more likely to benefit from exchanging information and observations with other experienced staff from their own or other settings. Consultation with Children's Services advisers and other specialist staff, such as psychologists and curriculum advisers can extend the knowledge and skills of staff who are maturing in the job. Those who have considerable experience are likely to benefit from networking with colleagues outside the setting and by participating in conferences and in-service training programs.

The effective supervisor will give some consideration to the form of supervision to which staff will be most receptive. For some staff, the one-to-one tutorial model might be the most effective way support their development. New and inexperienced staff are likely to benefit from supervisors who impart information, listen to concerns and anxieties and show support and understanding in a private consultation. An extension of the tutorial model is the supervisory group model where a small group of staff who are at a similar stage of professional development meet with the supervisor.

Both inexperienced and experienced staff may find the peer model of supervision more stimulating. Peer supervision involves the objective observation of a colleague's practice without making inferences, interpretations or assumptions about the interaction and then sharing and discussing those observations (Schiller, 1987). It is an appropriate form of supervision when staff relationships are based upon mutual trust and respect. Staff may choose to work in self-selected pairs or, alternatively, small groups of individuals may wish to participate in regularly scheduled peer conferences to discuss aspects of observed practice and interaction. The peer model provides an opportunity independent of the supervisor to discuss decisions, solve problems, share responsibility and support one another. Peer supervision can encourage staff to engage in reflective thinking about practice and therefore provide a continuing opportunity for professional development.

The team model of supervision enables members of particular teams—for example staff who work in a specific room—to evaluate the morale and task aspects of their performance in order to work more effectively. When leaders share supervisory responsibility with the team, they need to ensure that the group possesses the necessary professional knowledge and skills, especially the essential communication skills, to manage this delicate task, as well as a willingness to request outside help if the problems identified are beyond the resources of the group.

This book focuses on the need for developing more qualified leaders in early childhood who will facilitate the professionalisation of the field by raising the standard of care and early education through the consistent provision of quality services. One way of developing leadership potential is through improved supervision of both students and existing staff. The position of deputy, sometimes called second-in-charge, offers considerable scope for the leader to become a mentor to a suitable member of staff, and for that person to gain valuable on-the-job training and experience, which will nurture emerging leadership potential.

## THE LEADER'S ROLE AS MENTOR

Over the past few years, many educators—including those working in early childhood—have espoused the value of mentoring as a means for supporting professional growth. Unfortunately, the proliferation of early childhood award-bearing courses and increasing numbers of students has resulted in poorer quality training. For example, the worldwide trend towards increases in lecture-based training with concomitant reduction in tutorial opportunities, coupled with drastic cuts in the number of supervised hours that students spend in early childhood settings, means that many novice graduates begin work ill-prepared to meet the needs of young children and families. At the present time, being trained does not guarantee quality practice (Cummins, 2004). Mentoring is a leadership strategy for optimising learning and professional development (Rolfe-Flett, 2002), and is viewed as a viable strategy for the professionalisation of early childhood staff (Martin and Trueax, 1997).

Mentoring is a way of overcoming some of the shortcomings of current approaches to training early childhood practitioners by offering ongoing on-the-job training and professional development opportunities. It is a professional development strategy that meets the needs of novice and experienced practitioners (Bellm and Whitebrook, 1996). Mentoring is a peer support strategy that is based on processes of review and reflection that enable both mentor and mentee to feel valued (Law and Glover, 2000). When colleagues mentor each other, they support a culture of learning in the profession and throw a spotlight on quality practice.

When early childhood leaders take on the responsibility of mentoring another individual, they enter a special ongoing personal relationship with that person which is based on the development of rapport, mutual trust, respect and openness to learning. Mentoring is not a supervisory relationship; it is an opportunity for colleagues to engage in reflective dialogue that can enhance feelings of empowerment and success (Cummins, 2004) and promote dispositions towards lifelong learning (Weaver, 2004). The mentor becomes a critical friend in a supportive and non-threatening professional environment.

The quality of the relationship between mentor and mentee is fundamental to its success. Successful mentors display:

- empathy and understanding;
- an interest in lifelong learning and professional development;
- sophisticated interpersonal skills;
- cultural sensitivity;
- understanding of the role of the mentor; and
- considerable early childhood expertise.

Other important attributes include authenticity, gentleness, patience, consistency, positive attitude, teachability and enthusiasm (Hurst and Reding, 2002).

Certain skills are associated with effective mentoring, including:

- active listening;
- effective observations;
- reflective conversations;
- awareness of different learning styles; and
- adult/teacher development.

According to Hurst and Reding (2002), a good mentor leads through example, guidance and communication, and supports by being an advocate. If undertaken inappropriately, mentoring can result in the perpetuation of an authoritarian leadership style—the 'I lead, you follow' model (Ebbeck and Waniganayake, 2003). The intended outcome of mentoring is not to control or impose one's ideas, values and behaviours on another, but rather to encourage mentees to explore possibilities and collaborate in an array of decision-making opportunities.

Smith and Ingersoll (2004) found that some forms of mentoring activities were more useful than others. These included having a mentor from the same field, having common planning time or time for collaboration with others, regular and supportive communications with administrators and being part of an external network.

One of the dangers of mentoring is that mentees become compliant through perceived powers of mentors who may have control over important aspects of employment, such as pay awards or promotion. Mentors therefore need to set up a supportive framework of expectations, targets and assessment timelines that is neither overly ambitious nor undemanding (Law and Glover, 2000), and both mentors and mentees need to be clear about goals and obligations.

Leaders also benefit by acting as mentors. New understanding and insight can be achieved, better relationships can be developed, professional competence and careers can be enhanced, and professional renewal and re-energisation can be experienced.

> ... *aspiring leaders need to be mentored by other early childhood leaders with recognised expertise* ...
> **Associate professor, early childhood**

The early childhood profession has endorsed informal and formal mentoring as a key leadership strategy because it focuses on helping practitioners to realise their professional potential. Most early childhood practitioners are passionate about their work, and are keen to help others learn by sharing their own knowledge, understanding, practice and expertise. Weaver (2004) comments that the early childhood profession has developed a culture of problem-solving, goal-setting, assessment, continuous improvement and mentoring. She sees mentoring as a means of raising self-awareness and self-assessment in a collaborative, non-threatening atmosphere.

Formal mentoring programs are being set up in many early childhood organisations around the world. To be effective, such programs need the input of high-quality trained mentors. Structured mentor training contributes to the development of leadership capacity because it produces heightened awareness of the complexity of the profession. Successful mentors are recognised for their knowledge and expertise, as well as for their ability to critically examine and reflect on their own and others' practice.

## THE LEADER'S ROLE AS COACH

Coaching in early childhood is another collaborative process designed to promote practitioners' ability to provide quality services (Hanft, Rush and M'Lisa, 2003). Coaching is 'the facilitation and management of day-to-day team processes, and involves listening rather than administering' (West, 2004:60). Effective leaders use coaching to help teams to achieve goals and objectives and to help individual team members to achieve their potential. Coaches teach others to find their own answers to facilitate change (Drever, 2002) by listening, supporting, advising, guiding and suggesting. Through coaching, practitioners can deepen their learning, improve their performance and enhance the quality of provision in settings.

Coaching and mentoring share many similarities, and both are vehicles for analysis, reflection and action. However, there are important differences. Mentoring is a longer term, protected relationship in which a more experienced colleague enables a less experienced colleague to make significant transitions in professional knowledge, understanding, skills, experience and opportunities. Mentors usually have had direct experience of the roles and responsibilities of the mentee, and wisdom is shared and received (Huang and Lynch, 1995). On the other hand, coaching is a process that may not be based on direct experience of others' occupational roles, and coaches do not necessarily benefit from the activity. In early childhood, coaching tends to be related specifically to maximising practitioners' potential within a specific timeframe, while at the same time achieving a balance between professional aims and objectives and individuals' personal needs.

Coaching is an ongoing but time-specific partnership that begins with individual practitioners' personal and professional goals and uses reporting, exploring and choice to help them move forward. A good coach can help early childhood practitioners improve their confidence and self-esteem; relationships with children, parents and colleagues; communications skills; stress and time management; and to balance work and personal life and personal and professional direction and purpose.

A coach is someone who acts as a catalyst for early childhood practitioners to find the answers themselves by asking challenging and thought-provoking questions and focusing attention on the action that is needed for realising potential. A coach doesn't tell someone what to do, but helps them to challenge assumptions and explore different perspectives and alternatives. An effective coach can help early childhood practitioners develop greater self-awareness, purpose, wellbeing and professional competence, thereby empowering them to use their skills and abilities better and improve job satisfaction.

### REFLECTIONS ON LEADERSHIP IN PRACTICE

I have a life coach and he's brilliant. Generally, I find it hard to set goals in my life and I tend to procrastinate, putting off doing things that are difficult or unpleasant, and these issues have cropped up at work too. A friend recommended that I contact this particular coach. I have met with him a couple of times and I phone him up when there is something that I really need a push to get on with. He asks me questions and won't let me get out of answering them properly, and he sometimes suggests another way of seeing the problem. I found that talking to him has helped me see solutions to situations that I hadn't thought of. Knowing he is there and that I need to report back on my progress means I get on with doing the things that need to be done. It's worked for me in my personal life and I now use his strategies for dealing with issues at work. My manager noticed that I seem more assertive and confident in tackling certain work difficulties, especially delicate communications with colleagues and parents, and I feel a lot more satisfied with the state of my personal and professional life.

**Deputy supervisor, day nursery**

Coaching can be conducted in a number of different ways and media—for example, in one-to-one meetings or group coaching sessions in person, on the telephone or by email. This means that leaders can coach people outside their own setting and at times that are convenient. The length and frequency of coaching sessions are decided together to meet individual needs and schedules.

Goleman, Boyatzis and McKee (2002) observe that leadership is a competency that can be developed through coaching. For them, leadership development is self-development. They argue that the self-knowledge accessed through coaching helps leaders improve their confidence and skills, clarify their values and guiding principles, and strengthen their initiative to reach their goals. Leaders who believe in themselves can achieve whatever they want to achieve.

Early childhood leaders and experienced practitioners have a wealth of expertise and experience to offer in coaching because they possess the required contextual knowledge and understanding, as well as the appropriate communication and interpersonal skills and techniques to successfully engage in the process.

## THE DEPUTY: A SPECIAL OPPORTUNITY FOR LEADERSHIP IN AN EARLY CHILDHOOD TEAM

The position of deputy or second-in-charge has the potential to be a valuable training ground for becoming a formal leader of an early childhood setting. However, there are a number of features of the role which make it as challenging as that of the official leader.

This is an administrative position that is often characterised by role ambiguity and possible conflict, and where the level of responsibility fluctuates between shared and sole responsibility. It is a situation where the deputy is sometimes the official leader (on a short-term or longer term basis when the designated leader is absent) and sometimes a member of the team. The position often is filled by a staff member chosen by the leader. This is a good example of a situation where the principles of delegation should be applied by the leader to ensure that the most suitable staff member is selected for the task. The demands of the position call for sensitivity, flexibility and understanding on the part of the incumbent, the leader and the rest of the team.

The main roles of the deputy include:

- supporting the leader by stimulating cooperation and collaboration of team members in the operation and administration of the setting;
- supporting the team in achieving its goals while maintaining positive working relationships; and
- meeting one's own needs for affection, belonging, self-esteem and competence.

At times, these may appear mutually exclusive and contradictory, as well as impossible to achieve. However, the essence of the position is the provision of commitment to the delivery of efficient and effective early childhood services. It is not about fulfilling power needs by controlling the team or sabotaging the leader's efforts or getting involved in politics. It is an opportunity to play a positive role at an administrative level for those staff members who are interested in achieving their full potential.

The position of deputy is an opportunity to gain a broader perspective on the operation of an early childhood setting and the early childhood industry, and to develop a broader background of skills and experience in terms of career openings. Any staff member who is interested in shared decision-making and responsibility, team-building, managing conflict, building trust and supporting the administrative structure of a setting is a potential candidate for a deputy position because these are the skills demanded in the position. Taking on the role of deputy is important from the perspective of professional career development because it is a designated position and aspiring leaders often are expected to have some experience at this level of responsibility.

Changes in early childhood organisational structures are likely to result in alterations to the leader's roles and responsibilities. An emphasis on early childhood leaders' contribution to long-term planning, staff training and development and policy formulation can leave little time for any leader to have a significant input into the day-to-day running of a setting. The deputy will have increasing responsibility for daily operation, administration and service delivery. This scenario may witness designated administrative leaders becoming more isolated from the daily concerns of settings. It may be the deputy's responsibility to maintain the link between the leader, the team, the children and parents, and to keep the leader apprised of the current status of the setting by providing information and advice on the tasks, resources, opportunities and problems.

As with other aspects of working in early childhood, there has been little opportunity for orientation or training for those people who undertake deputy positions. Most people have to 'learn on the job' in order to discover what the job is actually about, what roles and responsibilities are entailed and what skills are needed. In some cases, the deputy has to fulfil allocated duties as well as take on extra duties associated with this administrative position. It is not surprising that many people in these positions experience high levels of stress and loss of morale when they think that their performance is not up to standard, or if their relationships with their colleagues appear to deteriorate. The deputy and the designated leader need to understand the key factors for successful leadership, the relationship between leadership and team performance, and the communication skills that are essential to undertake the role effectively.

There are a number of challenges associated with the position of deputy. Apart from the lack of opportunity for training, the absence of a standardised job description or specification creates problems for leaders and their deputies.

Some leaders willingly share authority, power, information and provide a time allocation for the extra administrative duties assumed by the deputy. In this situation, they are afforded a genuine experience of the leadership position during the leader's absence. Other leaders are not interested in any real delegation to the deputy, refusing to share real responsibilities and information, and expecting any extra duties to be absorbed as part of the normal workload. The deputy becomes a token leader in the designated leader's absence. There is little uniformity in the provision of financial remuneration for those staff who accept the extra responsibilities associated with this position. The absence of formal channels of communication between the leader and deputy can lead to difficulties in the mutual understanding of roles and responsibilities and expectations about financial remuneration for the higher duties.

The following support is necessary for a deputy to be successful in the position:

- appropriate training and orientation for the position so that a complete understanding of the range of administrative duties is developed;
- a standardised job description that is associated with appropriate and mandated levels of financial remuneration;
- allocation of an additional minimum time for administration in addition to planning time;

- an operational definition of the parameters of delegated authority;
- the mandatory employment of a reliever in the leader's absence;
- ongoing involvement with the leader on certain policy and decision-making issues; and
- ongoing opportunity to participate in the wider early childhood profession.

Without such support, the potential for conflict between the leader and the deputy is considerable. Potential sources of conflict identified include:

- lack of leader support for decisions made in the leader's absence;
- few clearly defined roles and responsibilities;
- different ways of doing things;
- insufficient information provided;
- unwritten expectations;
- different values, ethics and interpretations of situations; and
- the leader feeling threatened by the deputy's initiatives.

Lack of role definition and authority appear to create the potential for conflict with the rest of the team when the deputy is elevated to the position of responsibility in the designated leader's absence. Two major difficulties are identified here.

First, the team may not accept and challenge the deputy's decisions and authority in the leader's absence. This sometimes relates to a difference of opinion about the necessity for a qualified—as opposed to experienced but unqualified—staff member being nominated as deputy. One of the major problems faced by designated leaders, including the deputy, is that they may not be recognised by the staff on unofficial levels as the leader. Someone else may have been subtly chosen by the staff as the unofficial leader. Such a person may be given unofficial power, the right to make decisions on behalf of the staff group and draw unquestioning support from the staff on an informal basis.

A deputy, as with a designated leader, needs to earn the respect of staff by demonstrating relevant expertise, skills or knowledge and by gaining the support of staff through their recognition of the desirability and benefits of personal characteristics, resources and relationships in the early childhood context. Simply having an official position of leadership does not necessarily mean that the staff group will acknowledge and support the person in that position. In some cases, authority over, respect by and support from staff is earned through the way in which one fulfils the role.

Second, there is the issue of maintaining confidentiality. There have been instances when a member of the team has confided in the deputy who then considered that there was a moral obligation to inform the leader. This is an example of an ethical dilemma for which a professional code of ethics should provide guidelines. An apparent breach of trust can have destructive outcomes on the future relationship with the team, with the deputy being rejected as a member of the team when no longer in the leadership position. The impact on the deputy's relationship with the team as a result of the varying levels of authority associated with the position is an important concern.

Although there are other difficulties associated with this position, there are many positive aspects to the role. Participation in a team in this capacity helps to build self-esteem and enhances job satisfaction through the opportunity to provide input at a different level. The chance to demonstrate and develop leadership potential, gain experience and knowledge, and change people's perception about personal capacities are positive outcomes of accepting the extra responsibility.

Awareness about the possible pitfalls and pressures of leadership responsibility is important because it allows individuals to develop the knowledge and skills necessary to undertake the position in the future. In terms of the overall team, a competent deputy is essential to act as a backup in any emergency or unplanned absence by the leader. It is a logical and rational way of sharing the responsibility for helping the team to work effectively.

## BRINGING IT TOGETHER

Effective supervision, mentoring and coaching are on-the-job opportunities to advance the professional development of both leaders and early childhood practitioners. Creating a climate for personal and professional growth is critical for ensuring ongoing quality in early childhood service provision. Such opportunities and experiences can help improve practitioners' confidence, communication, respect for others and teamwork, and develop broader professional perspectives. The most effective on-the-job professional development experiences provide both the motivation and opportunity to learn from positive role models, mentors and coaches in supportive, encouraging environments.

# CHAPTER 10
## INITIATING AND IMPLEMENTING CHANGE

*An effective leader can harness the necessary expertise to push forward
an agenda for reform and change that has been jointly constructed.*

Senior lecturer, early childhood

THIS CHAPTER EXPLORES

- **the role of change as a crucial leadership challenge**
- **types of change in organisations**
- **change and the individual**
- **sources of resistance to change**
- **dealing with resistance to change**
- **effective implementation of change**
- **helping staff cope with change**
- **developing leadership for change**
- **features of successful change programs**

Change is one of the few certainties in life. It is a natural phenomenon
in all aspects of our lives. Given that human beings experience so much
change in their day-to-day lives, it can be difficult to understand why
the process of change presents such a threat to some people. Indeed,
one of the realities of change is that it will be resisted by many of us.
Change occurs in individuals, organisations and societies. Change at
any one of these levels will necessitate change in the others. Decisions
usually involve change because the process of implementation requires

change in individual attitudes and skills, as well as organisational policies and procedures. Therefore, change is an inevitable, ongoing process.

Change is also necessary. Growth is a result of change and illustrates the capacity of an individual or organisation to respond to the environment, to adapt, to be flexible, to question traditional or established practices, methods or ideas in order to develop new knowledge and ways of applying that knowledge. It is a means of creating opportunities that sustains individual and organisational survival.

The early childhood field continues to experience acute and chronic change where pressures for rapid and extensive changes have occurred over an extended period of time. Much uncertainty and unpredictability still exists for practitioners as the profession attempts to accommodate rapid social change and develop services and programs that are adaptive, flexible and responsive to community needs. Early years practitioners need to see themselves as active agents of change who both initiate and respond proactively to demands and need for change.

While some members of the field perceive the present situation as challenging, stimulating and ripe with future benefits, others view current events as a threat to themselves and the profession, to be avoided and resisted at all costs. In both responses to change, emotions are aroused. Positive emotions tend to be associated with positive responses, with change perceived as beneficial and a challenge. Negative emotions tend to be associated with negative responses, with change perceived as stressful and destructive. The leader has to ensure that their early childhood service is viable under current and anticipated future conditions, and meets the needs for support and strengthened team morale.

The role of the leader has become instrumental in managing change in organisations, with leaders regarded as orchestrators of change. The leader has the ultimate responsibility for managing change. As with leaders in other fields, early childhood leaders are expected to ensure efficient use of resources to meet present demands, while at the same time finding ways to guarantee the long-term survival and effectiveness of early childhood services. In terms of change, effectiveness means the ability to adapt to changing circumstances (Carnall, 1995).

The planning for and implementation of change are amongst the major challenges facing today's leaders in early childhood (Ebbeck and Waniganayake, 2003). Leadership for change requires:

- vision and inspiration;
- careful planning;
- decision-making skills;
- effective communication;
- confident conflict management; and
- sensitive handling of people involved in or affected by the change.

The extent to which change is well planned, sensitively handled, appropriately timed and sufficiently resourced or a loosely conceived, loosely implemented program of action will depend on the leader's understanding of the process of change and its implementation in an organisational setting.

For those early childhood practitioners who have not thought about the essence of change, the following general points are useful for understanding where and how it fits into personal and professional life. Change:

- is inevitable;
- is necessary;
- is a process;
- occurs in individuals, organisations and societies;
- can be anticipated and planned for;
- is highly emotional, and can cause tension and stress;
- is resisted by many people;
- can be adjusted to by individuals and groups with the support of the leader;
- entails developmental growth in attitudes and skills, policies and procedures; and
- is best facilitated on the basis of diagnosed needs.

When considering change, the leader must recognise that the organisation does not exist solely for the purpose of testing out new ideas. Prior experiences with ad hoc approaches to change, where change has been introduced for change's sake, have left many of those involved feeling ambiguous about or resistant to future change. This is because organisational effectiveness and viability rarely are enhanced through ad hoc changes.

Successful organisations have become so because their leaders have ensured that they have adjusted continually to the demands—both in terms of opportunities and constraints—that their social, political and economic environments have made on them. These leaders understand that the organisation exists to benefit its mission and to achieve its objectives. Therefore, change should only be considered if it is thought to be effective in furthering the organisation's mission and objectives.

Organisational strength is a function of the mix of and balance between two major forces: bureaucratisation and innovation. Bureaucratisation refers to the need to establish ritual, routine and predictable ways of doing things, and is a means of ensuring organisational stability. Rules and regulations, standard procedures, division of labour and the internal structural hierarchy are examples of bureaucratic forces. Over-emphasis on the traditional and established ways of doing things can result in a failure to perceive the need for change, a lack of action or inadequate action which comes too late. Sometimes organisations continue to uphold policies and practices not because they are the most effective or efficient ways to do things now—or even because they were the best ways to do things in the past—but simply because they *were done* in the past.

Innovation refers to organisational responses to any environmental demand and is the force that gives the organisation its adaptability, flexibility and responsiveness. Changes in structure (for example, new staff groupings), communication channels and processes (such as who reports what to whom, when and how) and changes in behaviour (such as in leadership style) illustrate innovation in an organisation. Over-emphasis on innovation can lead to a haphazard approach to change, premature change and blind imitation of certain policies and practices of similar organisations (an attitude of 'if they're doing it, it must be right, so we'll do it too'). The leader must ensure that decisions which are sufficiently innovative are based upon diagnosed needs as well as adequate bureaucratisation in order to meet the demands of task performance and team morale.

## TYPES OF CHANGE IN ORGANISATIONS

Change in organisations occurs in a variety of ways and involves different levels of significance for those affected by the change. Organisations, including early childhood settings, are dynamic in that their people, hierarchies, structures and systems are continually evolving. The pursuit of new knowledge and experiences, more efficient methods and more effective functions by the members of any organisation produces *incremental change*, where small modifications are introduced into and absorbed by the system on a day-to-day basis. These small changes often go unnoticed until a substantial difference is discerned by a staff member. Simple changes to the early childhood curriculum or routines are examples of incremental changes to which little attention is given. A series of incremental changes, whether planned or unintentional, can result in a major organisational shift in an unwanted direction if it is not adequately monitored.

*Induced change* results from a conscious decision to implement a change in people, processes, programs, structures and systems. Participation in a conference or in-service training can stimulate the desire to change an aspect of an early childhood service, such as the parent program, the curriculum or the staff's behaviour management practices. Induced change can involve different levels of significance. It can be routine, to meet a crisis, innovative and, more rarely, transformational.

*Routine change* is very common and is effected by the leader and team members on a daily basis in response to problem situations. The aim is to restore the status quo. Routine changes are designed to improve quality, to meet the needs of children and parents, to enhance cooperation between staff and to reduce conflict.

*Crisis change*, as the name suggests, is any response to an unexpected occurrence in the setting. Due to time constraints, the leader is likely to make a quick decision without consulting the team members. Team members usually do not object to the demands of change in a crisis, and are willing to accept an authoritarian decision by the leader in order to meet the needs of the situation. An exception to this is where the leader has procrastinated about or deferred necessary decision-making. Staff members may not be supportive of an executive decision under these circumstances. Crisis change can occur as a result of unexpected staff resignation, illness or absence, unexpected changes in physical or financial conditions or unexpected needs of children. Failure to recognise the need for change can precede and precipitate a crisis change.

*Innovative change* results from creative problem-solving or trial and error, where the leader and team members are seeking easier, faster and more successful ways to further the mission and meet objectives. Innovative change is more likely to occur under the team leadership of a highly supportive, committed and goal-oriented staff group. Altering a service's opening hours to meet the needs of local parents and children is an example of innovative change. Decision-making for innovative change involves initiation and implementation. Initiation includes knowledge awareness, the formation of positive attitudes towards the change and the actual decision to change. Implementation includes the initial introduction and planned execution of the change plus continued, sustained implementation of the change. However, Hasenfeld (1992) cautions that the decision-making process for the initiation and implementation of change rarely follows a rational and logical sequence from problem recognition to evaluation of alternatives to the adoption of a solution. Early childhood practitioners need to combine understanding about decision-making processes with awareness about factors that can make innovative change appear a chaotic event.

*Transformational change*, where the form of an organisation is radically altered, occurs at crisis point when the survival of the organisation calls for drastic action. This type of change is most likely to occur if the organisation fails to respond to the demands of the environment due to an over-emphasis on either bureaucratisation or innovation. The necessity for routine, minor crisis and innovative changes may have been ignored by the leader and the team. It is interesting to note that transformational change is occurring in the early childhood field with the creation of new services such as the multidisciplinary children's centres in England and extended child care in primary schools. The pressures on staff involved in transformational change are enormous, and the potential for stress and burnout is high.

## CHANGE AND THE INDIVIDUAL

Effective leaders understand that any organisational change can have a major impact on the lives of those involved or affected by it. It is not uncommon for people to react to change with anxiety, uncertainty and stress—even those who are fully committed to change. The magnitude of the change will determine the amount of stress that is generated. Stress and its management are very important for change to be implemented successfully. Conflict is often the impetus for change, and should not be avoided in professional situations. However, both conflict and stress need to be managed intelligently by the leader because there are definite links between these and self-esteem and performance. While some stress can challenge and motivate individuals, too much stress lowers performance and self-esteem. Leaders need to develop the art of managing stress levels in such a way that optimal performance and associated high levels of self-esteem are produced in the individual.

Change at work can challenge the individual's sense of professional self that has been constructed over time through their interaction with the task and with colleagues. The competent accomplishment of tasks becomes routine with experience and, for many staff, change threatens their sense of competence and mastery of the situation. This may lead to staff questioning the meaning of their work. These factors can evoke defensive reactions to suggestions of change as well as active and passive opposition and resistance to the implementation of any change. It is the leader's responsibility to overcome this tendency by presenting any impending change in ways that permit staff members to see it as a new opportunity that is consistent with existing views about self, and which does not threaten routines or question their established perceptions about work.

Leaders also need to be aware that any personal concerns or lack of confidence about their ability to facilitate change in the organisation are likely to result in the adoption of a more autocratic style of leadership which will decrease the team's ability to respond positively to the change. In addition, individuals with positive self-concepts and high levels of self-esteem are more likely to have a positive attitude to change and to respond to the demands of change in a creative way. This is important in understanding change, because change is inevitable. A person who perceives change as an opportunity for growth and development will approach a new situation with confidence and enthusiasm and is willing to learn new skills to become competent in the new situation. Knowing that change is inevitable, energy and time are put into preparing for change. Personal effectiveness and creativity are enhanced, and a more positive attitude to future personal and organisational change is developed. To survive the demands of constant change, organisations need to create a culture of learning and communities of lifelong learners where individual members are receptive to each other's ideas and are committed to learning and growing together.

### REFLECTIONS ON LEADERSHIP IN PRACTICE

Our team wanted to instigate High Scope as part of a government initiative. The lead person was the manager but she encouraged different people to take the lead on different aspects. She showed leadership because she supported each group member to sustain this area of practice.

**Early childhood course leader**

Where individuals believe that change will threaten their security, or demand skills that they cannot attain, or where they erroneously believe that change can be avoided, forestalled or even stopped, energy and time are put into opposing and resisting change. In such a situation, stress levels escalate and conflict within the organisation can increase. A corresponding deterioration in performance, relationships with other staff and self-esteem is inevitable. Withdrawal and alienation from the team and organisational goals are eventual outcomes of this process. Here, the leader needs to work with such individuals to develop self-esteem and confidence to meet the demands of the new situation. As well, the leader needs to assist these individuals to understand the role of change in organisational survival as well as individual survival.

### REFLECTIONS ON LEADERSHIP IN PRACTICE

I have seen some very innovative educational programs being implemented in early childhood settings. For example, the head teacher and teaching staff rewrote the Foundation Stage curriculum with an emphasis on skills. The changed curriculum also required moving one teacher out and replacing her with someone new. It was very impressive how they worked together constructively to make such a huge change happen.

**Primary adviser**

A commitment to personal and professional development on the part of all staff members is essential to meet the requirements for change in the early childhood profession. Effective leaders accept that staff members have the right to be cautious about anything new, but they do not have the right to become complacent or apathetic, to stagnate or to become inept. Furthermore, nobody has the right to stop others from growing and developing. Professional development programs help foster self-esteem and create individuals who are more resistant to threat. The leader needs to encourage all members of staff to develop dispositions for lifelong learning so that resistance to change is minimised and they are therefore able to approach change with interest and enthusiasm.

## SOURCES OF RESISTANCE TO CHANGE

Every early childhood setting is unique, and therefore will experience resistance to change from different sources. However, there are some common sources of resistance which can be identified, and it is the leader's responsibility to pinpoint these and to find antidotes or ways of overcoming them. The following sources of resistance to change have been identified in early childhood settings:

- *fear about personal future* in a changed environment. This is a major source of resistance. Individual staff members fear the unknown and may be anxious about losing their jobs, having their salary reduced, losing status, the inability to perform a new job, taking on new responsibilities, undergoing new training, changes in social relationships or possible relocation;
- *ideological factors*, such as changes in values and belief systems. These may affect goals and objectives, such as working as a member of a multi-disciplinary team;
- *individual personalities* such as negative and pessimistic staff members with low self-esteem and people who prefer routine and predictability;
- *misunderstandings* about the need for, the purpose of, and the scope and the ramifications of the change;
- *lack of trust in the leader* where the staff do not believe that the leader has their best interests at heart;
- *different assessments or points of view* about the proposed change and its effects on the established team culture;
- *self-interest*—'what's in it for me'—where an individual perceives the change to involve loss of benefits or little personal pay-off;
- *lack of knowledge* to understand the proposed change;
- *new technologies* that require new skills or different ways of doing the job;
- *lack of ownership* where change is imposed from outside;
- *excessive change* in the immediate past or demands for sudden change.

Today, many early childhood settings are run upon cooperative management lines using joint and consensual decision-making styles, thereby making resistance to change less likely to occur (Ebbeck and Waniganayake, 2003). However, effective leaders will be aware that some staff may engage in covert and subtle ways of resisting change that can sabotage its efficient implementation.

## DEALING WITH RESISTANCE TO CHANGE

The way in which the leader approaches staff resistance to change is an important issue in implementing any change. Fighting resistance—trying to overcome it with arguments, information, data and power—is usually not successful because the resistance goes underground. 'Leading with a gun'—that is, using force to deal with resistance—is likely to produce a desire for revenge, where staff may wait for an opportunity to get even. A better way to handle resistance is to get it out in the open and encourage the full expression of concerns. The aim is to encourage staff to start expressing their fears, unease and anxieties directly to the leader and to each other, thus preventing any attempts at subterfuge and sabotage.

The following methods of dealing with resistance are useful for leaders of early childhood services because they draw on communication and problem-solving skills that are usually well developed in practitioners in order to deliver services.

### COMMUNICATION AND EDUCATION

These methods can be used prior to and during the implementation of a change where lack of, or inaccurate, information increases stress levels and hinders staff members' perceptions of the benefits of the change. If individual staff members understand the rationale behind the change, they may be persuaded to accept it. An important outcome of communication and education is that staff may assist with the implementation phase by providing accurate information to other staff members. Unless some other staff can be involved in communicating with and educating team members, it can become a very time-consuming activity for the leader, especially if large numbers of people are involved.

### PARTICIPATION AND INVOLVEMENT

These methods can be used prior to and during the implementation phase where a leader wants to ensure team commitment to the proposed change, where the leader needs more information to design the change or where there are large numbers of possible resisters. The team is invited to provide advice to the leader and to help design and activate the change. Participation helps reduce stress and fears, and acts as a motivator by increasing self-esteem. Resisters are more likely to contribute if they believe that they can have some control over the process. Participating and involved staff can contribute to integrating all the available, relevant information into the proposal which will assist in refining and enhancing commitment to the final outcome. The only disadvantage is that poorly supervised participants may design an inappropriate change which can be costly and time-consuming to rectify should it be implemented. The leader needs to monitor the team's direction and contribution to ensure that the change is consistent with the setting's mission and objectives.

## FACILITATION AND SUPPORT

These methods can be used where staff openly resist change. While this is time-consuming, costly and may be unsuccessful, it is the only option a leader has to deal with adjustment problems. Attention is focused on staff members' concerns about task performance and relationships. The leader employs listening, conflict-resolution, problem-solving and stress-management skills to strengthen the level of trust in the group. Acknowledgment of and empathy for the difficulties of undergoing change are essential. Support through training and access to other resources needs to be made available.

## NEGOTIATION AND AGREEMENT

These methods can be used where it is obvious that someone is going to forfeit certain current benefits or experience extra burdens, or when the team has a lot of power to resist the change. The leader needs to offer incentives to actual or potential resisters, or work out some form of tradeoff where special benefits are guaranteed if the change is not blocked. One difficulty can be that early childhood leaders may have little to offer in terms of special incentives and benefits because they may not have the power or resources to provide financial and time-in-lieu rewards. Prestige in terms of nomination for the position of deputy or second-in-charge may be a reward for some staff members.

## PREPARING FOR CHANGE

This is the process of motivating staff to change by making them aware of the need for it and preparing them to be receptive to the change. The staff must be persuaded that the present situation is ineffective and that they have a professional responsibility to respond to the situation to restore the expected level of effectiveness. A sense of psychological safety can be tapped by leaders who convey confidence in the staff's ability to cope with the change. The leader must address any barriers to and sources of resistance to change at this point.

A common mistake many leaders make is to introduce change when the team is not sufficiently prepared for and receptive to change.

Staff often go through stages of coping with change. First, they may deny that a need for change exists and may try to defend the status quo. Much energy can be devoted to resistance if staff members have not been prepared adequately for the change or given enough time to adjust to the realities of the situation. As staff come to perceive that change is inevitable and necessary, with sufficient support from the leader they begin to let go of the past and focus on the future. Staff will then start to adapt to the new requirements but may find this period frustrating as they may not have the level of skill and competence to meet the new demands. Ongoing mutual support from the team and the leader is essential to move the staff through this stage and to ensure the long-term success of the change. Finally, as the change is incorporated into the personal repertoire of the staff and into the organisational system, it is accepted as a normal and routine part of work.

## EFFECTIVE IMPLEMENTATION OF CHANGE
This refers to the developing of new attitudes and behaviours on the basis of diagnosed need, new information or cognitive redefinition where new ways of looking at old information are adopted. The essence of changing is to ensure that the staff engage in the new behaviour or situation and start to experiment with the change. This is a transitional stage where learning, risk-taking and creativity are required. The more the staff interact with the change, the faster it will be integrated into accepted, normal patterns at work. The leader needs to provide feedback about how well the staff are doing in effecting improvements in achieving the mission and objectives, improving the strategies, tasks, structures and team culture.

The leader can set the conditions for the successful implementation of a change by following three steps. Change should be understood by leaders as a people-oriented process which involves specific groundwork to prepare people to be receptive to change, action to implement change and ongoing activity that stabilises change by the development of positive attitudes and behaviours.

## STABILISING AND EMBEDDING CHANGE
This occurs when the staff have accepted the change to a point where they support it as a normal part of daily life. The leader needs to stabilise and sustain the change by restoring a sense of equilibrium to the work environment but at a higher level of effectiveness. The

process of stabilisation helps eliminate feelings of chaos and lack of control that some staff experience during change. The leader needs to provide support for the change, reward the staff for their efforts to meet the demands of change, and review and evaluate the effects so that any adjustments can be made. Efforts need to be made to ensure that staff members are supported in the rebuilding of their self-esteem. If the conditions are not stabilised following the introduction of a change, the staff might revert to the old way and the change will be short-lived or abandoned. The leader's inability to sustain and embed the changed circumstances accounts for many attempts at change that fail.

## HELPING STAFF COPE WITH CHANGE

Fear and uncertainty about change can lower staff morale and lower their performance level. However, staff members can be supported through periods of change by a sensitive leader who can ease adjustment to new demands and enhance self-esteem in the process. The following guidelines for early childhood leaders which have been adapted from suggestions by Schrag, Nelson and Siminowsky (1985) are called the 'Six Cs of Change'.

### CHALLENGE

Help staff to perceive change as a challenge, not a threat, by developing staff morale and open communication, and encouraging a mutually supportive team approach to work.

### COMMUNICATE

Keep staff informed. Fear of the unknown, lack of information or misinformation can lead to resistance and lack of trust in the leader. Empathise with staff members' real experiences and problems with change. Don't ignore or trivialise them.

### COMMITMENT

Involve staff in the diagnosis of the need for change, as well as the planning, design and implementation of the change. Participation and involvement in decision-making and problem-solving ensure a high level of commitment. In this way, staff 'own' the change and do not feel as if it has been imposed from above or from outside.

### CONTROL

Help staff members feel that they are not powerless in the face of change and that, through participation and involvement, they will be able to influence the course of the change. Allow for some flexibility to incorporate staff ideas and feedback. Train staff in the skills of negotiation.

### CONFIDENCE

Build confident, resilient staff who do not read any implications about their worth into change. Help staff to realistically identify and feel comfortable with their strengths and weaknesses. Focus on promoting self-awareness and self-acceptance while at the same time encouraging staff members to engage in personal and professional development.

### CONNECT

Network with other individuals and organisations who are undergoing change to help staff develop an awareness of the inevitability of change and a more sophisticated approach to adapting to change. Extend the team's support network by linking up with colleagues and peers in the field. Ask for outside assistance if necessary.

## DEVELOPING LEADERSHIP FOR CHANGE

Leadership for change is a key role for early childhood practitioners who are committed to the provision of high-quality services for the community. While many of the factors that relate to effective leadership have been outlined in previous chapters, the demands of facilitating change in the early childhood field require several additional abilities. Hersey and Blanchard (1988) suggest there are three general skills that leaders need in order to facilitate change in an organisation:

- *diagnosing* (a cognitive skill with which the leader assesses the gap between the present situation and future needs);
- *adapting* (a behavioural skill in which the leader modifies behaviour and other resources to solve the problem of meeting future needs); and
- *communicating* (a process skill used by the leader to communicate clear objectives and direction to others).

Effective leaders should take into account the organisation's previous history of change when considering the timing of it. Positive or negative experiences with change in the past, as well as the length of time that an organisation has been experiencing it and the significance or magnitude of change that has been required, affect the organisation's readiness to accept further change. The organisation's previous experience can act as a barrier to the implementation of necessary changes.

Given that the early childhood field is experiencing a period of continuous change, with many workers poorly prepared and few skilled agents of change, high levels of resistance to demands for further change are to be anticipated. Effective leaders will analyse the critical barriers and plan any innovation in small, unintimidating steps that help minimise stress levels of those who are involved with or affected by the change. To implement a change successfully, the leader will:

- ensure that the team clearly understands the need for and the benefits of the change;
- communicate the objectives so that the team has a clear sense of purpose;
- provide broad guidelines for achieving the objectives (such as a step-by-step plan);
- encourage team participation to clarify the needed change and provide detailed information relevant to the change; and
- provide feedback and some form of reward for those who participated in the implementation of the change.

The essence of the leader's role in facilitating change is to set, clarify and focus on the values underpinning the needed change, to support the team's task accomplishment through calculated risk-taking and problem-solving, to design processes and procedures that will support manageable action, and to support people in the development of confidence and skills. This is not an easy task, but it is an essential one. Change is about learning by both the leader and the team. It is possible that some changes will not be achieved, or will be short-lived. Effective leaders will not be deterred by failure or avoid becoming involved with possible future change, but will reassess the situation and try again. Commitment to change in order to further the professionalisation of the early childhood field is another hallmark of the effective leader.

> **REFLECTIONS ON LEADERSHIP IN PRACTICE**
> Our service was given a new identity when a new manager took charge. She developed courses and events to meet local government targets and existing known community needs. Her leadership skills are not reflected in her job description or salary and that needs to be reviewed. But her leadership has improved her own job prospects alongside the enhanced quality of our service.
>
> **Teacher, early excellence centre**

## FEATURES OF SUCCESSFUL CHANGE PROGRAMS

To complete this study of leadership and change, effective leaders need to be able to identify the following characteristics in their plans to implement change and increase the probability of success:

- clear objectives that provide a sense of purpose for the team;
- a realistic and limited scope—start small and build up as small changes are successful and the team becomes more receptive to change;
- informed awareness by team members about the role of change in personal, professional and organisational development and survival;
- selection of appropriate intervention strategies that are consistent with the organisation's culture;
- good timing and appropriate pace—ensuring change is not introduced too early or too late, too slow or too fast;
- a sense of ownership through the participation of all involved, especially resisters;
- support from key power groups, especially top management;
- involvement of existing power structures such as the deputy and lobby groups;
- open assessment or diagnosis before initiating change;
- support of the majority of staff to minimise resistance;
- support of competent staff to optimise the probability of success;
- training and other necessary support available;
- a framework where new policies, procedures and practices can be integrated with existing and established ones;
- a protocol for continued evaluation;
- adequate rewards to reinforce the change, such as feedback and public recognition.

## BRINGING IT TOGETHER

Some early childhood services have been criticised for their apparent inability to respond to the demands of change. While the field has been responsive to change on the basis of crisis, it appears that it still can improve its capacity to engage in innovative change—that is, where early childhood leaders exhibit the motivation to overcome obstacles, to counteract sources of resistance to change and to mobilise both internal and external resources that can support change. The traditional conservatism of the early childhood field may jeopardise its long-range survival and viability. However, if attitudes to change become more positive and practitioners feel confident about voicing their opinions and experiences of imposed and self-initiated changes, the future can hold exciting possibilities for children, parents and the staff who are associated with early childhood services.

# CHAPTER 11
## LEADERSHIP AND THE
## RESEARCH CONNECTION

*Effective leaders possess a desire to know more and they want to pass on their knowledge widely to others in the early childhood field and/or the public arena.*

Associate professor, early childhood

**THIS CHAPTER EXPLORES**
- **research and what it can offer those who care for and educate young children**
- **reasons why research is under-utilised by early childhood practitioners**
- **encouraging a research culture in the early childhood profession**
- **action research as a guide to decision-making and problem-solving**

The early childhood field has begun to develop its own research ethos, culture and community with specific research agendas that focus on the application of findings to care and educational settings. Some settings already undertake high-quality research themselves and, in partnership with government departments and higher education organ-isations, some practitioners have acted as consultants to external research studies. However, many early childhood practitioners still appear hesitant to define research as a part of their professional roles and responsibilities. Historically, the field relied on academic staff from a variety of disciplines within universities and colleges to pursue new knowledge and apply it to child care and early education. A division between research and academic staff and early childhood practitioners led to the latter becoming recipients of others' advice and consumers rather than producers of research. Today, however, practitioners need to understand research processes and become more active in their own early childhood research community (Keyes, 2000).

With their reluctance to regard themselves as intellectuals with a responsibility and capacity for scientific inquiry, early childhood practitioners themselves have perpetuated the perception that they are a lower status group, mainly concerned with practice rather than theory. However, with the increasing numbers of practitioners who hold a range of accredited qualifications and the growing professional development opportunities that cultivate inquiry-based research skills, the nature of the early childhood practitioner is changing. The field now has the potential to grow its own researchers who can lead professional reform and develop informed confidence through research into practice (Anning and Edwards, 1999; Ebbeck and Waniganayake, 2003).

Part of being an effective leader is the ability to understand and apply research findings to early childhood services, and the ability to design and implement a research project within a service. Research, especially action research, is considered to be one of the most effective ways to optimise the care and education of young children, as well as improve the professional image of the field. Numerous writers have recommended that early childhood practitioners themselves should set appropriate research priorities. They also challenge leaders in early childhood to identify and strengthen the professional image of the field through the scientific application of research findings to care and educational settings for young children. Early childhood leaders and practitioners themselves can make a critical contribution to professional transformation by engaging in research that links practice to professional knowledge.

If early childhood practitioners continue to opt out of the research role, they will deny themselves a valuable tool for change, and will not be empowered to influence others to think and act. This will diminish their ability to initiate and implement change on their own behalf and from their specialised knowledge base. Such a continued lack of involvement in research will diminish the field's credibility as a true profession, especially if the nature of early childhood practitioners' work is derived from a knowledge base that has been generated by researchers outside the profession.

Researchers from many other disciplines such as psychology have a goal of increasing knowledge and are mainly interested in what is, not what ought to or could be. The early childhood field has a responsibility to meet the challenge of effecting change, and needs to go beyond the descriptive to the predictive and appropriately responsive. However, many practitioners also tend to resist changes that are guided by research findings. This is because much of the tradition of, and many of the practices in, early childhood are based on professionally socialised attitudes, beliefs and values which are ingrained and hard to change under any circumstances, let alone on the recommendation of research conducted by an 'outsider' who would be unlikely to empathise with the field's idiosyncratic constraints.

Moyles (2003) queries whether early childhood practitioners are pedagogues or pedabogues. She defines a pedagogue as one who is concerned with theory of education, teaching and instruction, whereas, a pedabogue is one who displays a fear of professional inquiry, discourse and discussion. She challenges early childhood practitioners to scrutinise and question traditional and accepted practice by developing basic research skill such as self-evaluation, analysis, reflection and articulation. When practitioners use critical reflection as a research tool, they can free themselves from constraints of traditional knowledge and practice. This can allow them to work more effectively, and to transform both practice and the profession (MacNaughton and Smith, 2001).

Due to a limited sense of ownership of research by the early childhood field, a gap exists between those who conduct research and those practitioners who could and should use the findings in their work with children and families. Practitioners have a vital role to play in initiating and implementing change in any society where informed action is based on critical inquiry and reflective judgment. In assuming responsibility for conducting research, early childhood practitioners need to shift away from traditional conceptual simplicity, which is concrete, particular and not necessarily valid, to a scientific interdisciplinary approach to knowledge and thinking, which is theoretical, general and rational.

Unfortunately, the field—like other systems of education—continues to suffer from a poor understanding of and subsequently a limited interest in, the relationship between research and innovation and change. An uneasy relationship continues between individuals engaged in practice in the early childhood field and those engaged in research

(Katz, 1995a). Early childhood leaders and practitioners need to participate in a range of collaborative multi-disciplinary research projects to avoid finding themselves caught between the push for change and the pull of tradition, and becoming reactive to the variety of trends and counter-trends. However, the field throughout the world continues to undergo rapid change, and is under pressure to address many pressing problems faced by children, families and professionals. The greatest challenge facing the field today is to find new ways to encounter and understand early childhood development, care and education, and to be innovative in the application of new knowledge to assist early childhood practitioners, administrators and leaders to improve the quality of service and enhance the quality of life for children, families and professionals.

A number of specialist references are available for practitioners who wish to undertake research and understand how to use research in practice. MacNaughton, Rolfe and Siraj-Blatchford (2001) cover a range of traditional and newer approaches to qualitative and quantitative research methods in early childhood. Crosser (2005) explains how to use research, details what research tells us about selected key issues, and connects research to practice through case study scenarios. Fraser et al. (2003) and Lewis et al. (2003) examine issues that arise during the research process and illustrate the process of carrying out research with children and young people through research narratives. Such publications are useful tools for assisting early childhood practitioners to identify more closely with the research aspect of their work.

## WHAT IS RESEARCH AND WHAT CAN IT OFFER THOSE WHO CARE FOR AND EDUCATE YOUNG CHILDREN?

Research is a basic tool for advancing knowledge and stimulating change in attitudes, values and practice—all of which are essential means for progressing the early childhood field. Research can help explain the current status of the field by looking at and reflecting upon the past. It also contributes to the impetus to develop new ideas and directions. Research is a means of evaluating the impact of a variety of ecological contexts upon children's development and learning, as well as professional practice. It can be used to influence the design of broad social policies. In short, research can provide early childhood practitioners with a comprehensive, systematic, rational basis for understanding child development both in a broad sense, and for practical action. It is also a means to stimulate staff development through increased professional learning.

The demands on early childhood practitioners are high because they are required to provide quality services to meet the range of needs of children and families in ways that are inclusive and socially and culturally relevant. Early childhood is recognised universally as a prime time for growth, development and learning, with society holding certain assumptions and expectations regarding the types of experiences young children need to be exposed to and shielded from. Early childhood practitioners are expected to extend their contribution to the development and welfare of children by meeting parents' needs for information, support and education. The practitioner is charged with the responsibility for making decisions about the experiences that will optimise young children's development and learning in diverse settings, and they are expected to be responsive to the challenge of constant change in society. The key question concerns the basis on which early childhood practitioners make decisions about young children and their families, and the information they use to do so.

There are a range of sources of information and strategies that practitioners use in order to engage in responsible decision-making and be responsive to the challenge of change. Increasingly, the leader of an early childhood setting has a large impact on the sources and variety of information that are available to staff, particularly those with little or no training. It is interesting to note that educators in general, and early childhood practitioners in particular, are reluctant and hesitant to use research as a basis for decision-making, but tend to rely upon other sources of information as guidelines and reference points. Some of these sources have a number of disadvantages and are likely to result in poor-quality and perhaps even inappropriate decisions for children, families and professionals.

One of the most common sources of information for decision-making is personal opinion and intuition. This involves the use of a subjective viewpoint, which is usually derived from personal values and experience, as a guide to action and decision-making. Such an approach needs to be treated with extreme caution. Under this broad umbrella of knowledge about development, care and education, early childhood practitioners use a number of common expressions to rationalise their decisions. Among the more popular references are 'intuition', which may or may not have some basis in theory but which is often little more than a gut feeling that the exponent cannot justify on rational and logical grounds; 'common sense', which can be vague and often incorrect and fallible; 'in my experience', which may have been limited and/or unrepresentative of general experience; and 'in the best interests of the child/parent/staff member', which usually describes a personal opinion or dogma.

This subjective approach as an information source for decision-making tends to be unhelpful because it is influenced by the prevailing moral and social climate, personal values, convictions and stereotypes, the psychological characteristics and personal histories of the decision-maker, and other political and ideological considerations. What is being used as a basis for decision-making in this approach are personal mythologies about development, care and education. Inexperienced early childhood practitioners are prone to relying on this source of information as a basis for action that is often well-intentioned but non-professional (Vander Ven, 1988).

Tradition, or the justification of decisions and action by reference to historical or established practices, is another major source of information used by early childhood practitioners, often to create barriers to and resist suggested changes. In this approach, expressions used include 'That's the way I was brought up and it didn't hurt me', 'We've always done it that way' and 'Why change something that's working well. Leave well enough alone!' Early childhood practitioners need to recognise that considerable differences exist from one period of time to another, as well as from one place to another. Attitudes and practices that were fashionable at one time or in a particular place lose popularity as more information becomes available and societies change. While traditional and established practices may have been defensible at one time, exponents of some of these approaches rarely appeal to rational, logical or scientific evidence as the basis for their claims. Rather, bold assertion of subjective assumptions and preconceptions about what is 'the best way' is the strength of the argument, and there is usually little room for debate. Fear about the uncertainty of change may evoke the tendency to hang on to what is known or familiar. However, practitioners who use this as a basis for their decision-making are likely to find themselves in a vulnerable situation professionally because their ideas and practices are out of touch with the rest of the community and the field.

Reference to 'the expert' as a source of information for decision-making is a common strategy used by early childhood practitioners.

There are many experts who have contributed to scientific knowledge about and understanding of development, care and education, such as Bowlby, Bronfenbrenner, Freud, Katz, Piaget, Spodek and Tizard, to name just a few. Then there are other experts who have professional credentials and background, but who often rely on their personal charisma or reputation to capture the imagination of ordinary people. These experts, such as Dr Benjamin Spock and Dr T. Berry Brazelton, are able to exert influence on knowledge, understanding and practice in the popular culture. In the main, their contribution has been helpful and informative; however, it is essential that early childhood practitioners who have had a tendency to defer to the 'experts in the field' do not simply take for granted the wisdom of these so-called experts from other disciplines, such as psychology, sociology, biology and history. Instead, they should closely examine the sources of their information and recommendations.

While early childhood practitioners have assumed that the interests of the field can be represented by contributions from more prestigious individuals and groups of professionals, the training of these experts leads to different perspectives on early childhood settings, and takes decision-making and change out of the hands of practitioners. Moreover, the majority of experts still tend to be men, who are likely to have a very different perspective on the issues that are important to the overwhelming percentage of women who constitute the field. In addition, an expert's information and recommendations can be derived from a mixture of personal opinion and intuition, guess-work and informed hunches, folklore, work with small numbers of clinical cases and often the experience of rearing their own children. The proportion of reliable and valid scientific information from which claims are asserted may be small.

Research is another major source of information used as a basis for decision-making that is available to but under-used by early childhood practitioners. As described earlier, research is the systematic investigation of a problem or issue. For a service provider, research is a form of audit, examining and evaluating the system as a basis for good practice and benefiting consumers. The information and knowledge derived from research has certain characteristics that give it advantages over other sources of information. It is:

- *empirical*—conclusions are based on direct observations of relevant phenomena or from verifiable experience available to all;

- *systematic*—data are collected according to an explicit plan not on an ad hoc basis, dependent on personal biases or tendencies;
- *basic and applied*—the purpose of basic research is to develop a base of knowledge upon which theory can be built. Applied research is often designed to answer practical and useful questions, solve specific problems or provide information that is of immediate use;
- *qualitative and quantitative*—qualitative studies can provide descriptive data whereas quantitative data enable comparisons between groups or conditions. Qualitative data, used in conjunction with quantitative data, can help practitioners understand what the numbers mean. Quantitative research usually is controlled: studies are designed in such a way as to rule out all possible explanations except one;
- *public*—the methodology and findings of studies are available for public scrutiny so that the work can be critically assessed and subsequently replicated by other researchers.

Research can provide early childhood practitioners with valid and reliable information on which they can confidently make new decisions, reaffirm previous decisions and initiate change. Such changes will not be on an ad hoc basis or 'change for change's sake', but will be changes based on a rational and logical basis. Unfortunately, some disheartening research (Gibbs, 1990) indicates that the attitudes of those beginning early childhood studies change very little once they are in the profession. Early childhood practitioners need to be encouraged to value and incorporate research as a source of decision-making in order to avoid becoming rigid, stereotyped and outdated in their attitudes. The outcome of an inquiry- or research-based practice should enhance professional development and effectiveness because personal bias will be reduced and mistakes minimised.

Research, however, does not provide magical answers and there may be no one right answer to the questions asked or the problems posed. The answer more often than not may be 'it depends'—that is, factors such as the individual, the type and composition of the group, the type of intervention and the local conditions will affect the interpretation of research outcomes. In addition, more questions and problems will be generated for future investigation than will be resolved by research. In this way, however, the pool of knowledge relevant for early childhood practitioners will be expanded.

In Chapter 2, the relationship between stage of professional career development and leadership was explored. As mentioned, Vander Ven

(1988) argues that early childhood practitioners who are at higher stages in professional career development, such as stage 3—informed, stage 4—complex and stage 5—influential, use more complex and sophisticated sources of information in their daily practice. They tend not to rely on common sense, their personal experience or simplistic applications of basic empirical knowledge and theory, but rather demonstrate progressive thinking by using an interdisciplinary knowledge base (underpinned by scientific research), which is interpreted in the light of clinical experience.

Although early childhood practitioners may not perceive themselves as researchers, in practice they are researchers because they continually process information gathered as they work with children and families. Using data collected prior to, during and following decision-making, they construct their own implicit theories on which to base future action. These grounded theories are extracted out of their own experience and practice, and are not developed and tested by researchers for other disciplines. An effective leader in the field will base practice on information gained from scientific research as well as the intuitive theories that have been constructed from personal experience.

## WHY IS RESEARCH UNDER-UTILISED BY EARLY CHILDHOOD PRACTITIONERS?

The current situation in many early childhood settings, where practice may not reflect what research has discovered about development, care and education, is one which needs to be transformed quickly if the field is to gain professional credibility and status within the community. Given the slow progress of the adoption of a research orientation by the early childhood field, it is evident that research needs to be encouraged by leaders within the field, politicians and the general public. Unfortunately, the field's limited awareness of and interest in research is a major obstacle to the meaningfulness and application of any research findings and recommendations.

It is evident that a gulf exists between research and practice in the field which results in research having seemingly little impact on early childhood services. Practitioners continue to undervalue the need for and the benefits of new knowledge in relation to the improvement of professional practice. This situation would be unthinkable in other professions, where it is an inherent expectation that professionals keep abreast of current research and developments in practice. Imagine how a medical practitioner or an engineer would be perceived if they were ignorant of, disregarded or discounted new research findings and failed to incorporate them into their work! It would be considered totally unacceptable by other members of the profession, consumers and the general public. However, relatively few members of the early childhood profession consider it a professional responsibility to keep up to date with the relevant research and other literature. Yet the role of a leader is to communicate vision and implement ideas with the support of the team. Leaders of early childhood services appreciate that well-designed research is a reliable source of information where many of those new ideas can be found, developed, transformed or created.

It is not difficult to identify some of the reasons why research is under-utilised by early childhood practitioners. Several of these are outlined below.

First, the professional socialisation in pre-service training these days includes a very brief focus on the role and value of research. Basic attitudes and values towards research have not been nurtured in the preparation of early childhood personnel. The emphasis has been on skill development for the practical aspects of working with children and operating services with little attempt to develop the skills required to understand and conduct research. The predominantly practice-oriented interests of early childhood practitioners appear to have acted as an inhibitor to basic research in areas related to early childhood.

Second, early childhood practitioners are often unaware of the different approaches to research due to the practical orientation and limitations of current training. For some practitioners, the lack of training is the obstacle here. Many staff simply lack knowledge about what research is available because in general they do not subscribe to or read research-oriented journals, do not purchase theoretically and conceptually demanding textbooks or borrow them from libraries, and do not attend staff development opportunities that have a research orientation. The personal libraries of early childhood practitioners are more likely to be made up of popular literature on practical aspects of child development and psychology, with some dated texts from pre-service training courses.

There also appears to be an inability on the part of researchers to communicate research findings to practitioners—when early childhood practitioners do read research reports, they often complain that the theory, findings and recommendations are incomprehensible and therefore irrelevant. Because they lack training and skill in research methodology, the technical and abstract language of the researcher is difficult for the practitioner to understand and interpret. Researchers need to adapt their findings to the language of the practitioner to encourage their application. However, many researchers find this a difficult task given their limited familiarity with the practical contexts of early childhood services, and would prefer to pursue their own research interests rather than become a translator for a group of professionals who do not appear receptive to what research has to offer.

Researchers tend to write for a specific audience—that is, other academics and colleagues in higher education. Academic journals, in which most research is published, are favoured by researchers because publication in such journals is related to career advancement. Such journals are not easily available to practitioners unless they are enrolled to study in higher education degrees. Other possible audiences—such as practitioners in the field, the general public, the press and media, and policy-makers at local and national levels—are perceived by many academic researchers to have less status compared with their colleagues.

Early childhood practitioners also tend to distrust research findings and new ideas, and often refuse to accept them because they find personal security in the known and familiar. The ongoing demand for change has produced some negative attitudes to change—especially change that resulted in discontinuities in practice. Consequently, some practitioners have become suspicious about adopting innovations too quickly. Some practitioners are resistant to change and view change and innovation as unnecessary. Research findings alone are unlikely to stimulate change in established practices that have been derived from attitudes, values and beliefs built up over many years.

The implementation of research findings and new ideas involves extra work for practitioners who already have demanding jobs. Early childhood practitioners who wish to implement the results of research may find it necessary to persuade committees of management, school governors or employers of cost-effective benefits; may need to devise new strategies and techniques; and may need to clarify and restructure their value systems. All of this takes time and energy. Time is the most valuable but also the most scarce resource for many practitioners, who argue that this is one reason that they are not able to keep up with or implement new developments.

Early childhood practitioners consider themselves to be autonomous and may use their traditional right to independence to justify poor practice. Some practitioners are suspicious that academic researchers (who are assumed to have little knowledge of and experience in working with young children and their families, or who may have lost contact with the field) are trying to dictate what should be done in early childhood services. Consequently, they choose to ignore the contribution that research can make. A lack of collaboration between researchers and practitioners has created an additional problem of 'ownership', where practitioners are not involved in the production of research and therefore do not have a sense that it relates to them. Genuine collaboration could enhance ownership and help to diminish any perceived threat to autonomy.

Some early childhood practitioners consider their work to be a practice-oriented art rather than a theoretically based science. Their dislike of theory, which is articulated throughout pre-service training, continues into workplace attitudes. Some practitioners find theory diffi-cult to grasp because they have not developed sophisticated conceptual and analytical skills. This cognitive limitation is linked to an inability to comprehend the relevance of theory to practice. They do not under-stand that theory and research are sources of knowledge that can be used as guides to practice or as a resource, but alone are not sufficient to act as a foundation or directive for curriculum or program design.

The present training and career structures for the early childhood field still do not emphasise the skills of understanding, implementing and producing research as an integral aspect of professional leader-ship. The field needs more intelligent consumers of research as a basis for nurturing producers of research. However, unless early childhood practitioners themselves take responsibility for extending the boun-daries of knowledge and ideas in their own field, the present reliance on professionals outside the field to conduct research and shape its future will continue—a factor which will impede the budding profes-sionalisation of the early childhood field.

The existence of the above obstacles to interest in and incorporation of research into decision-making and change will not deter the effective early childhood leader, who—while acknowledging these structural difficulties—will work towards overcoming them through the creation of a special ethos or atmosphere in settings where research is valued for its contribution to the early childhood service and the professional learning and development of staff.

## ENCOURAGING A RESEARCH CULTURE

There are many disincentives to consuming and producing research in the early childhood field. In order to address this problem, leadership needs to come from within the profession, from individuals who are innovative, flexible and creative and who combine these attributes with disciplined thinking based on accurate sources of information. Effective leaders need to make research and reflection an inherent part of their own activity and encourage their staff to do the same. One way to elevate the status of research as a source of information for professional decision-making and the initiation of change is to foster a culture where research is valued.

What is a 'research culture'? It is really a matter of personal and professional attitude. It can also be described as an environment in which intellectual interest and scientific curiosity exist and are evident. A research culture is evidenced by a prevailing atmosphere throughout the early childhood profession, at training and at service level, where individuals are motivated to seek additional knowledge which forms the basis of choices in practice, whether they be by researcher, practitioner or parent. A research culture values theoretical and research-based knowledge which relates to child development and learning processes, interactional and instructional methods, and human resource management.

The strategies described below can be implemented to create and enhance a research culture in the early childhood profession:

First, it should be acknowledged that the early childhood profession is distinctive, unique and possesses its own traditions, values, assumptions, experiences, practices and training, and is therefore capable of extending its own knowledge base without relying on other professionals to fulfil this role. A shift in attitude is necessary—that is, from one of deference to the opinions of experts and authorities from other professions to a healthy, questioning scepticism of the input from others and increasing respect for the contributions from members of the early childhood field.

A greater acceptance of pluralism should be encouraged in the theoretical perspectives on which research is based. To date, research in early childhood has come mainly from a psychological perspective— in particular, developmental and educational psychology. In order to gain a deeper and broader understanding of the social reality of development, care and education, other perspectives—for example, sociology, ecology, biology, anthropology, history, philosophy, politics, curriculum theory and economics—need to become as familiar to early childhood practitioners as the psychological viewpoint. The early childhood field needs up-to-date information on a wide range of issues, problems and techniques to advance the provision of a range of quality services that will meet the needs of a changing society.

A research orientation should be supported in training programs at all levels for students and staff so that research becomes an accepted and valued part of the professional culture. In this way, potential members of the field will develop the skills to be intelligent consumers of research and to perceive their role as one which may include the production of research. In addition, the fact that more practitioners are completing higher research-based degrees as part of their own staff development has begun to change the face of the field from a predominantly practice-based orientation to one of evidence-based practice in which there is a perceived balance between the scientific and practical needs required to meet the early childhood endeavour.

Early childhood practitioners should be encouraged to become involved in collaborative research (Potter, 2001). The gap between researcher and practitioner can be narrowed if more practitioners become involved in research, not only as postgraduate students, but as equal partners in multi-professional teams which undertake research. The inclusion of practitioners in research teams can sensitise them to the entire research process in a way that promotes effective use of resources and improvement of practice. Collaborative investigations by researchers and practitioners begin with a dialogue concerning values, beliefs, assumptions and local conditions in order to establish the basis of the research project. Individual responsibility, initiative and direction can be handled through responsible delegation by the team leader.

Collaborative research teams can overcome the problem and effects of lack of 'ownership' in the research endeavour. Lack of involvement in research can lead to important findings remaining unknown and consequently not being applied in appropriate circumstances by practitioners. Collaborative processes are a means of promoting communication and understanding between researcher and practitioner, and help to ensure that research findings using a minimum of jargon are made available and presented in simple and intelligent ways, so that they are easily understood by decision-makers and consumers.

From their day-to-day practice, early childhood practitioners gain intimate knowledge about and understanding of questions and problems that need to be addressed in a systematic investigation. These practitioners can provide the clear link between real-life issues and the needs of the field, and the research questions that are defined for examination. Reflective practitioners and leaders use their drive and initiative to conduct the necessary research themselves, or to establish a collaborative, multi-disciplinary team that includes practitioners and experienced researchers. While the research activities of developing, testing and confirming scientific knowledge are not pursuits that can be carried out in spare time at work, early childhood practitioners need to be encouraged to engage in action research which can be conducted in various settings.

Research needs to be perceived as a routine problem-solving exercise that can contribute to new knowledge and understanding, as well as to practical outcomes.

These strategies will not change the prevailing culture of the early childhood profession overnight, but an effective leader can signal the need for change in this area by focusing on the positive outcomes of valuing research as much as practice. Keyes (2000) encourages practitioners to become more active in the research community because of the added value brought about by systematic inquiry into practice. Collaborative research plays an important role in enhancing critical reflection and co-construction of professional understanding because it offers practitioners opportunities to engage in conversations about curriculum, pedagogy and change in knowledgeable and meaningful ways (Potter, 2001).

Early childhood practitioners who want to engage in research can begin to do so by making the time and space to:

- reflect on their practice;
- talk about pedagogy—that is, learning and teaching;
- relate professionally and collaborate with colleagues; and
- use evidence-based practice as a means for improving quality.

A research culture can develop when practitioners appreciate that:

- research is a professional responsibility for those working in learning communities such as early childhood settings;
- collaborative inquiry is fundamental to the development of settings as professional learning communities;

- collaboration is a way of ensuring that knowledge, understanding and good practice are shared; and
- evidenced-based practice builds on success and improves quality.

A research culture can be stimulated by early childhood leaders who support staff to accept some responsibility for defining questions to be investigated by themselves or other researchers, for verifying research results reported in professional literature, and for ensuring cogent interpretation and practical application of relevant recommendations.

## ACTION RESEARCH AS A GUIDE TO DECISION-MAKING AND PROBLEM-SOLVING

Action research is a recognised means of professional development for early childhood practitioners. It is a tool for bridging the gap between research and practice that enhances professional learning and fosters reflective practice. Evidence indicates that educators and administrators would make better decisions and become more effective practitioners if they were willing and able to conduct action research in their places of work (Campbell, 2002). Indeed, action research has been linked to quality improvement in the services provided for young children (MacNaughton, Rolfe and Siraj-Blatchford, 2001; Crosser, 2005). Early childhood practitioners who are able to conduct this type of research in their settings are able to demonstrate creative leadership in their ability to diagnose and respond to problems and the need for change in a systematic manner. Action research has been suggested as a vehicle for increasing professionalism because, through the process of conducting action research, practitioners begin to value research and develop a professional culture that values reflection.

The term 'action research' refers to a way of thinking that uses reflection and inquiry as a way of understanding the conditions that support or inhibit change, the nature of change, the process of change and the results of the attempt to change. Action research entails action disciplined by inquiry and combines the research procedure with a substantive act (Hopkins, 1990). The goal is to improve practice, which is an ongoing concern for all members of the profession. In order to optimise a successful outcome for action research undertaken by early childhood practitioners, the problems chosen to be explored need to be significant for the leader and the team in terms of the mission, objectives and quality of the service. The problems must be manageable within a realistic timeframe, and appropriate for the research skills of the people involved. A healthy attitude within the team to problem-solving, risk-taking and experimentation is also helpful, and needs to be tempered by the leader with realistic expectations about the unpredictability of change and the probability of immediate success.

Wadsworth (1997) and Kemmis and McTaggert (1988) give clear, practical descriptions of action research for human service professionals. The following steps briefly outline the action research process and cycle.

1 *Identifying problems of mutual concern.* The present problems are brought into focus through the processes of observation and reflection by all members of the team.
2 *Analysing problems and determining possible contributing factors.* The ability to diagnose the determinants of a problem is required. The existing situation is monitored using recorded, uncensored and uninterpreted observations from members of the team.
3 *Forming tentative working hypotheses or guesses to explain these factors.* At this point, questionable assumptions are eliminated. Decisions are made about the form and method of interpretation of the data that are to be collected.
4 *Collecting and interpreting data* from observations, interviews and relevant documents to clarify these hypotheses and to develop action hypotheses. Accurate details of events need to be recorded in order to avoid erroneous or superficial influences.
5 *Formulating plans for action and carrying them out.* Plans are experimental, prospective and forward-looking, and may involve the acquisition of new skills or procedures in order to implement the plans.
6 *Evaluating the results of the action.* The processes of observation and reflection are used to critically assess the effects of the informed action and to make sense of the processes and issues that unfolded during the implementation phase. Collaborative reflection provides an opportunity to reconstruct meaning out of the situation and establishes the basis for a revised plan.
7 *Introducing a revised cycle from step 1 to step 6.*

Because becoming engaged in action research can be perceived as yet another role and responsibility to take on, and another demand on the already heavy workload of early childhood practitioners, it is important that some non-research-related considerations be highlighted. Although some practitioners initiate projects that could be called action research, these are often abandoned for a range of reasons. It appears that recognition by would-be researchers of the importance of other factors in the success of action research projects is an essential aspect. Borgia and Schuler (1996) outline what they call 'The 5 Cs of action research', which refer to some other important components related to successful action research:

- *commitment* (giving and taking time, developing trust with participants);
- *collaboration* (sharing, giving, taking, listening, reflection, respect);
- *concern* (developing a support group of critical friends, risk-taking);
- *consideration* (reflection about and critical assessment of one's professional actions); and
- *change* (working towards growth, development and improvement in a nurturing, supportive environment).

Without support, encouragement and commitment from colleagues and research project participants, undertaking action research can be a threatening and demoralising experience. It is the interpersonal aspect of action research that makes it particularly relevant for early childhood practitioners, given the philosophical focus on the importance of positive and constructive interpersonal communication and relationships for all of the children and adults who are concerned with early care and education services.

Although some academic researchers regard action research conducted by other professionals (for example, early childhood practitioners) in their own environments as deficient in sound methodology and competent research skills, there is little doubt that skill in action research can contribute to improvements in practice and raise the critical consciousness of those involved. One of the major benefits flowing out of action research is enhanced staff professional development because of the focus on practitioner learning (MacGilchrist, Myers and Reed, 1997). In accepting the responsibility to systematically research solutions to common problems and goals, mutual respect and teamwork can be enhanced. Action research provides another opportunity where professional leadership can be demonstrated by any member of the team. However, the designated leader retains the major responsibility for convincing the team of the necessity for and usefulness of action research as a means of problem-solving and responding to the need for change.

> ### REFLECTIONS ON LEADERSHIP IN PRACTICE
> Early childhood practitioners display leadership when they engage in action research and then disseminate its findings at an in-service, conference or through publication.
> **Associate professor, early childhood**

One final aspect related to undertaking action research, or indeed any type of research, is awareness of and adherence to the ethical principles underpinning research involving children and adults. Those conducting research need to appreciate their moral obligations to those participating in or affected by any research project, and strike a balance between the pursuit of knowledge and understanding and the rights of children and adults who are included in the project. Cohen, Manion and Harrison (2000) suggest that ethical issues in research can stem from a range of areas, including the nature of the specific issue under investigation, the context, research procedures, data-collection methods and the uses of data. The following principles are in general use in academic research departments, and provide guidelines for would-be researchers about the kinds of ethical considerations that need to be addressed before beginning any research project.

- *Informed consent.* Participants should be made aware of the focus of the research and any features of the research which might affect their decision to take part in the project. In the case of children, informed consent should be obtained from parents or adults who act in loco parentis.
- *Openness and honesty.* Participants should be made aware of the specific purpose of the research. Deception is regarded as unacceptable, unprofessional and unethical behaviour.
- *Right to withdraw.* Participants should be informed at the beginning of the study that they may withdraw at any time and may choose not to engage in specific aspects of the study, answer specific questions or provide specific information.

- *Protection from harm.* Participants must be protected from experiencing physical or psychological harm during the project. While it is unlikely that early childhood research would result in physical harm, some research may focus upon sensitive or delicate issues which participants may find stressful. Researchers have an obligation to minimise stress arising out of research projects and to provide support to alleviate such stress.
- *Debriefing.* Participants have a right to have access to oral or written information about the procedures, processes and results following the conclusion of any research that they participate in.
- *Confidentiality.* Unless participants give specific consent regarding identification, researchers must ensure that confidentiality of the identity of individuals and organisations is maintained during the project and in any ensuing publications.
- *Ethical principles of professional bodies.* Where professional bodies, such as the National Association for the Education of Young Children and the Australian Early Childhood Association, have published their own guidelines and principles, these must be consulted and adhered to in the design and conduct of any research project.

The above principles are designed to protect both participants and researchers from potentially difficult situations that can arise in undertaking research. Early childhood practitioners who wish to become involved in research are encouraged to develop, interpret and extend such considerations as are appropriate for early childhood settings.

## BRINGING IT TOGETHER

Research activity is an effective way for early childhood practitioners to improve the quality of their services and to shape their image and reputation. Continued professionalisation of the field requires a revitalisation of the knowledge base and the rationality and justice of practice (Moyles, 2003). Some would go so far as to argue for a total reconceptualisation of the field. Early childhood practitioners need to establish their own research base that reflects a balanced multidisciplinary and collaborative inquiry by practitioners into theoretical and practical concerns. In addition to fostering a positive attitude to research through valuing a research culture, the profession could elevate the status of research by encouraging the development of professional learning communities who focus on the idea and practice of shared knowledge. While it is acknowledged that research is a slow but effective tool for change and progress, early childhood practitioners need to acquire knowledge about and skill in research technology so that they can command sufficient authority and respect to play a central role in the professionalisation of their own field.

# CHAPTER TWELVE

# BUILDING SHARED UNDERSTANDING
# WITH PARENTS AND THE PUBLIC

*Finding ways of working with parents in genuine ways and as partners
is one of the biggest challenges of my work.*

Nursery officer, day nursery

**THIS CHAPTER EXPLORES**
- **the importance of working with parents as partners in the early
  childhood team**
- **parent involvement in early childhood settings**
- **obstacles to partnerships with parents**
- **leadership in the public domain**
- **participation in professional organisations**
- **research and writing**
- **networking with other professionals**
- **becoming political and using the media**

As the early childhood field continues to respond to the demands of
significant change in a range of areas, many practitioners have
reported a sense of uncertainty about their future roles with children
and families in the community. This uncertainty will remain until
agreement is reached between the early childhood field, academic
training staff, government regulating bodies and unions about the
models of care and education that best meet the needs of children and
the community, minimum mandatory qualifications and associated

awards (which may help eliminate many of the current inequities in the staffing of early childhood settings), and the roles and responsibilities that early childhood practitioners are expected to undertake. As long as the field is perceived to lack clear direction in the debate over its future, public support cannot be expected. Early childhood practitioners themselves need to be more politically active in articulating their views and concerns in order to help shape their own destiny. We need to build a shared understanding about practitioners' roles and responsibilities in nurturing young children and their learning through quality service provision.

In the past, early childhood practitioners have readily accepted government action on behalf of children and families. Yet, when government policies fail to reflect the experience and opinions of the field, some ambivalence about where the actual responsibility for policies and planning lies is evident. The onus for representing the views and desires of the early childhood field in terms of the appropriate use of its expertise in the community must be taken up by the present leaders of all early childhood settings. These people are the 'active proponents' of early childhood (Ebbeck and Waniganayake, 2003:168), responsible for public relations with the range of people that they come across in their position including parents, other professionals and the general public.

### REFLECTIONS ON LEADERSHIP IN PRACTICE

Leaders in early childhood are people who have a 'public face' and who are committed to participating in professional activities in ways that achieve recognition and respect from parents and members of the wider community.

**Associate professor, early childhood education**

At the grass roots level, the early childhood profession needs leaders who take on the responsibility of informing parents about the important role that early childhood practitioners have to play in the growth and development of young children. Every practitioner needs to take responsibility for helping raise the status of early childhood.

**Director, early learning centre**

Community understanding about the types of high-level skills and unique expertise that are required to satisfy the complexities of the early childhood practitioner's role is clearly linked to professional recognition by the wider community. Therefore, it is essential that leaders consider how they will accomplish this aspect of their leadership role. Practitioners need to perceive parents as allies rather than adversaries. Parents, through their contact with and involvement in early childhood settings, can provide feedback and information that assist in enhancing community understanding of the roles and responsibilities associated with working in these settings. Helping parents to understand the profession's vision and objectives is the first step towards increasing public awareness of, and eventually support for, early childhood services.

## WORKING WITH PARENTS AS PARTNERS IN THE EARLY CHILDHOOD TEAM

A strong connection between families and providers of early childhood services is essential for creating quality learning environments for young children. Research continues to show that, when families are involved positively in their children's early learning and education, their children demonstrate higher levels of achievement, better attendance and display more positive attitudes and behaviour. In addition, families who receive positive and frequent messages from early childhood practitioners tend to become more involved in their children's early education and care (National Association for the Education of Young Children, 1999; Hiatt-Michael, 2001). The Effective Provision of Pre-school Education project (EPPE) revealed that the most effective settings had developed positive contact, information-sharing and relationships with parents, and that parents were often involved in decision-making about their child's learning (Taggart, 2003). This research also indicated that children did better in settings where educational aims were shared with parents. Consequently, many early childhood practitioners have responded positively to such research findings as well as to community expectations and demand for increasing parent involvement in settings.

*Parents have a lot to offer my setting. They don't need a special skill or language, they just need to be ordinary people who will chat, help, share, read a story and sing songs with us.*

Teaching assistant

Parent involvement and programs for parents form a core part of early childhood service delivery, and periodic interest has been shown in themes of:

- *partnership* (a philosophy of shared child-rearing);
- *continuity* (the promotion of consistency between the conditions and experience of setting and home); and
- *parent education* (the professional responsibility to support and educate parents to enhance children's wellbeing, and parental enjoyment and competence in the parenting role.

Although not new in focus, the resurgence of interest by early childhood practitioners in helping parents to understand their children and the parenting role in ways that are advantageous to them both signifies a move towards a holistic approach to professional practice with children and families and an affirmation of the traditional role in programmatic work with families. This additional responsibility for parents, as well as children—including those with special educational needs—underlines a marked shift in roles and responsibilities for early childhood practitioners.

Parental involvement in early childhood services has been regarded by many experts in the field as a crucial element in the provision of quality programs (Draper and Duffy, 2001; Page et al., 2001). However, many practitioners report that it is a source of tension and one of the most difficult aspects of their role. Although parental participation in services increasingly has been encouraged over the past 30 years, the accumulating research evidence is a compelling argument for continuing to strengthen parental involvement, from the typically token level to a level of genuine partnership, in any service related to the care and education of young children. In addition to benefits for children, parents' involvement as members of the early childhood team means that they can act as advocates for children, families and services. Early childhood practitioners who include parents in genuine decision-making in settings have taken a political step towards initiating innovative change in the field.

*Parents need to know what goes on day to day in the nursery so they don't get confused or panicked by what they hear in the media these days. The best way to find out what goes on is to spend some time here.*
**Manager, day nursery**

Early childhood practitioners historically have defined their client group broadly, and have considered their relationship with parents as an added dimension to their practice (Ebbeck and Waniganayake, 2003). Teachers especially have long recognised the significant influence of the family on the care and education of young children, and have attempted to support parents in their own growth and development (Caddell, 2001). These days, parents are as much the clients of early childhood practitioners as are their children. Given that it is the goal of every professional educator to assist the client to achieve a more meaningful experience in life, the potential for early childhood practitioners to demonstrate leadership in work with parents is high.

Some parents, as members of committees of management, also act as employers. This situation can increase misunderstanding about lines of authority, communication channels, roles and responsibilities of parents and practitioners—especially if the parent's children attend the setting. Parents and practitioners tend to have different expectations, perspectives, views and experiences about young children. Where a shared understanding is achieved, their roles become mutually affirming, reciprocal and interdependent. For such a complex relationship to succeed, specialised training needs to be offered to practitioners to enable them to work effectively with the diversity of communities, family circumstances, parents, carers and staff members who make up the team within an early childhood setting. The lack of training focused on working collaboratively with parents contributes to the anxiety and frustration that practitioners experience in this role.

## WHAT IS PARENT INVOLVEMENT IN EARLY CHILDHOOD SETTINGS?

Part of the difficulty of involving parents in early childhood settings revolves around the apparent confusion among early childhood practitioners about what the term actually signifies. While practitioners have always involved parents in some capacity, usually at a token level, they have generally retained their traditional autonomy (Ebbeck and Waniganayake, 2003). More recently, differing attitudes and beliefs have dictated that closer and more meaningful links between parent and practitioner be established. While the prevailing philosophies have changed with the times, they have initiated changes in the relationship between parent and practitioner, some of which have been adopted willingly while others have sparked some resistance.

Demand for parental involvement at more than a token level, such as providing an extra pair of hands, arose in the 1960s when governments in Western societies focused on the idea that democracy should be extended beyond politics and formal government in the lives of ordinary people to include participation in decision-making by those affected by the ultimate decision. Early childhood practitioners initially were reluctant to incorporate the full spirit of the partnership approach to working with parents because they believed that they were the experts when it came to children and early childhood services. This belief slowed the process of change, but eventually practitioners adopted a compensatory approach to parental involvement in which deficit models of family life were responded to with the provision of interventionist strategies.

*I have learned a lot from the parents because they have known the child from birth and I have only known this child for a few weeks.*
**Early childhood teacher**

The 1970s saw a new philosophy which convinced early childhood practitioners that they could enhance their professionalism in the eyes of parents by improving communication and developing positive relationships. The focus was 'informed interest', where it was believed that parental involvement was a matter of communication and contact. The philosophy of communication gave way to the philosophy of accountability in the 1980s, where parents began to be perceived as consumers of a service who possessed rights and responsibilities which early childhood practitioners were obliged to meet. Parental involvement at this time was focused on consulting and discussing policies, procedures and practices with parents or their committee representatives; however, there was little real partnership or collaboration.

As the 1990s approached, parents' rights to have control over decisions that affected the lives of their children were clearly affirmed. Early childhood services were challenged to facilitate effective participation by and accountability to parents. Effective participation was defined as 'active management' of services, rather than tokenistic expression of opinion. The management structures of early childhood services began to reflect a partnership approach between parents, practitioners and other staff. This nascent partnership orientation gave priority to liaison, involvement and the sharing of responsibility for child-rearing between home and the setting.

*When children see practitioners and parents working together, they feel more secure.*

**Nursery officer**

The push towards the adoption of a true philosophy of partnership gathered momentum in the 1990s, with early childhood practitioners recognising that they had both shared and complementary goals with the parents associated with their setting. Practitioners generally have accepted that both they and parents are experts when it comes to children and families, but that each brings a different type of expertise. This shift to a partnership approach emphasised the impact that both home and setting have on young children, as well as the need to coordinate the efforts of parents and practitioners through non-hierarchical, collaborative relationships. The willingness of early childhood practitioners to share power and responsibility with parents in a partnership of equals is another illustration of team leadership to achieve the setting's mission and objectives.

*If parents don't have any real experience of what happens in the classroom, they can't really make any judgment about the quality of provision.*
**Early childhood teacher**

The partnership approach to parent involvement stresses cooperative rather than joint activity and permits parents to decide upon the level of involvement that is appropriate in terms of their priorities and commitments. The Pen Green Centre for Under 5s, in Corby, England and the Reggio Emilia pre-schools and infant toddler centres in Italy are excellent examples of settings where parents and practitioners have developed and are engaged in powerful partnerships. Such working relationships are based on and valued by equal but different contributions from, and shared accountability of, parents and practitioners. These settings take a whole-family, multi-disciplinary approach to early education and care. They may offer parents a range of training opportunities and different ways to contribute. Practitioners have time to help parents understand how their children learn and parents help practitioners find out more about how their children learn. Parents spend time observing their children in the settings and collect practical information about their children at home to share with practitioners. There is extensive use of documentation of children's learning and progress. In this way, practitioners and parents enjoy mutually supportive, collaborative partnerships based on shared goals and understanding. The partnership has been borne out of meaningful contact, connection and communication.

The following values and beliefs are fundamental for the development of a partnership approach to parental involvement. Parents are:

- experts on their own children;
- significant and effective teachers of their own children;
- skilled in ways that complement those of practitioners;
- different but have equal strengths and equivalent expertise;
- able to make informed observations and impart vital information to practitioners;
- inherently involved in the lives and wellbeing of their children;
- able to contribute to and central in decision-making;
- responsible and share accountability with practitioners.

These values are useful guidelines for early childhood practitioners who wish to establish a collaborative relationship with parents, or assess the extent to which their relationship with and involvement of parents is that of a partnership.

### REFLECTIONS ON LEADERSHIP IN PRACTICE

When I lived in another country, my two children went to child care there. One morning when we arrived at the centre, I was told that my children were to go outside and join the other children until a relief teacher arrived. It was bitterly cold and we had walked for 30 minutes to get to the centre. I didn't think it was appropriate for my children to go outside immediately. The director wasn't there and the deputy did not want to discuss the matter with me. My children were crying and I was trying to pacify them and getting upset myself. The cook came to my aid and spoke to my children, calmed them down. I had to go to work and was very upset. Later that day, the director phoned me and invited me to come and talk to the staff about the morning's events. I was taken to the staff room, there were coffee and pastries and the staff who were involved in the incident that morning were there. The director explained that she wanted us all to have an opportunity to discuss the morning's happenings openly and work out some strategies for how best to handle situations such as this if it were to happen again. She left us and went to play with the children. The staff and I had a difficult time getting started, with the staff apologising. At the end of about an hour, I walked away feeling that my concerns had been listened to. In this incident, both the cook and director displayed leadership. The cook showed courage in coming forward and getting involved in a situation that she didn't have to but she put the bond she had developed with me and my children to effective use in defusing a conflict situation. The director was decisive in taking action immediately and creating a situation of empowerment to allow all voices to be heard. Both individuals recognised the importance of parent–staff communications.

**Senior lecturer, early childhood and parent**

Desforges and Abouchaar (2003) outline a number of key findings from the literature regarding parent involvement, including a range of strategies that are suitable for creating parent partnership involvement and contribution. Examples of activities for promoting a partnership with parents include inviting parents to:

- attend and participate in staff meetings to assist, for example, in reviewing and making decisions about early childhood philosophy, goals, policies, standards, expectations, curricula and programs;
- work in conjunction with an experienced staff member on special skill-development projects with their own or other children;
- develop activities related to parent-initiated needs and interests, such as parent education programs;
- volunteer their expertise for special program activities, such as in music, movement, stories and multicultural perspectives;
- contribute to criteria for and the process of staff selection; and
- contribute to reviewing budgets and fundraising.

Where, however, does this partnership approach leave early childhood practitioners? How can professional expertise be used? What is your professional standing with colleagues, peers, other professionals and the community when partnership means that you are mutually responsible and accountable with a person who is also a consumer and a secondary client of the setting? Could professional efforts to maximise parental involvement and influence undermine the leader's efforts to achieve the early childhood setting's mission and objectives for implementing culturally and developmentally appropriate curricula and practice according to the values and beliefs of the profession?

Evidence suggests that parents' ideas about how children develop and learn are by no means clear or straightforward (Bruce and Megitt, 1999). Parents, like early childhood practitioners, have their own widely differing implicit theories about children, which have been constructed largely from their own family of origin experiences and as they have lived with and cared for their own children. Early childhood practitioners have developed theories on the basis of their own experience in a similar way to parents, but usually have interpreted this experience in the light of knowledge and skills gained during professional training and the experience of working with large numbers of children in a variety of settings. Parental theories and professional theories about what is the right way to work with children leads then to differing perspectives on policies, procedures and practice. Early childhood practitioners need to bring all their expertise to finding a common ground between the two perspectives.

*I need parents' help with monitoring the children's progress.*
**Nursery officer**

The answer to the dilemma of finding a pathway to partnership with parents is to negotiate a cooperative agreement concerning the planning and implementation of the early childhood service. In this way, practitioners accept the responsibility to meet other people's needs (that is, those of the parents) by making their expertise available to the parents for their consideration. Practitioners also meet their own needs by recognising the value of training, experience and philosophy as information sources for making decisions about how, when and where young children's development and learning can be facilitated. The leader who effectively creates a partnership with parents in early childhood services possesses the confidence to articulate a philosophy concerning care and early education while simultaneously acknowledging parental rights, information, theories, expectations, problems and pressures.

In this way, the perceived complementary expertise of both parent and practitioner can be brought to meet the needs of the situation in mutually agreed ways. The practitioner's role is to begin to develop a partnership by welcoming all parents (Vickers and Ashton-Jones, 2003), respecting all parents, building up trust, encouraging dialogue with parents about alternative perspectives on children's development, and learning to point out different ways of responding to or intervening in issues related to care and education. It is also essential to seek parents' own ideas about how they might wish to share the care and education of their young children (Elliott, 2003). Once established, the partnership and shared understanding can be consolidated through regular home visits, diaries, chat sessions, short talks, workshops or whatever type of contact best meets parents' needs and interests. The success of this approach will depend on the early childhood practitioner's skills to contact, connect and communicate with the parents.

Communication practices are the key to successfully negotiating relationships with parents (Hughes and MacNaughton, 2002). Fostering shared understanding and a partnership with parents requires the ability to:

- clearly and unambiguously explain issues in an egalitarian as opposed to a paternalistic style;
- remain non-judgmental and overcome stereotyped and/or prejudiced attitudes in interaction;
- listen with understanding to parents' views and acknowledge their feelings;
- respond in ways that will enhance the perception of team spirit and relationship;
- respond professionally where personal feelings are managed and expressed appropriately;
- confidently assert one's professional opinion;
- recognise and respond to conflict appropriately; and
- involve parents as active and equal members of the decision-making team.

## OBSTACLES TO PARTNERSHIPS WITH PARENTS

Developing skills to work effectively in partnership with parents takes time and experience. Lack of time—for both parents and practitioners— is a big obstacle to building the respectful relationship that is required in a shared understanding and partnership. Given that relatively little formal training has been available for developing skills related to this aspect of early childhood practice, it is not surprising to find that some practitioners give perfunctory recognition to this extra responsibility.

Katz (1995a) and Vander Ven (1988) recognise the fact that the type of relationship developed with parents and the level of parental involvement in early childhood settings appears to be determined by the stage of professional development that a leader has achieved. Vander Ven suggested that it is not until stage 3—informed practice, when practitioners have made a strong career commitment to the early childhood field, that they develop the awareness of the necessity for working collaboratively with parents. For Katz, it is not until practitioners have reached the consolidation stage that they are able to respond sensitively to parental needs and expectations concerning the program.

A shift in maturity, as well as a broader perspective, is considered to be the stimulus for identification with parents and families as well as children. At earlier stages of career development and professional maturity, relationships with parents are more likely to be authoritarian and paternalistic, token in nature and from a deficit perspective—that is, where parents, even those who are considerably older than the staff member, are not thought to possess the knowledge and skills necessary for bringing up their children. This approach is unlikely to empower parents to develop skill and competence in their own lives.

One of the effects of parents' lack of professional knowledge in terms of their involvement in early childhood settings is that practitioners may implement forms of support and opportunities for involvement which do not match parental needs, expectations and characteristics. The initiation of any change in an early childhood setting should be on the basis of diagnosed need (discussed in Chapter 11). Effective leadership of parents entails understanding parental needs in order to tailor initiatives that are related to particular stages of parenthood, specific needs expressed by parents, and the social and cultural characteristics of parents as well as parents' levels of educational achievement (Desforges and Abouchaar, 2003). Any dimension of practice with parents should be subject to a process of objective evaluation to ensure that both the processes and the outcomes are appropriate for the parents. Evidence indicates that some undesirable but unintentional effects may result from poorly designed and implemented experiences for parents. There is little point in putting energy into parent support, resourcing, education or partnership if it is not what the particular group of parents wants. Early childhood practitioners should provide parent programs that meet parents' expressed or objectively assessed needs and not rely on their subjective perception of their role in relation to parents.

If early childhood practitioners wish to define parents as members of the team that provides quality care and education for young children, the ways in which parents are involved need to be collaborative in nature. A reciprocal relationship, such as in a partnership, can ensure that the staff and the curriculum of a setting are sensitive and responsive to the needs and norms of the children and parents who use it. However, both parents and practitioners need assistance to understand the parameters of their respective roles as they begin to explore the effects of the equal balance of power in the partnership. Collaborative parent–practitioner relationships can be the starting point for growth and change in parents, early childhood practitioners and the services they deliver. Of all the people practitioners interact with, it is parents who will play the leading role in determining the recognition of the professional status of the early childhood field.

## LEADERSHIP IN THE PUBLIC DOMAIN

To this point, leadership has been discussed in the micro-context of interaction with the staff and parents who are associated with an early childhood setting, with leadership effectiveness being evaluated in terms of child wellbeing, goal-attainment related to program responsiveness, and adult morale and personal development. Little reference has been made to leadership activities outside settings in the public domain. However, this aspect of leadership cannot be ignored because of the pressing need to develop and exercise leadership at local and national levels. In other professions, leadership usually is defined as an integral aspect of organisational sustainability and is evaluated in terms of its effectiveness both within the organisation and within the external environment in which the organisation operates. Once early childhood practitioners are encouraged to extend their concern beyond the direct care of children, they can move to a position where they can begin to use their communication skills to champion the rights of children and adults in early childhood settings in the wider context. The leadership activities that are relevant for the wider external environment in which early childhood services operate are addressed below.

In general terms, leadership activities that are related to the broader context can be described as *advocacy*. Advocacy is a term that has been used in the early childhood field to stimulate practitioners' perception of their personal responsibility for raising the profile of children and families and the early childhood profession in the eyes of the community. While advocacy is perceived as one of the key functions expected of early childhood leaders (Ebbeck and Waniganayake, 2003), it still is not clearly or widely understood by some members of the field. The word 'advocacy' has tended to conjure up images of politics and protest for many practitioners, who have yet to understand and identify with the political element of their role.

Becoming politically aware simply entails understanding how the policies of the public, private and voluntary sectors affect the lives of children, families and the early childhood profession. Early childhood leaders keep up with local policy and other issues, understand who is involved and how the political scene operates at the local level, and network with key people to champion individual settings or the profession within the community (Moyles and Yates, 2004).

*Once I was so angry about proposed cuts to our funding that I wrote a letter to my local member. I got a reply but I don't think my letter made much of a difference. I think that more people needed to stand up and express their opinion about something that was going to impact on not only our setting.*

**Head teacher, nursery school**

Responding to that understanding with committed action is the first step towards demonstrating the political dimension of leadership. With early childhood services constantly under the threat of closure, restriction and withdrawal of funding, it appears that survival may depend on the abilities of some members of the field to engage in those activities, called leadership or advocacy, which will bring key issues to a wide audience. Sometimes this requires creativity in approach, skill in respectfully and constructively articulating issues and concerns, and persistence (Ebbeck and Waniganayake, 2003).

Early childhood leaders also appreciate the need to keep up with national government policies and changes as they affect settings and the profession, and to network with relevant politicians in order to raise the profile of children and the early childhood profession and keep them visible and high on the political agenda (Moyles and Yates, 2004).

*It's become a paper war . . . there are so many government papers and documents that I need to read to keep up with changes initiated by the government, sometimes I feel the weight of information overload but I know being well informed is part of my responsibility to the children and families that I work for, so somehow I make the time to go through them.*

**Head teacher, early excellence centre**

Given the political attention that early childhood has received over recent years, it is essential that leaders are confident about voicing and sharing their expertise and insight with key people in the public domain as a means of moving the field forward.

*I think more politicians should be invited to speak at our annual conference. They need to explain their policies to us and we need to be able to hold them accountable by asking questions and expressing our views on their policies.*

**Early childhood teacher**

Once early childhood practitioners understand that advocacy is merely a shorthand term for bringing professional leadership knowledge and skills to benefit children, families and the profession, they can begin to engage in some of the wide range of activities that are required to enhance the status of children and families and the professionalisation of the field. This must be understood as a long and slow process of change that requires high levels of self-confidence and assertive ability to overcome the obstacles and setbacks to initiating change. Activities that are related to this dimension of leadership include participation in professional organisations, research and writing, networking with other professionals, and becoming political and using the media. These activities take time, effort and the development of special knowledge and skills in order to become influential in the arenas that have the power to make decisions and change policy. While advocacy is the responsibility of every member of the early childhood field, it is a particular responsibility of leaders because they have a broader perspective of the current needs in the field.

Collaboration with other relevant professional organisations has been recommended as one way to solve the complex problems in early childhood service provision (Edgington, 2000). Involving members from organisations concerned with advocating for children and families may facilitate systematic problem-solving which appears to be difficult for one group alone. For example, bringing together members from childcare, teaching, health and social services or from private, public and voluntary childcare organisations who share similar concerns about services for children seems logical, desirable and time-efficient. Collaborative activity requires that participants share mutual aspirations, a common conceptual framework, agreed goals and agreed outcomes of the project. To be an effective collaboration, responsibility must be delegated and control shared.

Collaboration with other professional groups is a means rather than an end in terms of addressing issues in early childhood care and education. A united collaborative multi-professional group can speak with more weight and command more respect from the decision-makers than one organisation alone. It is an effective means of using the knowledge, expertise and perspectives of the individuals with a variety of backgrounds who make up the early childhood field, as well as a way of encouraging them to take responsibility for and to contribute to policy-making and planning issues.

## PARTICIPATION IN PROFESSIONAL ORGANISATIONS

As a leader, it is important not only to join but also to become active in the organisations that are concerned with early childhood services. With the publications, seminars and conferences offered by professional organisations, such as the Australian Early Childhood Association, the British Association of Early Childhood Education, the Association for Childhood Education International and the National Association for the Education of Young Children, opportunities are provided for continuing professional development. They are also arenas where problems or issues that are of concern to early childhood practitioners are identified, discussed and responded to. Professional organisations are often the vehicles by which groups of practitioners bring issues of concern to the attention of the wider early childhood field, parents, unions, politicians, business and the media. However, they rely upon the efforts of their membership to be effective. The larger the number of people whose views are represented by the organisation, the stronger and more effective will be the impact of their actions.

As well as professional associations and unions, there are advisory boards, committees and working parties at local, state and national level where an early childhood member can be influential in accomplishing change. By becoming a member of one of these organisations, individuals can represent the perspective of the early childhood field. Such organisations provide direct access to influencing decision-making and change.

> *I see it as part of my professional responsibility to sit on the Early Years Development and Childcare Partnership. It takes a lot of time because I also sit on working parties and other sub-committees that are established to deal with particular issues. But I also learn a lot about what is happening in the field so I am empowered and better prepared to deal with changes that impact on my setting.*
>
> **Head teacher, infant school**

In addition, membership of professional organisations increases the opportunity for professional contact with colleagues. This is an important function, given the isolation in which most early childhood practitioners work. Those in positions of leadership often complain that they have less access to support in their settings than other members of the team because of the need to keep some distance from staff in order to retain authority. In addition, the narrower perspective of team members compared with that of the leader means that team members are unable to empathise with the leader. Contact with colleagues who are able to understand the leader's position and provide the emotional support that may not be available at setting level is available through membership of professional organisations and is a way of initiating and building a support network.

## RESEARCH AND WRITING

The role and advantages of research as a source of information for decision-making and change were discussed in Chapter 11. However, research is also important for leadership in the public domain because it is a recognised means of gathering the facts and information that carry weight in arguments for change. The use of research findings gives substance and credibility to issues, and helps decision-makers to focus on the key concerns and to consider different alternatives. Professional organisations, such as those identified above, usually have research interests and can provide support for and access to relevant research findings. However, as stated previously in Chapter 11, it is not sufficient to be a consumer of other people's research. Leadership requires that commitment be made to produce research that has been initiated from the early childhood practitioner's intimate knowledge of the current needs and concerns of the field.

*After visiting the Reggio Emilia pre-schools, we were interested in researching the impact of changing the way we organise lunchtime for the children and the team had an opportunity to access funding from the Education Action Zone. We planned how we would undertake the action research, then carried it out over a term and wrote a report. Doing a systematic investigation of a change and writing it up really clarified our understanding of the impact of the change.*

**Early childhood teacher**

The next step is to disseminate research findings, ideas and concerns in ways that will reach and be understood by the intended audience. Something as simple as leaders writing about their current concerns in the setting's newsletter is a way of informing parents and activating their interest in supporting continued effort to address the issue. Many organisations and local authorities have set up websites where practitioners can share examples of best practice and become involved in discussion groups. Writing letters to politicians, government ministers and the editors of newspapers and magazines is another way of providing leadership on behalf of children, families and the profession. Publication in a professional journal requires greater effort and skill, which may need to be acquired through further study, but it is not outside the capabilities of many early childhood practitioners. The real purpose of writing is to express an informed opinion on a critical issue in clear, understandable and accurate ways.

Whereas writing can be done during or outside work hours, speaking—the alternative means of communicating a point of view—requires specific time commitments, usually away from the setting. This may be more difficult for early childhood practitioners who are required to maintain strict child-to-staff ratios during working hours, and who may find the extra demands on their personal time too burdensome. However, this activity should not be avoided.

*I was invited to do a presentation about my approach to numeracy for three- and four-year-olds to my local network that meets in the late afternoon a couple of times a term. At first, I didn't want to do it;*

*I thought people would know more than I do. But the Adviser was really encouraging and gave me some tips. There were fifteen people there and it went really well, they asked lots of questions and I could answer them! It was scary but a really worthwhile experience and I feel more confident about talking to others now.*

Early childhood teacher

Opportunities to express a point of view arise informally with parents, staff, colleagues, members of the local neighbourhood and community, friends and formally at meetings, seminars and conferences and with employers. Speaking formally or informally is another way of informing others and building support for an issue, and should not be overlooked by early childhood practitioners—especially those with leadership responsibilities.

**REFLECTIONS ON LEADERSHIP IN PRACTICE**

When the kindergarten was under threat of closure, the director was required to convince the funding body that the kindergarten and its activities were worthy of retention. It was the responsibility of the director to prepare and answer questions about an extensive written report that represented the setting and its activities in a positive light.

Director, early learning centre

## NETWORKING WITH OTHER PROFESSIONALS

Leaders who act as advocates on behalf of the early childhood profession need the support of others—such as parents, the general public, politicians and administrators—to help them achieve their goals. However, achievement of goals is likely to be more efficient if the leader engages the support of, and acts in collaboration with, members of other professional groups who have an interest in early childhood. Change can be accomplished more effectively if it is supported by a range of professional groups rather than appearing to be the concern of a single professional group. Networking with colleagues from related professions gives access to a greater range of knowledge and skill that can strengthen the weight of any argument. Moral support, encouragement and feedback also can be provided by colleagues outside the early childhood profession, which can help strengthen the resolve and commitment essential to pursue the issue of concern.

Networks can be informal, where individuals with common interests and goals link up to share information and to plan action on a regular basis. They can also be formal networks, where committees or working parties are formed with official representation from professional organisations, institutions or agencies. The advantages of establishing and participating in a network system are that isolation is broken down, awareness of others' interests and activities is increased, barriers to communication are decreased and misunderstanding and miscommunication are diminished. Successful networking takes time. Practitioners will require all their skills in communication and interpersonal relationships to build the cooperation of others.

*The Foundation Stage Learning and Development Network has brought practitioners together from the different sectors across Cornwall in a constructive and learning environment. Teachers and childcare practitioners realised that they shared similar concerns and there was a feeling of all of us being in the same boat. People understand each other more now.*

Early childhood team leader

### REFLECTIONS ON LEADERSHIP IN PRACTICE

While there is usually a defined position of leader, it is important to recognise that other positions in settings have elements of leadership which, if supported by the leader, can allow for effective cooperation and networking between different professionals and services. Cooperation and networking between practitioners and different professionals enhances quality service provision and develops leadership capacity.

**Head teacher, early excellence centre**

The strength of networking is in the development of trusting relationships, where allies and supporters can be called upon when required to add impact to activity. Early childhood practitioners who establish strong networks with colleagues from other professions can encourage these other professionals to assist in raising the status of early childhood in the community. Networking is another way of reaching out to the community to enhance understanding of and enlarge support for the profession's vision, mission, goals and concerns.

## BECOMING POLITICAL AND USING THE MEDIA

It is encouraging to observe that few members of the early childhood profession continue to maintain that children and politics do not mix. Unfortunately, the lengthy failure to perceive the connection between early childhood services and politics accounts in part for the slow and extended process of professionalisation in the field today. While practitioners increasingly have acted as advocates for children and families, a narrow conceptualisation of the role of power in politics and a general unwillingness to become involved in the political arena have meant that their achievements are probably far lower than they potentially could have been. Steering clear of politics has kept the status of the profession low. However, in order to meet the challenges of most early childhood career opportunities in changing times, practitioners today need to be politically aware and to make a difference to the lives of children and families.

Moving away from the traditional apolitical stance to becoming politically aware and active is likely to produce a number of benefits for the early childhood field. First, it informs governments about the needs and requirements of children and families. Second, it explains the crucial role that early childhood practitioners play in promoting child and family welfare. Third, it signals issues that are emerging as important concerns for those who are responsible for supporting children and families in the society. However, it is unlikely that early childhood practitioners who have not reached stage 4—complex, or stage 5—influential, in their professional career development (Vander Ven, 1988) will have gained sufficient intellectual independence to produce the kind of proactive orientation which is required to become politically active and influential.

Becoming political entails understanding the process of democratic government and legislature; knowing who are the local and national public representatives and what their platforms are on issues of concern to early childhood practitioners; knowing who their counterparts are; being able to identify the public servants who administer the government departments responsible for early childhood services; and being prepared to lobby by expressing an opinion personally or in writing to the appropriate government official. Lobbying is having a voice, speaking out and being heard as a way of stimulating action.

*We've tried to get the local politicians interested in early childhood issues by asking our members to send a standard letter that we provided to their local member, we've asked a couple of politicians to open new buildings or speak at annual general meetings and we've invited them to tour selected settings and speak with parents. When we have this type of close personal contact with them, they seem to appreciate our concerns more.*

**Early childhood teacher and**
**organisation representative**

Lobbying is the process of informing public officials and relevant others about the issues that confront early childhood practitioners on a daily basis. It involves getting the right information to the right person at the right time. If politicians and government officials are ignorant of the issues, they are unlikely to take any action. There are many other groups with loud voices and well-organised campaigns who will capture the attention of the policy- and decision-makers in government. If they are only partly informed or misinformed, they cannot be expected to make decisions which will be perceived as appropriate by those who are better informed on the subject of early childhood.

Persistence in attempting to make meaningful contact with public officials is essential. Those who are easily fobbed off will make little progress in getting a hearing. The long history of reticence by early childhood practitioners to speak out and articulate their contribution and concerns has meant that a weak basis of power—if it exists at all—is the starting point for attempts to influence the actions of public officials on behalf of children, families and early childhood staff. Given that early childhood practitioners still have a way to go in becoming politically powerful, one of the best ways of gaining the support of public officials is to invite them into early childhood settings and begin to establish a personal relationship with them. In this way, practitioners will be perceived as community experts on early childhood issues and their opinions will have more influence on government decisions.

Becoming involved politically means becoming involved in the decision-making process on issues that affect children, families and the early childhood profession. It means perceiving the political dimension in early childhood issues and acting in ways that ensure these issues command greater attention and priority within the community.

The media are an increasingly powerful tool that can be used to shape public opinion in our society. Most people, particularly women, are interested in news related to children and families, especially in the local community. Many media reporters are interested in the issues that are of concern to early childhood practitioners because these are topical issues that capture people's attention. However, the media are under-utilised by early childhood practitioners as a means of disseminating information and opinion to the public. In addition to providing information, early childhood practitioners can point out other aspects of concerns critical for children's services.

*I was invited to appear on a current affairs television program to comment on the value of play in early learning. The program unit spent a day filming at the setting and interviewing me. When the program was shown, they had cut out a lot of the pertinent comments I made and showed mainly gender-stereotyped play. The segment lasted about three minutes. I suppose even a short opportunity to talk about play helps the public understand its importance.*

**Director, early learning centre**

Regardless of the format chosen—a letter to the editor, a short article focusing on a particular issue for the local newspaper or an interview for television or radio—early childhood practitioners need to focus on using the media to keep issues in front of the public eye and to build up community awareness.

## BRINGING IT TOGETHER

Early childhood practitioners can increase the status of children, families and the field if they define part of their leadership role as reaching out to the community. The way in which contact with the local, national and even international communities is made can take a variety of forms, from working with parents and other professionals to accessing all the available channels of communication. Continued efforts by practitioners within the community can foster change in awareness and understanding about the fundamental importance of, and the vital role played by, early childhood services which will eventually benefit children and families and move the field along the pathway of increased professionalism.

# THE ETHICS OF LEADERSHIP

*There is a strong ethical dimension in early childhood practitioners'*
*daily work. We have to make fast decisions that sometimes are in*
*conflict with our values. Sometimes, meeting the needs of one child can*
*impinge on the needs of another leading to unsatisfactory outcomes for*
*children, parents and staff. It isn't an easy job at times because there*
*may be no right answer . . .*

Early childhood teacher

**THIS CHAPTER EXPLORES**
- **the importance of promoting and protecting children's rights**
- **advocacy and becoming a children's champion**
- **the importance of providing quality and economically viable services**
- **administering early childhood settings in accordance with the profession's ethical principles**
- **employing an early childhood code of ethics to guide the resolution of ethical dilemmas**

The changing world of leadership has forced the adoption of new perceptions about and understandings of this phenomenon by professionals in many fields, including early childhood care and education. The relationship between leadership, quality and organisational effectiveness has been well documented throughout this book. For those of us working with young children and their families, leadership has been recognised as possessing caring, educational and, more recently, moral aspects. Previous chapters in this book have explored some of the caring and educational aspects of leadership. In this chapter, the moral aspects of leadership in early childhood will be explored beyond the role of a code of ethics in guiding decision-making, which was mentioned earlier. It is important now to recognise the interrelationship between these three aspects of leadership. An effective leader—particularly one who is intimately involved and influential in the lives and welfare of children and families—needs to understand the impact of who they are, how they behave and their decisions on people's lives. Newman (2000) observes that underpinning all aspects of the leadership role in early childhood settings is the need to act ethically and to lead the team to do likewise. The continued professionalisation of the field is dependent upon members understanding and accepting that they have a responsibility to become politically aware and to act as advocates for children and families (Moss, 2001).

In attempting to explain the moral aspect of leadership, Sergiovanni (1999) outlines a morality-based style of leadership and likens the leader to a minister who must pay attention to management, politics and ethics. The leader's role is perceived as the bringing together of diverse people and influencing them to accept and adopt the values and beliefs, vision and the virtues espoused by the organisational ethos. Today, most early childhood practitioners endorse the inclusion of a moral aspect in their definition of leadership. Indeed, many would agree that leadership can be understood as a moral act which is guided by personal and professional values and principles about what is right and wrong, and in the best interests of individuals and groups.

In early childhood, leaders are considered to hold social responsibility for enhancing the potential of the children and adults with whom they interact, for protecting their welfare, for laying the foundations for lifelong learning, and for providing quality services which are relevant and responsive to the communities they serve. They are charged with a moral responsibility to act as advocates for children, families and the profession—that is, to be articulate, organised and skilful in acting as a voice for individuals and groups who may be vulnerable and powerless.

The National Association for the Education of Young Children (NAEYC) uses the notion of a children's champion (Ebbeck and Waniganayake, 2003) to describe the key role leaders play in the public arena. The NAEYC (1996) asserts that every early childhood practitioner can make a difference to the quality of children's lives by:

- speaking out on behalf of children at every opportunity—for example, with colleagues, family members, friends, the general public and politicians;
- doing something to improve the life of one child beyond their own family—for instance, volunteering at an out-of-school setting, or supporting learning by taking a child in need on a trip to the zoo, gardens, children's farm or museum;
- holding public officials accountable for making children's wellbeing and learning a national commitment in terms of actions as well as words—for example, investigating how public officials stand on issues affecting young children, families and early education and child care; supporting those who give priority to key issues for early childhood; challenging the status quo if it is not considered to be in the interests of children's wellbeing;
- encouraging organisations to which you belong to make a commitment to children and families, perhaps by sponsoring a children's service, purchasing needed equipment, helping to create inviting public spaces for children and families or setting up a neighbour- hood watch group; and
- urging others to become children's champions—to voice their opinions regarding the quality of children's lives, to participate in education and care activities and to release staff to give time to education and care settings.

In relation to the moral or ethical aspect of effective leadership in early childhood, four key areas need to be considered. These are:

- the promotion and protection of children's rights;
- the provision of a quality and economically viable service which does not compromise children's rights;
- the administration of a setting in accordance with the profession's ethical principles; and
- the employment of an early childhood code of ethics to guide the resolution of ethical dilemmas.

The understanding about, reflection on and resultant decisions related to such areas can produce leadership that corresponds to ethical practice in early childhood settings. These areas are considered to be part of the ethical domain because they are related to 'ideas about how people ought to behave, how people ought to treat one another, and what obligations people have to one another' (Mulligan, 1996:102). The implications of each of these areas in the ethics of leadership for early childhood practitioners are discussed below.

## PROMOTING AND PROTECTING CHILDREN'S RIGHTS

One of the primary and significant responsibilities of any adult—but especially leaders in early childhood settings—is to make decisions and act in ways that promote and protect the rights of young children, who generally are considered to be dependent, vulnerable and voiceless in contemporary society. Rayner (1995:196) claims that children's rights are more than 'claims of dependence . . . [they] . . . are ethical statements about the quality of a human life'. Discussion about the rights of children has had a prominent profile recently, with many countries giving at least tacit recognition to the importance of respect for children's rights (Lansdown and Lancaster, 2001). Parents and members of the general community agree that, in principle, children have a universal right to survival and development, although whose responsibility it is and the level to which such rights might be promoted and protected would be likely to cause some debate. The term 'development' refers not only to physical health, but also to the 'mental, emotional, cognitive, social and cultural development' (Franklin and Hammarberg, 1995:x) in which the principle of equality is inherent. However, although understanding about the rights of children has undergone significant change, it is evident that the rhetoric generally is not translated into action, with the importance of early childhood receiving little attention in terms of its contribution to success in later life.

The moral or ethical responsibility of early childhood practitioners in acting as a protector, advocate, facilitator, negotiator and champion becomes a high priority because their intimate knowledge about individuals and extensive experience with young children place them in the best position to know what is in the real interest of the child and their family. Given that young children are vulnerable, they need special support to allow them access to their rights. Therefore, those adults who work with young children need to be aware of, sensitive to and respectful of their rights and best interests, and to take on an enabling role (Lansdown and Lancaster, 2001).

While the recognition of the concept of children's rights has gained greater acceptance, debate has surrounded specific definition of what such rights might be. Although early childhood service provision has recently been raised in priority and status on the agendas of many governments, conflicting ideologies, lack of direction and political naivety within the profession mean that early childhood practitioners do not hold sufficient power or credibility to act effectively as advocates in promoting and protecting the rights of young children. During the 1990s, early childhood practitioners in a number of countries—among them Australia, New Zealand, Canada and the United States—recognised the importance of developing a code of ethics or standards of practice as a means of ensuring that children's rights were identified and enhanced. Such documents provided a clear statement of goals and values that early childhood practitioners could use to guide their decision-making and interactions in relation to young children. However, such codes appear to have had limited impact on encouraging advocacy. The Association for Childhood Education International currently is addressing the issues of owner-ship and comprehensiveness in the NAEYC Code in an effort to make the code more relevant (Freeman, 2004). However, Woodrow (2001) comments that codification is only one approach to raising ethics awareness, and suggests that more recent developments in the emer-gent fields of applied ethics and feminist ethics have expanded the range of resources helpful for encouraging the field's engagement in ethical thinking and conversations.

The United Nations Convention on the Rights of the Child, which has been ratified by almost 200 countries, provides a vehicle for those who work with young children to promote their rights. Early childhood practitioners have a responsibility to become aware of its contents, and to develop and implement policies and practice that are in line with its spirit. Early childhood practitioners continually are confronted with ethical choices about purpose, meaning, practice and relationships (Moss, 2001). Therefore, 'every educator . . . must come to realise that they . . . have a responsibility to work for children's rights and that they can do much on a day-to-day basis to support, extend and uphold chil-dren's rights' (Nutbrown, 1996:101).

## PROVIDING QUALITY AND ECONOMICALLY VIABLE SERVICES

The provision of quality and economically viable services that do not compromise children's rights is another moral or ethical challenge for early childhood practitioners. Recent images of parents as consumers whose purchasing power can influence the type of care and education offered within the community have been met with considerable concern. Research indicates that a number of factors influence parental choice of service, and that quality of service is a high priority only for those parents who are aware of quality matters. As well as offering a range of flexible services for young children and their families, pressure is also on early childhood practitioners to address issues of quality assurance and improvement, the rights of the consumer and value for money in service provision (Ebbeck and Waniganayake, 2003). Sometimes, such issues are incompatible with the rights and needs of young children in early care and education settings. The push towards becoming entrepreneurial and being responsive to the demands of a competitive market means that consideration of children's rights may be driven into the background when developing new and existing services. While it is essential that early childhood services be affordable and cost-efficient, these factors must be balanced against the ethical responsibility to protect children's rights. Ultimately, early childhood services cannot afford to sacrifice children's rights in order to meet short-term priorities and pressures because this may in fact have long-term effects on children's development as productive citizens.

There is a clear need for explicit principles and values which reflect the rights of children to high-quality care and education that fosters their development and acknowledges the role of their family. Quality is not a finite goal which, once attained, can be checked off a list of things to do. Quality is a complex ideal which early childhood practitioners continually pursue. Understanding of quality changes over time as understanding of young children's development, needs and rights grows. Quality in early childhood is related to high-quality professional practice where the rights and interests of the child are regarded as the highest priority. Unfortunately, statements about goals and values, and written documents such as a code of ethics, are professional guidelines that can be used only to assist in decision-making and conflict-resolution. Such documents generally hold no legal status, and those professionals whose behaviour does not conform to such guidelines are not subject to any legal or professional sanctions. Their power comes from the ethical obligation inherent in the early childhood professional's roles and responsibilities to promote and protect the rights of young children.

Many early childhood professional organisations, as well as statutory bodies, have put forward sets of quality indicators which can be used to assess the range of existing services. Alexander (1995:137) offers the following five central goals and values that are useful in determining to what extent children's rights come before other considerations.

- *Children come first.* Every child has a right to depend upon adults to provide the conditions that will enable them to reach their full potential. We all bear responsibility for all our children, and it is essential that parents and carers should receive the necessary support to ensure that their children receive the best possible start in life.
- *Children have a right to be recognised as people with views and interests.* They have the right to be listened to and to participate in decision-making about issues that affect their lives.
- *Children should have the opportunity to be part of a family and community,* to experience a stable learning and caring environment that enhances their esteem as individuals, their dignity and auton-omy, self-confidence and enthusiasm for learning, and respect for others that ensures they are free from discrimination.
- *Parents, carers and communities need to be supported in promot-ing the interests and welfare of their children.* Children need strong adults upon whom they can depend to provide love, security and the financial resources to ensure they can access an adequate stan-dard of living. Early childhood services must be rooted in local community infrastructures and provide real choice for families, particularly those on low incomes.
- *Children have the right to safe play environments* that provide a whole range of opportunities for autonomy, social development and recreational activity. Children and families also have the right to participate in the services provided by the retail, cultural and tourist sectors.

The services provided for children should start with, and be based on, the rights and interests of the child, not emerge from the interests of parents (although the common interests of parents and children must be recognised), or from those of professionals, the organisation, finances and educational fads.

## ADMINISTERING EARLY CHILDHOOD SETTINGS IN ACCORDANCE WITH THE PROFESSION'S ETHICAL PRINCIPLES

One of the indicators of quality is an effective administration or management structure (Pugh, 2001). Administrative or management competence is considered to be a necessary, but not sufficient, aspect of leadership. Nevertheless, effective and efficient administration requires that a leader make decisions and act upon ethical principles that have been accepted and endorsed by the early childhood profession. For early childhood, administering services in an ethical manner means transforming traditional power relationships into collaborative, consultative, communicative, respectful decision-making.

Effective administration or management of early childhood settings involves the four major functions of planning, implementation, operation and evaluation. Planning includes aspects of leadership, philosophy and involvement of others. Implementation includes ethical decision-making and creative problem-solving, as well as aspects of motivation, team-building and staff development. Operation refers to the knowledge base for the running of services, the choices made in relation to issues such as facilities, equipment, the use of space, room arrangement and scheduling, as well as financial management and record-keeping. Evaluation refers to the ongoing learning process that provides information about the effectiveness of services and informs the management of change. Each of these four functions can involve ethical issues and dilemmas—that is, moral decision-making that cannot be settled by reference to educational or developmental theory and research (Katz, 1995b) or statutory regulations.

Examples of common ethical or moral dilemmas faced by early childhood practitioners include:

- parents wanting their toddlers to be kept awake during the day because they say they can't get them to sleep at night;
- a father who requests that his son not be permitted to play with dolls, dress up in female clothes or play in the role-play area;
- parents who ask for their three-year-old child to be 'taught' reading and writing skills;
- passing on information to a parent about their child's behaviour, knowing that the parent is likely to punish the child for it at home;
- a mother who asks you to smack her child when he misbehaves in the setting;

- overhearing a child discuss with a friend the petty shoplifting that his mother encouraged him and his siblings to do;
- telling parents that their 'vegetarian' child ate a ham sandwich from another child's lunchbox;
- overhearing a child discuss abusive behaviour by one of his parents towards another;
- treating children differently because of their parents' non-traditional values;
- confronting a colleague about a breach of confidentiality; and
- implementing any practice or policy that you believe to be harmful to children.

Effective leaders understand their power and status in these areas, and the need to be guided by professional principles and values in order to deliver quality services. Where leaders understand their professional roles as administrators or managers, they will make responsible decisions that are guided by professional standards of practice and a code of ethics.

Staff selection, development and evaluation are areas that are central to the ethical administration of an early childhood setting. The quality of staff in terms of appropriate training and experience is critical for the provision of high-quality services in early childhood (Ebbeck and Waniganayake, 2003). It is important that those charged with employment of staff regard staff selection as an ethical responsibility, and as part of meeting the needs of young children. It is essential to provide professional training and development opportunities to all adults associated with early childhood settings because, the better the understanding that early childhood practitioners and support staff have about what constitutes quality in early childhood services, the goals of early care and education and child development, the more responsive early childhood services can be to children and families. This is part of the ethical responsibility to provide for children's rights to quality care and education.

In addition to training opportunities, early childhood practitioners need to be encouraged to regularly evaluate their performance and goals. Evaluation is an essential part of the ongoing learning process in which all professionals engage. The notion of reflective practice (Ferraro, 2000) as a basis for evaluation of individual staff members, the organisation itself and the pursuit of quality has been endorsed by many early childhood practitioners.

The process of reflection involves thinking about your own style of work in order to identify gaps in knowledge, understanding and skill as a basis for improving practice. Becoming reflective is part of being a lifelong learner. Reflective practitioners seek out and consider new information and ideas, draw on the opinions of others and use these resources as a means of developing new ways of working (Abbott and Pugh, 1998). Early childhood practice can be enhanced and extended through professional conversations and dialogues with colleagues and mentors, as well as through in-service training and other continuing professional development opportunities. The use of a professional portfolio can be very effective in structuring, gathering evidence and documenting learning, professional growth and improvement in practice. Claxton (2002) considers that the ability to be reflective is grounded in thinking about learning and understanding yourself as a learner. It involves becoming more strategic about learning by planning in advance what changes might be needed, revising and adapting those plans in the light of insight gained from monitoring and learning from experience.

Reflective practitioners take stock of themselves and the constraints of their working situation, seek out and use available resources, prioritise their learning challenges, review progress, make required modifications and ponder over how they can transfer or generalise their learning to other areas of their work. They reflect about their professional roles, values and goals and feel confident to discuss and debate issues of practice with colleagues, other professionals and parents. Becoming a reflective practitioner essentially involves evaluating what we do through a process of thinking about our earlier work, judging its effectiveness and developing an action plan for improvement it in the future.

However, reflection and evaluation are not value-free processes. Perceptions of what is important in early childhood services are based on professional and personal values. Behaviours, attitudes and attributes will be judged on the basis of such values. It is essential that leaders understand the value basis of reflection and evaluation and ensure that procedures and processes are consistent with the professional values and philosophies that guide the profession. Evaluation of staff, practice and services must be conducted within the context of social responsibility, children's rights and ethical decision-making.

Where early childhood settings are administered from an ethical perspective, it is likely that positive interaction and teamwork between staff members will be evident. The creation of effective early childhood teams appears to be related to the leader's ethical decision-making in relation to the employment of the best staff available and ensuring that all staff take part in regular training and a range of evaluation approaches. It is important that leaders make the principles and values on which they developed the administrative structure transparent for team members because this will help others to understand the valid basis of administrative policies and operations.

## EMPLOYING AN EARLY CHILDHOOD CODE OF ETHICS TO GUIDE THE RESOLUTION OF ETHICAL DILEMMAS

Being an early childhood practitioner in contemporary society means more than being appropriately trained for and experienced in the care and education of young children. It means adopting a particular mental set or attitude towards one's work. Members of the field increasingly regard themselves as professionals, with a distinct professional identity and growing professional self-esteem and confidence.

Professionalism continues to be a valued goal for members of the field throughout the world. Part of being regarded as a professional is the incorporation of certain attributes into one's professional identity. Katz (1995a) describes a number of attributes which are considered to be relevant for early childhood practitioners. Among these attributes is the adoption of a code of ethics by a profession. Effective early childhood leaders will appreciate that one of the products of becoming a professional—and indeed an ethical leader—is additional moral obligations and responsibilities to children, their families, colleagues, the community and society, and the profession.

The Australian Early Childhood Association (1991:3) defines its code of ethics as a 'set of statements about appropriate and expected behaviours of members of a professional working group [which], as such, reflects its values'. Katz (1995b:240) considers a code of ethics to be 'a set of statements that help us deal with the temptations inherent in our occupations' which provides guidelines for deciding what is right rather than expedient, good rather than practical, and what acts may never be engaged in or condoned under any circumstances. A code of ethics can be considered to be a vehicle for protecting the rights and welfare of those who may be dependent and vulnerable, as well as a means of protecting members of the profession themselves from making unsuitable decisions in relation to young children and their families. While leaders in early childhood settings might argue that they have an altruistic mission and vision, and naturally would act in the best interests of young children and their families, a code of ethics provides a focus for debate about philosophy, values and ethical issues, as well as being a tool for guiding the complex decision-making faced in day-to-day work with young children and their families.

There are several reasons why early childhood practitioners need a code of ethics. One is because they have considerable autonomy and independence over their behaviour and decisions. Decisions have to be made quickly, often without discussion with or reference to others. Such pressures may result in unsuitable behaviour or decisions which do not protect children's rights or which are not in their best interests.

*The parent of a special needs child challenged one staff member about the way she managed her child's behaviour. The parent doesn't understand that her child is just one child in a group of children, all of whom have needs and rights. The practitioner couldn't permit her child to continue with that behaviour because it could have resulted in injury to another child. She made the best decision she could at that time; in hindsight, she had other options but sometimes decisions have to be made fast.*

**Manager, day nursery**

In addition, a decision that can be rationalised and justified by reference to a code of ethics appears to carry more weight and credibility, and as such is less likely to be challenged than one that does not have such a solid underpinning. A code of ethics can guide and support the leader's decision-making and problem-solving and give a leader greater confidence in these demanding aspects of the work.

*Some aspects of the government guidelines for the Literacy Hour have not been appropriate for four-year-olds. We need to have credible reasons for implementing the Literacy Hour differently. There is research evidence we refer to but we want our professional values and insight into what works with children recognised by people like inspectors and advisers.*

**Early years teacher**

Another reason why a code of ethics is helpful is because many situations and incidents that occur in day-to-day work with young children contain inherent conflicts of value or interest, or pose an ethical dilemma. Fleet and Clyde (1993) define ethical dilemmas as situations that involve conflict between core values and difficult, even painful, choices that result in less than satisfactory outcomes.

*Some parents put a lot of pressure on us to teach the children to read and write in the nursery. They don't understand that many children are not ready for this and we don't want the children to experience failure. But if we don't respond to the parents' expectations, they remove the children and enrol them at a setting that will try to teach them those skills. What do we do? If we teach reading and writing too early, it is not in the best interests of some children. If we don't, the parents get upset and threaten to find a nursery that does.*

**Nursery officer**

Leaders often have to take ultimate responsibility for deciding on or supporting courses of action that will affect the lives of other people. Where a decision is required but where no mutually acceptable or satisfactory options appear to exist, effective leaders will refer to the code of ethics to determine overriding principles and values to help them work towards an optimal resolution of the dilemma.

*There has been a lot of discussion among the staff about management's decision to accept three-year-olds who are still not toilet trained. The key issue here is not to disadvantage any child. We have policies about inclusion and equal opportunities so they need to understand that the decision was based on the values endorsed in the policies.*

**Deputy supervisor, day nursery**

Finally, a code of ethics is necessary because the infrastructure of the early childhood profession contains a number of features that increase the likelihood of ethical dilemmas occurring in daily practice. These features include low status and power, a multiplicity of clients with potentially conflicting needs and interests, role ambiguity, and poor integration of knowledge base and practice (Fleet and Clyde, 1993). A code of ethics can assist early childhood practitioners, including leaders, to behave in ways and make decisions that do not compromise children, themselves and other parties and groups associated with early childhood settings. While a code of ethics cannot, and is not, intended to solve the individual and complex situations faced by early childhood practitioners in their work, it does offer a tool to guide reflection, behaviour and decision-making.

One of the limitations of many professional codes of ethics is that they provide no power to enforce the code or apply sanctions to members who choose not to endorse or comply with—or even flagrantly breach—the principles and values accepted by and for the professional group as a whole. Behaving in accordance with a profession's code of ethics tends to be a voluntary undertaking by individual members of that profession. For the early childhood profession, a code of ethics indicates the moral obligations and responsibilities of practitioners to individuals and groups who are associated with the field, and highlights moral issues related to working with those who are vulnerable. An effective early childhood leader will act as a role model for others by using the code of ethics to explore issues that arise in practice and will work to gain acceptance of and support for ethically appropriate rules and guidelines with team members. While not asserting power over non-compliance with or breaches of the principles reflected in the code of ethics by colleagues, a leader will accept the moral responsibility for raising such issues for discussion, and work towards positive resolution.

It is important for leaders to understand that a code of ethics—even without sanctions—can play an important role in improving the professional practice of early childhood practitioners. It can focus thinking and debate, thereby increasing understanding of, and unity of purpose within, the field. It can guide advocacy efforts and raise the professional standing of the field within the community. A code of ethics needs to be perceived as part of the resources available to leaders and all members of the field, and as such should be central to meeting the ethical challenges faced in day-to-day practice.

One final area in the discussion of the ethics of leadership relates to gender-specific leadership. The issue of gender-specific leadership was discussed in Chapter 2. However, in the area of ethical leadership, a gender-related but not gender-specific orientation has been identified (Desjardins, 1996). It appears that men and women may use different moral orientations in their approach to leadership and the way they respond to ethical dilemmas. Desjardins argues that moral orientation has two dimensions: a justice-rights orientation and a care-connectedness orientation. The justice-rights orientation emphasises objectivity and universality, and directs the leader to treat others fairly and avoid interfering with their rights. The care-connectedness orientation focuses on attachment and care, expressed as concern with providing for the needs of others, as guiding principles in moral decisions. Desjardins' work suggests that men appear to act more generally on the basis of the justice-rights orientation, with women more frequently being guided by care and connectedness values. It is important for an effective leader in early childhood—who is more likely to be a woman—to appreciate the two dimensions of moral orientation and to ensure that considerations of rights and fairness, as well as attachment and care, are employed when faced with ethical dilemmas and moral decision making.

## BRINGING IT TOGETHER

Effective leaders in early childhood appreciate their moral obligation to act with professional integrity in all aspects of their work. In exercising ethical leadership, consideration needs to be given to the clarification of personal morals and professional ethics. Effective leaders will be able to clearly articulate their value system and, as a consequence, others will perceive their behaviour as more predictable and credible. The leader's value system should be understood by those associated with the early childhood setting as providing a rationale for the broad goals of the service, ethical decisions and choices, as well as providing the basis for administrative and organisational aspects of settings. The ethics of leadership lie in the leader's attitudes towards the involvement and participation of others in issues that affect their lives. Ethical leadership is a process of working with people to achieve specific goals, and it is founded on trust, values, respect, communication, collaboration and empowerment.

# CHAPTER FOURTEEN

## BUILDING AND SUSTAINING LEADERSHIP CAPACITY IN EARLY CHILDHOOD

*Every early childhood practitioner has the potential to become a leader if they want to because most of the skills and qualities can be learned and developed. Leadership comes to some naturally but most of us learn to become leaders.*

Manager, day nursery

**THIS CHAPTER EXPLORES**
- the role of leadership in the quest for quality early childhood services
- the role of leadership in quality assurance and accreditation schemes
- the role of training in building and sustaining leadership capacity and professionalisation
- a selection of leadership training programs for early childhood practitioners
- suggestions for building, encouraging and sustaining leadership capacity in early childhood practitioners

As the research that documents the strong link between high-quality early childhood services and children's later social and educational success accumulates, early childhood practitioners need to be more articulate about their vital role in facilitating young children's development and achievement. It is time for practitioners to act on their own behalf to inform the public about their fundamental importance in children's development and education, their essential contribution to improving policy and decision-making in care, educational and welfare areas and the cost-effectiveness of their services.

While the importance of leadership is increasingly recognised within the field, it still is not considered to be a mandatory aspect of the administrative role of the manager, coordinator or director of an early childhood service, which explains in part the continued low status ascribed to those who work in such services. However, research evidence shows that early childhood practitioners can display leadership if they develop and use their skills efficiently to administer a responsive service and to initiate change in a methodical way. The type of leadership exercised by the designated administrator of an early childhood setting has continued to be identified in research findings as one of the critical factors in the level of quality of programs provided for young children, in terms of positive results for both children and staff (Bella and Jorde-Bloom, 2003; Muijs et al., 2005). The role of the leader and the manner in which that role is carried out has become central to the provision of high-quality services and to determining the level of professionalism that is accorded to the early childhood field. It is no longer acceptable for practitioners to be unprepared to exercise leadership effectively.

Jorde-Bloom (1992:138) defines the leader of an early childhood setting as 'the gatekeeper to quality'. She argues that the role is both critical and complex, requiring conceptual and practical skill in organisational theory and leadership, child development and early childhood programming, fiscal and legal issues, and committee, parent and community relations. While high-quality services have been associated with experienced leaders, other evidence reveals that training, rather than work experience, is the best predictor of quality early childhood services. However, in terms of the leadership aspect of the role, very little training has been available for those who have been employed to administer early childhood services. In fact, the majority of leaders report that they have learned 'on the job' with support from some in-service training. As a result, the quality of leadership is unlikely to indicate the hidden and undeveloped potential of many of those in administrative positions in the field.

In order to move the early childhood field along the pathway of professionalism, practitioners need access to the knowledge and skills required for effective leadership in settings and in the community. The profession is dynamic and characterised by growth, change and futures-orientation (Ebbeck and Waniganayake, 2003). It is therefore essential that all members of the early childhood field embrace a life-long learning perspective towards their own development, and regard leadership as a key aspect of this development. This book has addressed many of the essential issues in becoming a leader. However, the focus has been on knowledge and information, and books cannot train people! The next step is for the reader to put some of the ideas into practice and to begin to integrate the theory with professional practice. Support for the development of these nascent skills can be obtained from in-service courses and from undertaking further study in courses which provide a focus on leadership in the early childhood context. Leaders will be required to demonstrate an orientation and commitment to further professional training and development to be able to be responsive to change.

The introduction of quality assurance and accreditation schemes for early childhood services has produced further changes in the role of the leader. One of the basic premises of quality assurance and accreditation is that leadership is related to the quality of provision. The leader is responsible for ensuring a nurturing and educational environment for children, as well as fulfilling the responsibility for the recruitment, training and development of staff, the support and development of parents, and establishing and personifying the 'public face' of settings and the early childhood profession in contacts with other professionals and the general community. Leaders need to be able to meet these demands in a style that communicates a confident level of professionalism. The opportunity for community acknowledgment of a new level of professionalism in early childhood hinges on the development of the leadership abilities of practitioners.

The critical role of building and sustaining leadership capacity has been recognised by the increasing number of different training programs aimed at developing leadership in early childhood practitioners that are now available. Several such programs are described below.

## TRAINING PROGRAMS

Wheelock College's Institute for Leadership and Career Development in the United States was one of the first tertiary training organisations to address the need for leadership training. Its 'Taking the Lead: Investing in Early Childhood for the Twenty-first Century' program is a national initiative designed to build the leadership capacity of early childhood practitioners as a way of improving quality. Five key elements are incorporated into a program that supports the development of leaders in early child care and education (Alvarado et al., 1999). These are:

- *community partnerships*, where participants are trained to connect with community resources and respond to leadership opportunities through active involvement with a wide range of organisations and populations within their community;
- *cultural and community context*, where participants learn to create appropriately responsive initiatives that meet the needs of the cultural and community context;
- *relevant context*, where participants learn leadership skills and competencies that ensure success in any discipline or context;
- *mentoring*, where participants learn about the mutual benefits of mentoring and how to effectively mentor others' individual personal and professional growth; and
- *opportunities to exercise leadership*, where participants have opportunities to put theory into practice and continue their own development through developing teamwork.

The Centre for Early Childhood Leadership, National-Louis University, in the United States, has offered two leadership training programs of different lengths and intensities. 'The McCormick Fellows Leadership Training Program' was a two-year program that led to NAEYC centre accreditation. 'Taking Charge of Change', which is currently offered, is a more streamlined program lasting ten months. Both programs focus on building leadership capacity through personal transformation and professional development, where leaders learn to shift from one perspective to another—that is, look at the big picture while simultaneously being aware of the small details that influence reactions to any event. As leaders, they learn to view the same situation from different perspectives when making decisions, building systems, mentoring colleagues, evaluating actions and serving as agents of change.

Evaluation of the training programs by participants from 1993 and 2003 indicated that they experienced an increased sense of empowerment, a heightened sense of self-esteem and increased feelings of self-efficacy and confidence. Four clusters of skills were identified as contributing to better job performance in their management and leadership roles:

- interpersonal and communication skills;
- group facilitation skills;
- decision-making skills; and
- staff development skills.

The training programs also had an impact on career decisions in a field characterised by high staff turnover and burnout. Over 80 per cent of participants continued to work in the early childhood field, and over 90 per cent planned to be working in early childhood for the next five years. The training also acted as a catalyst for growth and change in that many participants went on to undertake additional accredited training.

In England, Moyles and Yates (2004) from the Centre for Research into Education and Teaching at Anglia Polytechnic University have developed a written manual entitled *Effective Leadership and Management Evaluation Scheme—Early Years* (ELMES-EY) in association with Essex County Council and Southend Borough Council. While not a training program, this manual aims to offer professional guidance and support for early childhood practitioners who find themselves in a new managerial role. Its format allows the practitioner to reflect upon and evaluate their knowledge and skills in four broad areas:

- leadership skills;
- management skills;
- professional skills; and
- personal characteristics.

The ELMES provides information and structure about what early childhood leaders and managers need to address in their day-to-day work.

The expansion and coordination of integrated children's services in England has created demand for professional training in leadership and management that meet the specialised needs of early childhood practitioners. The National College of School Leadership in England, in conjunction with the Pen Green Leadership Development Centre, has developed a new one-year National Professional Qualification for Integrated Centre Leadership (NPQICL), which is part of its articulated approach to meeting the leadership and management needs of those working in all phases of education. This particular training program has been designed to address the needs of emergent leaders within multi-agency early childhood settings. The program aims to develop leaders who can create an ethos of community partnership, working by coordinating coherent and seamless high-quality services for children and families. The training focuses on:

- *exploring the leadership experience*, involving clarification of values, principles and vision, developing an effective learning environment, exploring leadership styles and approaches and making things happen; and
- *leading across professional boundaries*, including developing professional practice and leading learning, managing change, innovation and development, building community and partnership and creating the future.

Participants are mentored and learn through the experience of leading and keeping a leadership learning journal.

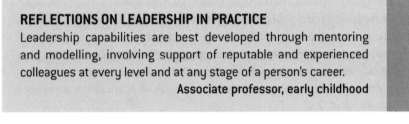

**REFLECTIONS ON LEADERSHIP IN PRACTICE**
Leadership capabilities are best developed through mentoring and modelling, involving support of reputable and experienced colleagues at every level and at any stage of a person's career.
**Associate professor, early childhood**

The above training programs highlight the recognised importance of the provision of leadership training designed specifically for early childhood practitioners. The early childhood field has acknowledged that, through the provision of systematic, intensive and relevant training, it can and needs to grow its own leaders from within and from the bottom up (Bella and Jorde-Bloom, 2003).

## BUILDING LEADERSHIP CAPACITY

Pechura (2003:118) offers a number of strategies that are helpful for managers, coordinators and directors who wish to build and sustain leadership capacity members of the team.

To begin the process of building leadership capacity in team members, it is important to:

- talk with other members of the team about leadership;
- ask other members of the team to take on leadership roles and responsibilities; and
- help other members of the team to exercise leadership successfully.

To encourage the development of leadership capacity, it is important to:

- give other members of the team opportunities to be leaders;
- encourage, support and involve other members of the team to be leaders;
- recognise the leadership efforts of team members;
- model and teach leadership skills; and
- build relationships that encourage leadership.

To sustain leadership capacity, it is important to:

- keep structures in place that foster leadership;
- showcase leaders in leadership roles;
- promote leadership with and among others;
- provide time and resources for others to be leaders;
- restate mission and goals for the setting;
- provide on-the-job, in-service or accredited leadership training for others; and
- encourage leadership through fun activities.

Such strategies can help develop an ethos where staff are groomed to take on higher levels of responsibility because leadership is distributed and delegated at different levels in settings.


## BRINGING IT TOGETHER

The ongoing and increasing interest in leadership in early childhood has emanated from research evidence showing that leadership contributes to the quality of early childhood services. Specifically, research shows that developing leadership in early childhood is important, and to successfully undertake this complex role requires special training and professional development (Muijs et al., 2005). In the current climate of accountability, the need for effective, professional leadership is high. Increasing the number of able early childhood leaders will contribute to enhanced professional competence, confidence and status within the community, which in turn may generate greater public and financial support for early childhood services. However, in order to build and sustain leadership capability, managers, coordinators and directors need to think about how their time can be structured to make space for leadership roles and responsibilities, and the types of resources that are needed to carry out leadership functions effectively. Focusing on embedding shared, distributed and collaborative leadership in settings may be one pathway to anticipating, preparing and supporting emergent leaders in early childhood.

# REFERENCES

Abbott, L. and Hevey, D. 2001, 'Training to work in the early years: Developing the climbing frame', *Contemporary Issues in the Early Years. Working Collaboratively for Children*, 3rd edn, ed. G. Pugh, Paul Chapman, London.

Abbott, L. and Moylett, H. eds 1997, *Working with the Under 3s: Responding to Children's Needs*, Open University Press, Buckingham.

Abbott, L. and Pugh, G. 1998, *Training to Work in the Early Years. Developing the Climbing Frame*, Open University Press, Buckingham.

Adair, J. 1986, *Effective Teambuilding*, Gower Publishing Company, Aldershot.

Adler, A. 1958, *What Life Should Mean To You*, Capricorn Books, G.P. Putnam's Sons, New York.

Albert, L. and Einstein, E. 1986, *Strengthening Stepfamilies*, American Guidance Service, Minneapolis.

Alexander, G. 1995, 'Children's rights in the early years: From plaiting fog to knitting treacle', *The Handbook of Children's Rights: Comparative Policy and Practice*, eds B. Franklin and T. Hammarberg, Routledge, London.

Almy, M. 1975, *The Early Childhood Educator at Work*, McGraw Hill, New York.

Alvarado, C., Chin, E., Copland, J., Elliot, K., Emanuel, B., Farris, M., Genser, A. and Surr, W. 1999, *The Many Faces of Leadership: Taking the Lead*, Centre for Career Development in Early Care and Education, Wheelock.

Andrews, D., Crother, F., Hann, L. and McMaster, J. 2002, 'Teachers as leaders: Re-imaging the profession', *Practising Administrator*, vol. 24, no. 1, pp. 24-7.

Annan, K.A. 2002, 'Foreword', *The State of the World's Children 2002: Leadership*, UNICEF, New York.

Anning, A. and Edwards, A. 1999, *Promoting Children's Learning from Birth to Five*, Open University Press, Buckingham.

Armstrong, M. 1994, *How to be an Even Better Manager*, Kogan Page, London.

Australian Early Childhood Association Inc. 1991, 'Australian Early Childhood Association Code of Ethics', *Australian Journal of Early Childhood*, vol. 16, no. 1, pp. 3–6.

Barbour, N. 1992, 'Meeting the child care needs of the 1990s', *Child and Youth Care Forum*, vol. 21, no. 5, pp. 297–8.

Bella, J. and Jorde-Bloom P. 2003, *Zoom: The Impact of Leadership Training on Role Perceptions, Job Performance and Career Decisions*, Centre for Early Childhood Leadership, Wheeling, Ill.

Bellm, D. and Whitebrook, M. 1996, 'Mentoring for early childhood teachers and providers: Building upon and extending tradition', *Young Children*, vol. 52, no. 1, pp. 59–64.

Bennis, W. 1989, *On Becoming a Leader*, Hutchinson, London.

Bennis, W. and Nanus, B. 1985, *Leaders*, Harper Row, New York.

Berk, L.E. 2002, *Child Development*, 6th edn, Allyn and Bacon, Needham Heights.

Blanchard, K. and Johnson, S. 2004, *The One Minute Manager*, Harper Collins Business, New York.

Bredekamp, S. 1992, 'Composing a profession', *Young Children*, vol. 47, no. 2, pp. 52–4.

Boardman, M. 2003, 'Changing times: Changing challenges for early childhood leaders', *Australian Journal of Early Childhood*, vol. 28, no. 2, pp. 20–5.

Borgia, E.T. and Schuler, D. 1996, 'Action research in early childhood education', *ERIC Digest*, EDO-PS-96-11, ERIC Clearinghouse on Elementary and Early Childhood Education, Washington.

Bowman, B. and Kagan, S. eds 1997, *Leadership in Early Care and Education*, National Association for the Education of Young Children, Washington.

Bruce, T. and Megitt, C. 1999, *Child Care and Education*, Hodder and Stoughton, London.

Caddell, D. 2001, *Working With Parents: A Shared Understanding of the Curriculum 3–5*, Learning and Teaching, Dundee.

Caldwell, B. 2003, 'Foreword', *Early Childhood Professionals. Leading*

*Today and Tomorrow*, M. Ebbeck and M. Waniganayake, MacLennan & Petty Pty Ltd, Sydney.

Campbell, A. 2002, 'Research and the professional self', *Becoming an Evidenced-Based Practitioner: A Framework for Teacher-Researchers*, ed. O. McNamara, Routledge Falmer, London.

Carlisle, H.M. 1979, *Management Essentials: Concepts and Applications*, Science Research Associates Inc., Chicago.

Carnall, C. 1990, *Managing Change*, Routledge, London.

——1995, *Managing Change in Organisations*, 2nd edn, Prentice Hall, Hemel Hempstead.

Clark, K. and Clark, M. 1996, *Choosing to Lead*, 2nd edn, Centre for Creative Leadership, Greensboro.

Claxton, G. 2002, *Building Learning Power*, Henleaze House, Bristol.

——2001, *Wise Up: The Challenge of Lifelong Learning*, Network Educational Press, Stafford.

Clyde, M. and Rodd, J. 1989, 'Professional ethics: There's more to it than meets the eye', *Early Child Development and Care*, vol. 53, pp. 1–12.

Clyde, M. and Rodd, J. 1993, 'A comparison of Australian and American centre-based caregivers' perceptions of their roles', *Advances in Early Education and Day Care*, ed. S. Reifel, JAI Press, Greenwich, CN.

Coady, M. 1991, 'Ethics, laws and codes', *Australian Journal of Early Childhood*, vol. 16, no. 1, pp. 17–20.

Cohen, L., Manion, L. and Harrison, K. 2000, *Research Methods in Education*, 5th edn, Routledge Falmer, London.

Cooper, C. 2004, *Shut Up and Listen. The Truth About How We Communicate at Work*, Kogan Page, London.

Covey, S.R. 2004, *The 7 Habits of Highly Effective People: Powerful Lessons in Personal Change*, The Free Press, New York.

Cox, E. 1996, *Leading Women: Tactics for Making the Difference*, Random House, Sydney.

Crosser, S. 2005, *What Do We Know About Early Childhood Education? Research Based Practice*, Thomson Delmar Learning, New York.

Cummins, L. 2004, 'The pot of gold at the end of the rainbow: Mentoring in early childhood education', *Childhood Education*, vol. 80, no. 5, pp. 254–60.

Curran, D. 1989, *Working with Parents: A Guide to Successful Parent Groups*, American Guidance Service, Minneapolis.

Davies, B. ed. 2005, *The Essentials of School Leadership*, Paul Chapman Publishing, and Corwin Press, London.

de Bono, E. 2004a, *Edward de Bono's Thinking Course*, BBC Books, London.

——2004b, *Six Thinking Hats*, Penguin Books, London.

Desforges, C. and Abouchaar, A. 2003, 'The impact of parental involvement, parental support and family education on pupil achievement and adjustment: A review of the literature', *Research Brief No. 433*, Department for Education and Skills, London.

Desjardins, C. 1996, 'Gender based teambuilding: Strengths men and women bring to leadership roles', *Proceedings of the Annual International Conference The Olympics of Leadership: Overcoming Obstacles, Balancing Skills, Taking Risks,* National Community College Chair Academy, Phoenix.

Dickman, M.H. and Stanford-Blair, N. 2000, *Connecting Leadership to the Brain*, Corwin Press, Thousand Oaks, CA.

Draper, L. and Duffy, B. 2001, 'Working with parents', in *Contemporary Issues in the Early Years: Working Collaboratively for Children*, 3rd edn, ed. G. Pugh, Paul Chapman, London.

Drever, P. 2002, 'The psychology of coaching, *InPsych*, April, pp. 24–5.

Ebbeck, M. and Waniganayake, M. 2003, *Early Childhood Professionals: Leading Today and Tomorrow*, MacLennan + Petty Pty Ltd, Sydney.

Edgington, M. 2000, 'Principles of effective collaboration', *Early Years Educator*, vol. 1, no. 10, pp. 2–5.

Edwards, C., Gandini, L. and Forman, G. 1994, *The Hundred Languages of Children: The Reggio Emilia Approach to Early Childhood*, Ablex Publishing Corporation, Norwood.

Elliott, R. 2003, 'Sharing care and education: Parent perspectives', *Australian Journal of Early Childhood Education*, vol. 28, no. 4, pp. 14–21.

Faber, B. 1991, *Crisis in Education*, Jossey-Bass, San Francisco.

Feeney, S. and Kipnis, K. 1991, 'Professional ethics in early childhood education', *Australian Journal of Early Childhood*, vol. 16, no. 1, pp. 40–2.

Ferguson, J. 2003, *Perfect Assertion*, Random House, London.

Ferraro, J. 2000, 'Reflective practice and professional development', *ERIC Digest*, ED449120, ERIC Clearinghouse on Teaching and Teacher Education, Washington.

Fleet, A. and Clyde, M. 1993, *What's in a Day? Working in Early Childhood*, Social Science Press, Wentworth Falls.

Franklin, B. and Hammarberg, T. 1995, *The Handbook of Children's Rights: Comparative Policy and Practice*, Routledge, London.

Fraser, S., Lewis, V., Ding, S., Kellett, M. and Robinson, C. 2003, *Doing Research with Children and Young People*, Sage, London.

Freeman, N. 2004, 'Ethics and the ACEI: Beginning the conversation', *Childhood Education*, vol. 80, no. 6, pp. 332–4.

Fullan, M. 1991, *The New Meaning of Educational Change*, Teachers College Press, New York.

Gardner, H. 1983, *Frames of Mind: Theories of Multiple Intelligences*, Basic Books, New York.

Geoghegan, N., Petriwskyj, A., Bower, L. and Geoghegan, D. 2003, 'Eliciting dimensions of educational leadership in early childhood education', *Australian Research in Early Childhood Education*, vol. 10, no. 1, pp. 12–23.

Gibbs, C.J. 1990, 'Student teacher opinions on educational issues—an initial survey, 1989', *Australian Journal of Early Childhood*, vol. 15, no. 2, pp. 38–42.

Giudici, C., Rinaldi, C. and Krechevsky, M. eds 2001, *Making Learning Visible: Children as Individual and Group Leaders. Project Zero Reggio Children*, Tipolitografia La Reggiana, Municipality of Reggio Emilia.

Goleman, D. 1996, *Emotional Intelligence: Why It Can Matter More than IQ*, Bloomsbury Paperbacks, London.

Goleman, D., Boyatzis, R. and McKee, A. 2002, *Primal Leadership: Realising the Power of Emotional Intelligence*, Harvard Business School Press, Boston.

Grant, L. 1997, '50 most powerful women in Britain. Part 2: The age of optimism', *The Guardian*, 27 May, pp. 2–4.

Greany, T. and Rodd, J. 2003, *Creating a Learning to Learn School*, Network Educational Press, Stafford.

Hall, V. 1996, *Dancing on the Ceiling: A Study of Women Managers in Education*, Paul Chapman Publishing, London.

Hanft, B., Rush, D. and M'Lisa, L. 2003, 'Coaching families and colleagues: A process for collaboration in natural settings', *Infants and Young Children*, vol. 16, no. 1, pp. 33–47.

Hartle, F. and Thomas, K. 2003, *Growing Tomorrow's School Leaders: The Challenge*, National College for School Leadership, Nottingham.

Hasenfeld, Y. 1983, *Human Service Organisations*, Prentice Hall, Englewood Cliffs.

——1992, *Human Services as Complex Organisations*, Prentice Hall, Englewood Cliffs.

Hayden, J. 1996, *Management of Early Childhood Services: An Australian Perspective*, Social Science Press, Sydney.

——1999, 'Delegation: Win–win strategies for managing early childhood settings', *Australian Early Childhood Association Research in Practice Series*, vol. 6, no. 1, Canberra.

Henderson-Kelly, L. and Pamphilon, B. 2000, 'Women's models of leadership in the child care sector', *Australian Journal of Early Childhood*, vol. 25, no. 1, pp. 8–12.

Hennessy, E., Martin, S., Moss, P. and Melhuish, E. 1992, *Children and Day Care . . . Lessons From Research*, Chapman Publishing, London.

Hennig, M. and Jardim, A. 1976, *The Managerial Woman*, Pocket Books, New York.

Hersey, P. and Blanchard, K. 1988, *Organisational Behaviour*, Prentice Hall, Englewood Cliffs.

Hiatt-Michael, D. 2001, 'Preparing Teachers to Work with Parents', *ERIC Digest*, ED460123, ERIC Clearinghouse on Teaching and Teacher Education, Washington.

Hill, M.S. and Ragland, J.C. 1995, *Women as Educational Leaders: Opening Windows, Pushing Ceilings*, Corwin Press, Municipality of Reggio Emilia.

Hopkins, D. 1990, *A Teacher's Guide to Classroom Research*, Open University Press, Philadelphia.

Huang, C.A. and Lynch, J. 1995, *Mentoring: The Tao of Giving and Receiving Wisdom*, Harper, San Francisco.

Hughes, P. and MacNaughton, G. 2002, 'Preparing early childhood professionals to work with parents: The challenges and diversity and dissensus', *Australian Journal of Early Childhood*, vol. 27, no. 2, pp. 14–20.

Hujala, E. and Puroila, A. eds 1998, *Towards Understanding Leadership in Early Childhood Context: Cross Cultural Perspectives*, Oulu University Press, Oulu, Finland.

Humphries, E. and Senden, B. 2000, 'Leadership and change: A dialogue of theory and practice', *Australian Journal of Early Childhood*, vol. 25, no. 1, pp. 26–31.

Hurst, B. and Reding, G. 2002, *Teachers Mentoring Teachers: Fastback 493*, Phi Delta Kappa International, Bloomington.

Johnson, D.W. 1996, *Reaching Out: Interpersonal Effectiveness and Self-Actualisation*, 6th edn, Prentice Hall, Englewood Cliffs.

Johnson, D.W. and Johnson, F.P. 2003, *Joining Together: Group Theory and Process*, international edn, Allyn & Bacon, Needham Heights.

Jorde-Bloom, P. 1982, *Avoiding Burnout: Strategies for managing time, space and people in early childhood education*, Gryphon House, Mt Rainier.

——1992, 'The child care centre director: A critical component of program quality', *Educational Horizons*, Spring, pp. 138–45.

——1995, 'Shared decision making: The centre piece of participatory management', *Young Children*, vol. 50, no. 4, pp. 55–60.

——1997, 'Leadership: Defining the elusive', in *Leadership Quest*, vol. 1, no. 1, pp. 12–15.

——2003, 'Thinking about your successor', in *The Director's Link*, Centre for Early Childhood Leadership, National Louis University, Wheeling, Ill.

Jorde-Bloom, P. and Sheerer, M. 1992, 'The effects of leadership training on child care program quality', *Early Childhood Research Quarterly*, vol. 7, pp. 579–94.

Jorde-Bloom, P., Sheerer, M. and Britz, J. 1991, 'Leadership style assessment tool', *Child Care Information Exchange*, vol. 87, pp. 2–15.

Kagan, S. 1994, 'Leadership: Rethinking it—making it happen', *Young Children*, vol. 49, no. 5, pp. 50–4.

Katz, L. 1995a, 'The nature of professions: Where is early childhood education?', in *Talks with Teachers: A Collection*, ed. L. Katz, Ablex Publishing Corporation, Norwood.

——1995b, 'Ethical issues in working with young children', in *Talks with Teachers: A Collection*, ed. L. Katz, Ablex Publishing Corporation, Norwood.

Katzenmayer, M. and Moller, G. 2001, *Awakening the Sleeping Giant: Helping Teachers Develop as Leaders*, 2nd edn, Corwin Press, Thousand Oaks, CA.

Kemmis, S. and McTaggart, R. 1988, *The Action Research Planner*, Deakin University Press, Waurn Ponds, Vic.

Keyes, C.R. 2000, 'The early childhood teacher's voice in the research community', *International Journal of Early Years Education*, vol. 8, no. 1, pp. 3–13.

Kinney, J. 1992, 'New thoughts on child care administration and leadership involving emerging information on the psychology of women', paper presented at the 1992 Conference of the National Association for the Education of Young Children, New Orleans.

Kotter, J. 1989, 'What leaders really do', *Harvard Business Review*, vol. 67, no. 3, pp. 103–11.

Lansdown, G. and Lancaster, P. 2001, 'Promoting children's welfare by respecting their rights', *Contemporary Issues in the Early Years: Working Collaboratively for Children*, 3rd edn, ed. G. Pugh, Paul Chapman, London.

Law, S. and Glover, D. 2000, *Educational Leadership and Learning. Practice, Policy and Research*, Open University Press, Buckingham.

Lewis, V., Kellett, M., Robinson, C., Fraser, S. and Ding, S. 2003, *The Reality of Research with Children and Young People*, Sage, London.

Loane, S. 1997, *Who Cares? Guilt, Hope and the Child Care Debate*, Mandarin, Sydney.

Lucas, B., Greany, T., Rodd, J. and Wicks, R. 2002, *Teaching Pupils How to Learn*, Network Educational Press, Stafford.

MacDonald, S. 2004, *Sanity Savers for Early Childhood Teachers: 200 quick fixes for everything from big messes to small budgets*, Gryphon House, Beltsville.

MacGilchrist, B., Myers, K. and Reed, J. 1997, *The Intelligent School*, Paul Chapman Publishing, London.

MacNaughton, G., Rolfe, S. and Siraj-Blatchford, I. eds 2001, *Doing Educational Research: International Perspectives on Theory and Practice*, Open University Press, Buckingham.

MacNaughton, G. and Smith, K. 2001, 'Action research, ethics and the risks of practising freedom for early childhood professionals', *Australian Journal of Early Childhood*, vol. 26, no. 4, pp. 32–8.

Martin, A. and Trueax, J. 1997, 'Transformative dimensions of mentoring: Implications for practice in the training of early childhood teachers', Conference Paper, China–US Conference on Education, July, Beijing.

Maslow, A. 1970, *Motivation and Personality*, Harper and Row, New York.

Maxwell, J.C. 1999, *The 21 Qualities of Leaders*, Thomas Nelson, London.

Mitchell, J. 1990, *Revisioning Educational Leadership: A Phenomenological Approach*, Bergin and Garvey, New York.

Morgan, G. 1997a, 'Historical views of leadership', *Leadership in Early Care and Education*, eds S. Kagan and T. Bowman, National Association for the Education of Young Children, Washington.

Morgan, G. 1997b, 'What is Leadership? Walking Around a Definition. Working Papers', The Centre for Career Development in Early Care and Education, Wheelock College, Boston.

Moss, P. 2001, 'Ethics in the nursery', *Every Child*, vol. 7, no. 3, pp. 6–7.

Moyles, J. 2003, 'The role of play in the foundation stage', Foundation Stage Conference, Cornwall Educational Development Service, Newquay, Cornwall.

Moyles, J., Musgrove, A. and Adams, S. 2002, *SPEEL—Study of Pedagogical Effectiveness in Early Learning*, Department for Education and Skills Report No. 363, London.

Moyles, J. and Yates, R. 2004, *Effective Leadership and Management Evaluation Scheme (Early Years)*, Research report for Anglia Polytechnic University, Essex County Council; The Schools Service, Southend Borough Council, European Social Fund.

Muijs, D., Aubrey, C., Harris, A. and Briggs, M. 2005, 'How do they manage? A review of the research on leadership in early childhood', *Journal of Early Childhood Research*, vol. 2, no. 2, pp. 157–69.

Mulligan, V. 1996, *Children's Play: An Introduction for Care Providers*, Addison-Wesley, Don Mills, Ontario.

National Association for the Education of Young Children 1984, *Accreditation, Criteria and Procedures of the National Academy of Early Childhood Programs*, National Association for the Education of Young Children, Washington.

——1993, *A Conceptual Framework for the Early Childhood Professional Development*, National Association for the Education of Young Children, Washington.

——1996, *After the Stand: Be a Children's Champion*, www.naeyc.org/ece/1996/06.asp.

——1999, *Building Parent–Teacher Partnerships*, www.naeyc.org/ece/1999/02/asp.

Neugebauer, B. and Neugebauer, R. eds 1998, *The Art of Leadership: Managing Early Childhood Organisations*, vol. 2, Child Care Information Exchange, Perth.

Neugebauer, R. 1985, 'Are you an effective leader?', *Child Care Information Exchange*, vol. 46, pp. 18–26.

Newman, L. 2000, 'Ethical leadership or leadership in ethics', *Australian Journal of Early Childhood*, vol. 25, no. 1, pp. 40–5.

Noone, M. 1996, *Mediation*, Cavendish, London.

Nupponen, H. 2000, 'Leadership and management: Into the 21st century', *Every Child*, vol. 6, no. 3, pp. 8–9.

Nutbrown, C. 1996, *Respectful Educators—Capable Learners: Children's rights and early education*, Paul Chapman Publishing, London.

Oberhuemer, P. 2000, 'Conceptualising the professional role in early childhood centres: Emerging profiles in four European countries', *Early Childhood Research and Practice* (Electronic), vol. 2, no. 2, pp. 1–3.

Page, J., Nienhuys, T., Kapsalakis, A. and Morda, R. 2001, 'Parents' perceptions of kindergarten programs in Victoria', *Australian Journal of Early Childhood*, vol. 26, no. 3, pp. 43–50.

Pechura, J.M. 2003, 'How principals build leadership capacity in others', *Leadership Capacity for Lasting School Improvement*, ed. L. Lambert, Association for Supervision and Curriculum Development, Alexandria, VA.

Potter, G. 2001, 'Facilitating critical reflection on practice through collaborative research', *Australian Educational Researcher*, vol. 28, no. 3, pp. 117–39.

Pugh, G. ed. 2001, *Contemporary Issues in the Early Years: Working Collaboratively for Children*, 3rd edn, Paul Chapman, London.

Rand, M.K. 2000, *Giving It Some Thought: Case Studies for Early Childhood Practice*, National Association for the Education of Young Children, Washington.

Rayner, M. 1995, 'Children's rights in Australia', in *The Handbook of Children's Rights: Comparative Policy and Practice*, eds B. Franklin and T. Hammarberg, Routledge, London.

Robbins, S. 2004, *Essentials of Organizational Behavior*, international edn, Prentice Hall PTR, Englewood Cliffs.

Rodd, J. 1987, 'It's not just talking: The role of interpersonal skills training for early childhood educators', *Early Child Development and Care*, vol. 29, no. 2, pp. 241–52.

——1989, 'Better communication = better relationships', *Day Care and Early Education*, vol. 17, no. 1, pp. 28–9.

——1996, 'Towards a typology of leadership for the early childhood professional of the 21st century', *Early Child Development and Care*, vol. 120, pp. 119–26.

——1997, 'Learning to develop as leaders: Perceptions of early childhood professionals about leadership roles and responsibilities', *Early Years*, vol. 18, no. 1, pp. 24–34.

——1998, *Leadership in Early Childhood: The pathway to professionalism*, 2nd edn, Allen & Unwin, Sydney.

Rodd, J. and Clyde, M. 1991, 'A code of ethics: Who needs it?', *Australian Journal of Early Childhood*, vol. 16, no. 1, pp. 24–34.

Rogers, C. 1961, *On Becoming a Person*, Houghton Mifflin, Boston.

Rolfe-Flett, A. 2002, 'Mentoring can optimise learning', *Training and Development in Australia*, vol. 29, no. 3, pp. 16–18.

Rosemary, C., Roskos, K., Owendorf, C. and Olsen, C. 1998, 'Surveying leadership in the USA early care and education. A knowledge base and typology of activities', in *Towards Understanding Leadership in Early Childhood Context: Cross Cultural Perspectives*, eds E. Hujala and A. Puroila, Oulu University Press, Oulu, Finland.

Rosier, M. and Lloyd-Smith, J. 1996, *I Love my Job, but . . . Child Care Workforce Attrition Study*, Community Services and Health & Industry Training Board, Melbourne.

Said, S. and Rolfe, J. 2001, 'Effective management of conflict in schools', *Educare News*, no. 122, pp. 22–3.

Sarros J.C. and Butchatsky, O. 1996, *Leadership: Australia's Top CEOs: Finding Out What Makes Them the Best*, Harper Business, Adelaide.

Schiller, J. 1987, 'Peer supervision: Learning more about what we do', *Australian Journal of Early Childhood*, vol. 12, no. 3, pp. 43–6.

Schiller, P.B. and Dyke, P. 1990, *Managing Quality Child Care Centres. A Comprehensive Manual for Administrators*, Teachers College Press, New York.

Schrag, L., Nelson, E. and Siminowsky, T. 1985, 'Helping employees cope with change', *Child Care Information Exchange*, September, pp. 3–6.

Schwahn, C., Spady, J. and William, G. 1998, *Total Leaders: Applying the Best Future-Focused Change Strategies to Education*, American Association of School Administrators, Virginia.

Sergiovanni, T.J. 1999, *Rethinking Leadership: A Collection of Articles, K—College*, Skylight Professional Development, Arlington Heights, Ill.

Sharp, P. 2002, *Nurturing Emotional Literacy*, David Fulton Publishers, London.

Smith, T.M. and Ingersoll, R.M. 2004, 'What are the effects of induction and mentoring on beginning teacher turnover?', *American Educational Research Journal*, vol. 41, no. 3, pp. 681–714.

Solly, K. 2003, 'What do early childhood leaders do to maintain and enhance the significance of the early years?', presentation on 22 May at the Institute of Education, University of London, London.

Southworth, G. 1994, 'School leadership and school development: Reflections from research', in Readings in Primary School Development, ed. G. Southworth, Falmer Press, London.

——2000, 'How primary schools learn', *Research Papers in Education*, vol. 15, pp. 275–91.

Spodek, B. 1987, 'Thought processes underlying preschool teachers' classroom decisions', *Early Child Development and Care*, vol. 28, pp. 197–208.

Steiner, C. 1999, *Achieving Emotional Literacy*, Bloomsbury, London.

Stonehouse, A. and Creaser, B. 1991, 'A code of ethics for the Australian early childhood profession: Background and overview', *Australian Journal of Early Childhood*, vol. 16, no. 1, pp. 7–16.

Sullivan, D. 2003, *Learning to Lead: Effective Leadership Skills for Teachers of Young Children*, Redleaf Press, St Paul, MN.

Sumison, J. 2002, 'Revisiting the challenge of staff recruitment and retention in children's services', *Australian Journal of Early Childhood*, vol. 27, no. 1, pp. 8–13.

Sylva, K. and Siraj-Blatchford, I. 2003, *Effective Provision of Pre-school Education*, Department for Education and Skills, London.

Taba, S. 1999, 'Lighting the path: Developing leadership in early education', *Early Childhood Education Journal*, vol. 26, no. 3, pp. 173–7.

Taggart, B. 2003, 'Focus on effective provision of pre-school education', *Sure Start Partners*, vol. 27, June/July, pp. 6–7.

Taylor, C. 2005, *Walking the Talk: Building a culture for success*, Random House, London.

Thomson, B. and Calder P. 1998, 'Early years educators: Skills, knowledge and understanding', in *Training to Work in the Early Years: Developing the Climbing Frame*, eds L. Abbott and G. Pugh, Open University Press, Buckingham.

Turner, S. 2003, *Tools for Success: A manager's guide*, McGraw Hill, London.

Vander Ven, K. 1988, 'Pathways to professional effectiveness for early childhood educators', in *Professionalism and the Early Childhood Practitioner*, eds B. Spodek, O. Saracho and D. Peters, Teachers College Press, New York.

——1991, 'The relationship between notions of care giving held by early childhood practitioners and stages of career development', in *Early Childhood Towards the 21st Century: A Worldwide Perspective*, ed. B. Po-King Chan, Yew Chung Education Publishing, Hong Kong.

Vickers, C. and Ashton-Jones, D. 2003, 'Putting out the "welcome mat": How open is your door?', *Classroom*, vol. 23, no. 4, pp. 22–3.

Wadsworth, Y. 1997, *Do It Yourself Social Research*, 2nd edn, Allen & Unwin, Sydney.

Walker, E.H. 1995, 'Teamwork in child care: A study of communication issues in forming a team', Masters Thesis, University of Adelaide, Adelaide.

Waniganayake, M. 2002, 'Leadership in early childhood: New directions in research', keynote presentation to Professional Development Conference, January, Melbourne.

Waniganayake, M., Morda, R. and Kapsalakis, A. 2000, 'Leadership in child care centres: Is it just another job?', *Australian Journal of Early Childhood*, vol. 25, no. 1, pp. 13–19.

Weaver, P.E. 2004, 'The culture of teaching and mentoring compliance', *Childhood Education*, vol. 80, no. 5, pp. 258–60.

West, M.A. 2004, *Effective Teamwork: Practical Lessons from Organisational Research*, 2nd edn, BPS Blackwell, Oxford.

Whalley, M. 1994, *Learning to be Strong*, Hodder & Stoughton, London.

——1999, Women as Leaders in Early Childhood Settings—A Dialogue in the 1990s, Unpublished PhD thesis, University of Wolverhampton, Wolverhampton.

——2001, 'Working as a team', in *Contemporary Issues in the Early Years. Working Collaboratively for Children*, 3rd edn, ed. G. Pugh, Paul Chapman, London.

Wonacott, M.E. 2001, 'Leadership development in career and technical education', *ERIC Digest*, No. 225, Columbus, Ohio.

Wong, C.S. and Law, K.S. 2002, 'The effects of leader and follower emotional intelligence on performance and aptitude', *Leadership Quarterly*, vol. 134, pp. 243–74.

Woodcock, M. 1979, *Team Development Manual*, Halstead Press, New York.

Woodcock, M. and Francis, D. 1981, *Organisational Development Through Teambuilding*, Gower Publishing, Adelaide.

Woodrow, C. 2001, 'Ethics in early childhood: Continuing the conversations', *Australian Journal of Early Childhood*, vol. 26, no. 3, pp. 26–31.

York-Barr, J. and Duke, K. 2004, 'What do we know about teacher leadership? Findings from two decades of scholarship', *Review of Educational Research*, vol. 74, no. 3, pp. 255–316.

# AUTHOR INDEX

# SUBJECT INDEX